Groupware, Workflow and Intranets

Groupware, Workflow and Intranets

Reengineering the Enterprise with Collaborative Software

Dave Chaffey

dp

Digital Press

Boston • Oxford • Johannesburg • Melbourne • New Delhi • Singapore

Library of Congress Cataloging-in-Publication Data
Chaffey, Dave, 1963–
    Groupware, workflow and intranets : reengineering the enterprise
with collaborative software / Dave Chaffey.
        p.   cm.
    Includes bibliographical references and index.
    ISBN 1-55558-184-6 (alk. paper)
    1. Groupware (Computer software)   2. Workflow—Management.
3. Intranets (Computer networks)   4. Reengineering (Management).
I. Title.
HD66.2.C48   1998   98-3741
651.7'9—dc21   CIP

British Library Cataloguing-in-Publication Data
A catalogue record for this book is available from the British Library.

The publisher offers special discounts on bulk orders of this book.
For information, please contact:
Manager of Special Sales
Butterworth-Heinemann
225 Wildwood Avenue
Woburn, MA 01801-2041
Tel: 781-904-2500
Fax: 781-904-2620

For information on all Butterworth–Heinemann publications available, contact our World Wide Web
home page at: http://www.bh.com

Order number: EY–W933E–DP

10 9 8 7 6 5 4 3 2 1

Printed in the United States of America

Contents

List of Illustrations

Figures

Tables

Acknowledgments

First of all my thanks go to my wife, Sal, who not only had to make do with a view of the back of my head for many evenings, but also provided me with an expert copy editor. My daughter Zoe helped in a way that only she knows how. Thanks also to my parents for their support.

From the publishers, I would like to thank Mike Cash, International Publisher of Digital Press, for initiating the project and Liz McCarthy, acquisitions editor, for her helpful advice and encouragement throughout the project. Reviewer Bob Rustici of Zero In Inc. provided detailed comments and additional material on video-conferencing for which I am grateful.

I would also like to thank colleagues from the University of Derby, particularly Simon Hickie for discussions and input. Finally I thank the many groupware and workflow vendors who provided me with product information. Special mention goes to Martin Geraghty of Staffware plc, David McCulley of InConcert Inc., Carl Rigby of AIT plc and Joanne Kilbride of Hatton Blue plc who provided me with product screenshots and technical information.

An Introduction to Collaborative Systems

Software to Promote Team Work

Today, many businesses are redefining the way they do business. This transformation involves breaking down old structures by building responsive cross-functional teams to meet customers' needs and face competitive threats. For these teams to operate effectively they need software that allows them to work together. The old method of an individual interacting only with the computer and its programs is gone forever. What is needed is software that allows team members to share ideas, information and tasks to help them complete business processes as efficiently as possible.

The software to bring about this new way of working is collaborative software. This has become one of the key enablers in restructuring the enterprise as part of *business process reengineering* (BPR), continuous improvement or total quality management programs. BPR is the radical redevelopment of the way a company operates. Existing processes are thrown out and new ones created. As Michael Hammer wrote in the early 1990s, "Don't automate, obliterate." By business processes we mean any activities performed by people or machines which transform inputs into outputs in the form of goods or services.

This book looks in detail at the two key types of collaborative software application—*groupware* and *workflow software*—and explains what they are, what benefits they give and how to bring them into your company. The increasingly important role played by the Internet and internal company Internet facilities, known as *intranets*, in providing collaborative facilities is also included.

Why This Book?

Despite the great promise of BPR and the use of collaborative systems in process management, many projects have failed to deliver what the business users wanted or failed to complete within time and budget. A recent survey put the amount lost in failed U.S. systems development projects at $80 billion!

Given these sobering statistics, the intention of this book is to go beyond a description of the types of groupware and workflow systems that are available and to explain how the development and deployment of these systems can be managed to ensure the potential is delivered. To achieve this, practical guidelines for managers are given in areas of:

▶ incorporating group functions into reengineering efforts

▶ evaluating where collaborative functions can be best used

▶ selecting the right software tool

▶ managing the stages of process analysis, design and implementation

This book covers groupware, workflow and intranet technologies together since there is increasing overlap between them. Today these technologies are often implemented together rather than separately. For companies seeking to reengineer or improve their processes both groupware and workflow software is commonly used, since they enable the people performing the processes to work together more effectively.

In This Chapter

Groupware, workflow and intranets are introduced in this chapter. We review why they are proving so popular, what their key functions are and the differences between them. A roadmap for the remaining chapters is provided at the end of the chapter.

What Is Groupware?

Groupware is software for enabling collaboration within and between companies. It spans a wide range of software that enables teams of people to work together efficiently. These teams may be "tight-knit" teams working on a new product launch or more loosely coupled teams made up of individuals from different parts of the business. You are probably familiar with one groupware function through using e-mail where people exchange information in an unstructured way. You may also have heard of groupware packages such as Lotus Notes or Microsoft Exchange, but what other functions beyond e-mail do these packages have to help you in your work?

Groupware provides functions to promote team work and improve efficiency through:

▶ increasing information sharing

▶ reducing communications overheads

▶ providing coordination

As such, *groupware* is software to enable group working or *computer supported cooperative work* (CSCW) which is the term used by academics researching this area. CSCW was first used in 1984 by Irene Greif, of the Massachusetts Institute of Technology, and David Cashman, of Digital Equipment Corporation, as the title for a workshop they were arranging. The term groupware covers a diverse range of products with varying functions and applications. The Gartner Group prefers the term *workgroup systems* (WGS) to define collaborative systems. They describe the properties of WGS as "a cohesive architecture based on distributed-logic client/server technology and inter-enterprise-capable, enterprise-class platforms for communications, collaboration, coordination and knowledge reuse."

Groupware is a big industry; a February 1997 survey by research firm Input of Mountain View, California, estimated that by the year 2000 there will be 40 million groupware users worldwide. Major groupware products such as Lotus Notes boast over 14 million users. The annual groupware market is measured in billions; it is estimated at $4 billion for 1998 by the New York research and banking firm First Albany Corporation.

Groupware Enables Teamwork in the Global Enterprise

One of the reasons groupware has become an essential business tool is that it can be used for collaboration in the global enterprise even when face-to-face contact is impossible. Employees can continue to communicate and work on joint projects even when they are in different locations or in different time zones. The *asynchronous* use of groupware is one of its key benefits. When considering the benefits of collaborative systems it is useful to categorize them according to which quadrant they lie in a grid showing how people can work together in time and space (Table 1.1). Chapter 3 considers these functions in more detail and also looks at options for synchronous groupware such as desktop video-conferencing and whiteboarding for remote meetings.

Table 1.1   *Different uses of collaborative systems classified in time and space*

	Synchronous	**Asynchronous**
Same location	Same time, same place Example: meeting support software	Different time, same place Example: workflow systems
Different location	Same time, different place Example: video-conferencing	Different time, different place Example: e-mail and discussion groups

Figure 1.1
Novell Groupwise
showing universal
in-box in left pane,
mail items in right
pane and mail
contents in
bottom pane

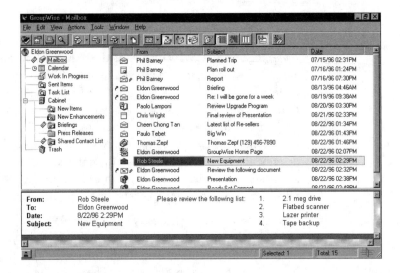

What Functions Are Provided by Groupware?

Groupware packages such as Microsoft Exchange, Novell Groupwise and Lotus Notes all provide a universal in-box in which all sorts of electronic information such as voice and e-mail, documents, spreadsheet data, graphics or animations are deposited for your attention by other team members. Figure 1.1 shows the in-box for Novell Groupwise, one of the well established groupware products.

The types of groupware function provided to create, access and share this information include:

▶ e-mail

▶ group discussions (threaded text based conferences)

▶ document sharing for joint authoring of reports

▶ electronic meetings software such as video-conferencing

▶ group decision support

▶ group coordination software for time management and scheduling

To enable access to the in-box, client software runs on the PC on each coworker's desk and is connected to a groupware server using a company network, intranet or the Internet.

From Groupware to Intranets

Since groupware means many things to many people, a brief history may be useful to highlight where its origins lie and help explain why it has so many

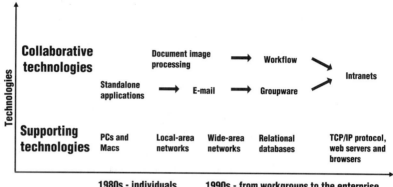

Figure 1.2
The evolution of collaborative and supporting technologies

different functions. Figure 1.2 shows how groupware has evolved from the introduction of the first PC. When the PC was first introduced it was used in a standalone mode with users finding the PC an easy way to organize their own personal information with limited sharing with others.

With the growth of local-area networks (LANs) it became possible to share information stored on file servers and to communicate directly via e-mail. These facilities, available years earlier in mainframe and UNIX systems, laid the foundation for PC based groupware products. As groupware has developed it has moved from a tool to help individuals communicate by e-mail through a workgroup based product to become an enterprise-wide method of communication, collaboration and communication.

Currently groupware is itself facing transformation as information sharing occurs through *intranets* which are based on well-known Internet technologies. These "private Internets" use low cost, easy to use web browsers such as Netscape Navigator to share information placed on a web server and accessed over the company LAN. The use of such intranets in Fortune 500 companies has reached over 90% in only a few years.

Such is the growth in use of corporate intranets for information sharing that the term *intranet* is now almost synonymous with groupware. The growth in use of intranets makes this an excellent time to introduce or extend groupware functions in your company since the cost of providing groupware functionality is falling rapidly.

What Is Workflow?

If your company struggles with processing and tracking information such as invoices, purchase orders or processing customer applications, then workflow can help. Workflow systems are a distinct class of software which automate business processes by providing a *structured* framework to support a process. Workflow systems help manage business processes by ensuring that tasks are prioritized to be performed:

⇨ as soon as possible

    ⇨ by the right people

        ⇨ in the right order.

This gives a consistent, uniform approach for improved efficiency and better customer service. For example, a standard method of dealing with purchase orders or processing insurance claims can be achieved using workflow systems. Workflow usually involves coworkers performing tasks sequentially as part of an overall process, so it is another important means of aiding collaboration. Workflow software provides functions to:

▶ assign tasks to people

▶ remind people about their tasks which are part of a workflow queue

▶ allow collaboration between people sharing tasks

▶ retrieve information needed to complete the task, such as a customer's personal details

▶ provide an overview for supervisors of the status of each task and the team's performance

A workflow application is used to structure a business process by specifying the order in which tasks need to occur. Figure 1.3 shows a process map of

Figure 1.3
Workflow definition for an employee hiring process displayed in the Staffware Workflow Definer

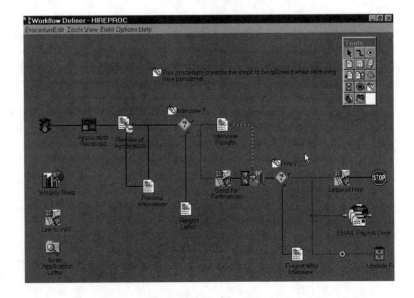

the workflow involved when hiring a new employee. The case is initiated when an application is received and the workflow ensures that a well-defined, repeatable review occurs. As each review marked by a "?" occurs, there is a decision point of continuing to the next stage or sending out a rejection letter. In this example the workflow application is integrated with imaging, with the application letter being scanned for later review.

The Growth of Workflow

Workflow did not originate as a method of group working, but rather as a way of reducing the time and cost of performing business processes and ensuring that tasks are performed consistently to improve quality. As Figure 1.2 shows, the growth in use of workflow was, like groupware, supported by the introduction of LAN and e-mail. Early attempts to automate office tasks through storing digital copies of documents such as customer letters or invoices led to the development of workflow. For example, sharing out processing of insurance claims between a group of staff is natural once these claims are stored in a digital form.

Document imaging processing is often an important part of a workflow system in these types of application. Workflow systems are also often integrated with *electronic document management systems* (EDMS) which are used to provide the corporation with all the procedures, guidelines and standards necessary for it to operate. EDMS are used to create, distribute and maintain this type of documentation.

The best way to understand workflow is through an example. Figure 1.4 illustrates some of the typical functions of a workflow system for processing an insurance claim. Processing a new claim starts with the claim form being scanned into the system so it is easily available as an image for future reference. The workflow system will then prompt the user to associate the image with a particular customer. This may involve automatically accessing information necessary to perform the task, for example, the customer policy details. These details are often stored on a separate existing or legacy system integrated with the workflow system.

The main workflow system function is to provide reminders to staff to do the right tasks at the right time. This is achieved through a workflow engine that manages a queue of tasks which need to be performed according to the task priority and who is available to complete it.

In this example, reminders are issued to check different aspects of the validity of the claim and contact the customer and other insurers when appropriate. Finally, the system will also provide status information for managers of the workgroup to show the status of individual tasks and the big picture such as the number of cases outstanding and average customer response time.

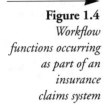

Figure 1.4
Workflow functions occurring as part of an insurance claims system

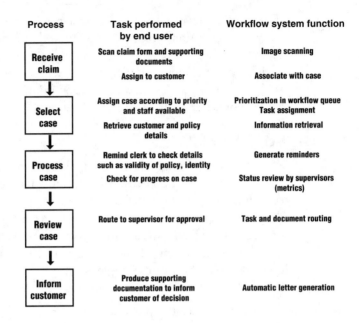

Process	Task performed by end user	Workflow system function
Receive claim	Scan claim form and supporting documents	Image scanning
	Assign to customer	Associate with case
Select case	Assign case according to priority and staff available	Prioritization in workflow queue / Task assignment
	Retrieve customer and policy details	Information retrieval
Process case	Remind clerk to check details such as validity of policy, identity	Generate reminders
	Check for progress on case	Status review by supervisors (metrics)
Review case	Route to supervisor for approval	Task and document routing
Inform customer	Produce supporting documentation to inform customer of decision	Automatic letter generation

When selecting workflow software two main alternatives are available to you:

▶ *ad hoc* or *unstructured workflow,* where users must perform tasks as they see fit, with limited prompting by the software. Collaboration on a product design is an example of this.

▶ *structured workflow* includes production workflow systems where the software is instrumental in managing the tasks and instructing the human operators what they are required to do. The insurance claims example is in this category.

These alternatives represent two extremes and in reality there is a continuum between structured and unstructured with so-called administrative systems lying between the two. Some products offer a combination of types, but usually their strength lies in one area. Chapter 4 examines the different types of workflow in more detail. To reflect the different roles between the computer and the business users in these types of situation the first type is often referred to as "pull" and the second as "push" workflow. Workflow systems are now often linked with other technologies such as computer telephone integration in call centers. Simple workflow routing functions are now being provided in groupware and intranet tools, and as this occurs they become more widespread. Chapter 4 describes the different varieties of workflow system and how they are constructed in more detail.

Groupware and Workflow—
What Is the Difference?

Confusion abounds when distinguishing between groupware and workflow. This arises since workflow is often considered to be a function or subset of groupware. This is true in that a simple workflow function such as routing of business forms between staff can be achieved using groupware. However, a large, mission critical workflow system such as that used by a bank to process loan requests is quite different in the way it is designed, built and used. For this reason, I believe the two must be considered as distinct products and they are described separately in Chapters 3 and 4. However, since many of the issues involved with their design and implementation are shared, these aspects are considered jointly in Chapters 6 through 9.

The two technologies are also treated separately by most academics and vendors, but the distinction is often made in an artificial way. Strictly defined, all types of groupware must involve an element of collaboration. This is not necessary for workflow systems—these are *sometimes* used by individuals undertaking tasks who are not directly collaborating with colleagues. However, I would argue that workflow systems are also collaborative in the majority of cases. When seen from a wider organizational perspective, the individuals are collaborating as they sequentially perform the activities of a business.

To summarize, workflow systems and groupware are both commonly used for collaboration. They are best considered as separate types of product since groupware is usually used in an ad hoc way while workflow imposes a more strict, structured way of working.

A Hardware Architecture for
Collaborative Systems

The infrastructure needed to bring in workflow and groupware systems to your company is described in Chapter 8, which explains the hardware architecture required to support the systems. Chapter 6 explains the best method of selecting software to meet your business requirements. The main components of a collaborative system are:

▶ Client software. This is the interface by which the end user accesses the software. Increasingly web based browsers are being used as groupware and workflow clients on a company intranet.

▶ Server software used to store group information, administer the system and provide links to other company systems. Again, this may be a web server or a database server.

▶ The infrastructure or plumbing of the system. This is based on local- and wide-area networking techniques.

▶ The application development environment which provides interactive programming tools to develop applications through the Application Programming Interface (API) of the package, which gives access to the middleware or intermediate software layers which enable different applications to interoperate.

Collaborative systems have grown in importance alongside the introduction of local-area networks and the client/server model of computing. The growth of client/server was closely linked with the trend to downsize from monolithic mainframes with arrays of user terminals with limited functionality. Cost savings were originally used to drive the introduction of these technologies. However, there is much debate about the high cost of ownership of client/server systems. The empowerment of the end user to develop their own applications and to use and share the data as they see fit is now considered to be the main benefit of client/server.

The client/server model involves a series of clients, typically desktop PCs, which are the access point for end user applications. The clients are connected to a server computer via a local-area network at one site of a company or use a wide-area network connecting different sites and/or companies. The server is a more powerful computer which is usually used to store the application and the data used by the user or shared with other users. When using PCs the application normally executes on the processor of the client.

There are many alternatives when deploying client/server. You can distribute data, processing or logic across both servers and client computers. This is only a thumbnail sketch of what client/server means. The advantages of the different varieties of client/server such as two-tier and three-tier and system management issues are covered further in Chapter 8.

Roadmap—How to Find the Information You Need

The book splits into two parts. In the first part, different types of collaborative systems are described plus the key terms and standards that are required to integrate the products. In the second part, practical guidance on building collaborative systems is given by looking in detail at each stage of their development.

Introduction to Collaborative Systems and Intranets

Chapter 2 provides the business background to the use of collaborative systems. The different functions provided by groupware and workflow and their applications are introduced in Chapters 3 and 4. Chapter 5 describes the latest use of intranets as a platform for providing groupware and workflow functions.

Chapter 2. Reengineering and Process Improvement Using Collaborative Software

▶ Business benefits and the different types of reengineering

▶ How do groupware and workflow support reengineering?

▶ Collecting metrics using collaborative systems

▶ Different methods of business reengineering

▶ Stages in reengineering

Chapter 3. Groupware Functions and Applications

▶ Key groupware functions: e-mail and messaging, text and video-conferencing, electronic meeting support, joint authoring and scheduling

▶ Applications of groupware

▶ Standards for integrating groupware products

Chapter 4. Workflow Management Systems

▶ Components making up a workflow system

▶ Different types of workflow systems

▶ Standards to integrate workflow products

▶ Applications of workflow systems

Chapter 5. Intranets and Internet based Groupware and Workflow

▶ Introduction to intranets—essential terms

▶ Setting up an intranet

▶ Groupware applications

▶ Workflow applications

▶ Problems of intranets

Building Collaborative Systems

Chapters 6 through 9 describe the steps involved with the introduction of collaborative systems and highlight what needs to be done to get the development right. In these chapters we look at how to build applications to help groups work together. Guidance on building groupware and workflow solutions is given by looking at the standard stages of a software development project from its start, when the right tool must be selected through analysis of the processes through to design and implementation of the system.

Chapter 6 looks at how to select the components of the system—what are the key requirements, what is available and which criteria you should use. Different products are compared in this chapter.

Chapter 7 considers in more depth how to analyze the business requirements of workflow systems. In particular it looks at methods of mapping the business processes so that they can then be used for designing workflow.

Chapter 8 looks at design factors important in building a system which end users will be happy with. These factors include performance, usability and security. Topics covered include the design of the hardware architecture, security and the human–computer interface.

Chapter 9 describes practical implementation issues such as testing and deployment options. How the users of the new system should be involved at each stage is an underlying theme to all these chapters.

Chapter 10 attempts to gaze into the future of how groupware, workflow and intranet systems may evolve from the current snapshot.

2

Reengineering and Process Improvement Using Collaborative Software

Why Reengineer?

Companies reengineer because of the promise of massive improvements in the efficiency of their business operations leading to improved business performance and better customer service. Promises offered include customer service index increased by 100%; time for issuing a loan reduced by 200%; staff needed for a process reduced by 300%. This chapter shows how groupware and workflow software can help in reengineering the enterprise.

So, how can collaborative software help reengineer the enterprise? The processes ripe for assistance are typically manual business processes which involve information processing when providing an internal or external customer with a service. Collaborative software is important to reengineering since the traditional hierarchies created in larger companies are usually broken down. The new, flatter structure with more process oriented teams needs software to support it. Of course collaborative software is not only used when companies are undertaking large scale reengineering, but can also be used with smaller scale improvements in the operation of a company.

Caution Required—The Reengineering Gamble

The logic behind the radical redesign or reengineering of processes is that while *small* adjustments and automation of existing processes may result in some performance improvements, these will be *small* in magnitude—measured in tens of percent. With BPR much larger gains, possibly of several hundred percent in performance, can be achieved. But reengineering also offers the largest risk.

Despite the promise of tremendous improvements, many reengineering projects fail; some surveys show the failure rate at 70 to 80%, so a cautious approach is necessary. The emphasis in the remainder of the book is on how to avoid the reversal of the big promises so improvements are delivered using groupware and workflow software and intranets. Trying for more limited improvements in processes through automation is also another way to limit the risk.

BPR was popularized in the early 1990s, and the term that is used to describe such business improvements will certainly change. Today BPR is being replaced by terms such as continuous improvement or process improvement to indicate that the lower risk option of gradually refining some processes is often best. However, improvement or redesign of business processes will certainly continue into the future.

In This Chapter

The use of collaborative systems to assist in both gradual process improvement and radical reengineering are both covered in this chapter. We start by considering how companies use IT, and in particular collaborative systems, to support their business strategy. We then look at how collaborative systems can support BPR and process improvement. Methodologies for the typical stages of a BPR program are related to the subsequent chapters on analysis, design and implementation. Overall, this chapter provides a framework for the remaining chapters which describe how to introduce collaborative systems into a workgroup or company. The important role of metrics in measuring the performance of processes is also examined in this chapter. It is shown how workflow systems are important in helping to collect metrics. Many of the issues discussed in this chapter are also covered by articles on the reference web site, "a business researcher's interests." This is recommended.

Web reference: http://www.brint.com

Implementing the IS Strategy

We will start by assuming that a company has an established business strategy and is looking to IT to help achieve its goals. An early decision when implementing the business strategy is whether to adopt and improve existing processes in a process improvement program or to completely reengineer them. With any new IS or groupware implementation there are three basic alternatives:

▶ **Automate existing ways of working**—Automate the existing working methods using computers to assist in performing tasks, but retaining the existing task structure. This is often referred to as doing bad things faster.

> ▶ **Improve key processes**—Base the office automation on the existing processes, but improve some key areas such as the most time consuming tasks or those involving customer service. This is process improvement.

> ▶ **Reengineer the business**—Make major modifications to the processes and the roles of the agents performing them. This often involves developing systems which work across functions rather than in a single traditional workgroup, which is the norm with automation.

Which of these is the right decision depends largely on the extent to which managers are prepared to take a risk. Although reengineering can potentially offer the largest gain, it also poses the largest risk. Often the intermediate option is best since this can give significant improvements in productivity, but without the higher risk of reengineering. Of course most companies who perform reengineering will previously have had the benefit of implementing an IT system to partially automate the business process. Through this they will have learnt from mistakes and identify processes which will particularly benefit from reengineering.

How Should IS Strategy Support Process Improvement?

Useful guidelines for developing an IS strategy to support process improvement have been developed by many of the large management consultants. Arthur Andersen Consulting recommends the following best practices for improving the management of information resources within an organization. Here, in the box "Guidelines for Supporting Process Improvement," I have applied the guidelines to show how collaborative systems can assist a company in restructuring its processes.

Web reference: http://www.arthurandersen.com (Describes global best practices initiative and /bp.)

How Can Groupware and Workflow Support Reengineering?

Collaborative Systems Can Support All Stages of Process Improvement

Each of the primary functions of groupware and intranets—communication, collaboration and coordination are important to BPR. With the introduction of matrix management and cross-functional teams in the reengineered company a superior means of communication and information sharing is required, and, of course, collaborative systems provide these. Davenport (1993) has also noted that group tools and e-mail are valuable in supporting the analysis and planning stages of BPR through helping communication across organizational and geographical barriers. For the new business processes to operate efficiently groupware and workflow will help the people involved with them communicate effectively.

Guidelines for Supporting Process Improvement

1. **"Develop and maintain an IT strategy that is integrated and aligned with the company's business goals."**
   Closely aligned business and IT strategies are necessary so that IT solutions are implemented to support business goals. Information resources should be made available through collaborative systems to support decision making at all levels within the company: strategic, tactical and operational.

2. **"Create and foster a customer focus for the IT organization and personnel."**
   Action Technologies considers customer focus in processes so critical that their workflow process model is defined through specifying a customer and a supplier for each sub-process (Chapter 7). This customer-supplier relationship puts the spotlight on customer service and can boost the quality of solutions delivered. Customer focus can apply to both internal or external customers.

3. **"Design an IT organization that maximizes support for the company's various business groups."**
   This guideline indicates that although processes and their supporting teams may seem to operate independently, it would be a mistake to think there are no links between these processes. Groupware is important in allowing information to be shared between different teams as well as within teams.

4. **"Use a centralized IT function to set enterprise-wide architecture standards."**
   This is important to ensure the adoption of common applications and standards throughout the company to reduce cost, but also to minimize technical problems of incompatibility between applications and promote information exchange throughout the organization.

5. **"Develop a clearly communicated process for integrating new technology into the business."**
   The final point emphasizes the importance of explaining through training why new collaborative technologies are being introduced and developing a plan so that there are no surprises for employees as new technologies are brought in to support processes. A culture can then be established where continuous change is familiar. It is then no surprise as new technologies are introduced to support changing business needs.

Management and monitoring of processes is also important to continuously refine them. Here, too, collaborative systems can help through automatic collection of metrics. The administrative modules of many workflow systems provide a powerful view of how well a process is functioning as is described later in this chapter.

Collaborative Systems Are a Catalyst for Change

In *Reengineering the Corporation*, Hammer and Champy (1993) identify a number of new technologies which are important to BPR, not only in providing a means of supporting processes, but also because they act as catalysts for change within companies. Collaborative systems don't figure as such in this list, but several supporting technologies do, such as tracking technology, decision support tools, telecommunications networks, teleconferencing and shared databases.

Hammer and Champy label these as "disruptive technologies" which can force companies to reconsider their processes and find new ways of operating. This is certainly also true for workflow and groupware systems and it is rare that a company that has the vision to undertake reengineering does not adopt some of the functions available in collaborative systems.

Hammer and Champy give examples of early experiences of reengineering by large companies such as Kodak which used group supported CAD/CAM software to perform concurrent engineering on their products and so slash new product development times. In another business function Ford used the introduction of a software system to reduce the number of staff in their accounts payable unit from 500 to 125.

Redesigning the Process Is More Important Than the Software!

It would be wrong to believe that improved process performance can only be achieved through the introduction of technology. While this will help, it is the fundamental redesign of the processes—the introduction of new ways of working—which is responsible for the greatest improvements. For example, when IBM Credit reengineered their process for financing hardware and software, they effectively moved from a six stage process handled by different staff to a one stage process by retraining and replacing specialists with generalists who performed all the original tasks. The six original stages, each involving different people were:

1. Log credit request

2. Check credit-worthiness via computer system

3. Specify special terms by modifying standard terms in another computer system

4. Price finance terms and set interest rate using spreadsheet

5. Collate information to verify quote

6. Issue quote letter

The new process, involving a single person was:

1. Credit issue

In reducing the number of stages the process was improved from an average of six days to four hours, which was close to the minimum theoretical time of 90 minutes which was recorded when a walk-through of the original process was conducted. Note that it would be possible to use software to help these separate staff collaborate and this would produce gains. However, much more significant gains were achieved by rethinking the process completely. So when introducing groupware and workflow systems, simple automation of existing processes may not give you the best benefit, although it will carry a lower risk than reengineering.

How to Reengineer

Many commentators on BPR, such as Hammer, Champy and Davenport, exhort companies to reengineer, but without giving detailed guidelines on how to achieve this. There is a growing range of literature which describes how to undertake BPR. Figure 2.1 shows Obolensky's recommended stages for reengineering. The first stages are involved with creating a vision for the company at a senior level and then planning the implementation. Then follows the stage of actually doing reengineering which covers activities described in this book such as process analysis, design and implementation. After the reengineered system is up and running, collecting metrics occurs so

Figure 2.1
Stages in Reengineering. Adapted from Obolensky, N. Practical Business Reengineering. *London: Kogan Page*

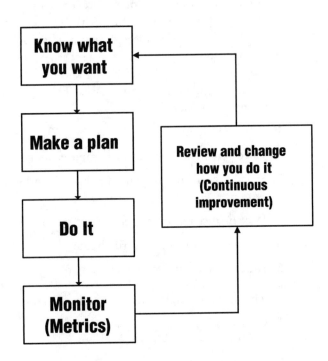

that the processes of the company can be continuously improved to keep up with or be one step ahead of the competition.

Reengineering Methodologies

There is no single well-known methodology for performing a BPR program in the same way that there are different methodologies for developing information systems. Rather than detailed, prescriptive methodologies, each systems integrator or management consultancy tends to have their own stated best practice. One of the better known is the Breakpoint BPR methodology developed by Coopers and Lybrand. It has three phases: Discover, Redesign and Realize:

▶ Phase 1 is the initiation, in which the project vision and communications strategy is developed, processes for redesign are identified and teams are built.

▶ Phase 2 is the redesign, modules are Mobilize, Analyze, Innovate, Engineer and Commit.

▶ Phase 3 is Mobilize, Communicate, Act, Measure and Sustain.

Mobilization of the workforce through promotion and education is important throughout to ensure that the vision and commitment is shared by all company staff. The Breakpoint BPR methodology shares high level similarities with other methodologies in that the major activities usually included are:

1. Development of strategic vision and communication to staff.

2. Development of a BPR or organizational change management plan.

3. Establishing new or revised processes and performance measures.

4. Implementation of improved process systems.

The order in which activities are conducted is open to variation. Some consultancies advise an initial analysis of existing processes or benchmarking before design and creation of new processes. Others say that dwelling on the current situation too much stifles initiative and the analysis should be more forward looking. The box "Ten Steps to Reengineering" shows the typical activities that occur in a reengineering project. Many of these are appropriate for a major implementation of a collaborative system. Of course some activities may not always occur and the sequence varies from case to case.

The Role of Process Metrics in Reengineering

When creating company vision and strategy the objectives of the company are often couched in grand phrases of "being the best" or "delivering world-class

Ten Steps to Reengineering

1. **Initiate BPR program.** Strategy identifies need for change so a project is initiated. The following need to occur:
   - Management buy-in necessary to promote vision, explain need for change to staff and provide continued support
   - Feasibility study and risk analysis to ensure benefits outweigh costs
   - Ensure IS function is integral to change team
   - Establish reengineering team (i.e., director level sponsor and stakeholders for each key process)
   - Appoint project manager and develop schedule

2. **Define scope.** Decide on extent or domain of reengineering ambition. Ask questions such as:
   - Are we going to reengineer or improve (redesign) our existing processes?
   - Where do we establish the boundary to reengineering?
   - If we redesign key processes, which ones and how do we phase them?

3. **Selection and procurement.** Select appropriate technologies and system integrators to assist reengineering (Chapter 6).

4. **Define baseline.** Understand existing processes through documenting and measuring to produce a baseline or "as is" model. Note that some reengineering gurus suggest this process capture stage is not performed by reengineering teams since it will block innovation or "new process thinking."

5. **Benchmark.** Benchmark to comparable "best of breed" organizations. This provides information on how others have updated their processes and also the technologies they are using to support them. Comparisons of your baseline processes may highlight a big gap with best of breed companies.

6. **Establish pilot process or domain.**
   - Identify processes involved (one or many).
   - Identify functional areas involved.
   - Identify users impacted.
   Often the processes with great potential for improvement are also high risk since they are complex, mission critical, probably involve customer contact and service and may be high cost and high visibility. You will need to balance risk against gain.

7. **Process analysis and redesign.** Start detailed process analysis and redesign (Chapter 7).
   - Identify problem processes, perhaps using Pareto analysis.
   - Develop ideas for new processes through brainstorming and more structured group techniques such as nominal group techniques where the alternatives are assessed in a structured way using GDSS such as GroupSystems (Chapter 3).
   - Develop scenarios and use-cases (i.e. activities and players making up processes).
   - Produce a wish list of capabilities for new process and corresponding Business Rules.
   - Rapid organizational prototypes of modified processes should be developed.
   - Possibly simulate new process with software.

8. **Engineer.** Develop new or revised business process through analysis, design and development of supporting information system including integration with legacy systems (Chapters 7 and 8).

9. **Implement.** Integrate new or revised processes into the organization. A change management program should manage organizational change (Chapter 9), reengineering is notorious amongst staff as a threat; this needs to be countered through involvement and education of the benefits of change.

10. **Continuous improvement.** Monitor process through metrics, leading to continuous improvement.

customer service." Moving towards these aims is only possible if you use measures to compare against your own baseline position, or against competitors before reengineering. A wide variety of metrics have been developed and whole books have been written on how to devise and collect them. The aim here is to indicate how different types of metrics may be used in a project which involves the introduction of a collaborative system. Metrics are reviewed from three main perspectives:

▶ High level measures such as critical success factors used to ensure the aims of principal business processes are consistent with corporate objectives

▶ Benchmarking to understand how your company compares with another in the same sector

▶ Detailed metrics describing the efficiency of a process are built into collaborative systems to reduce the cost of collection of metrics and provide managers with easy access to metrics

When to Use Metrics

Metrics can be used at all stages in a reengineering program as shown in Figure 2.2. Initially they can be used to help define the existing processes. They can be used in combination with simulation to choose the best of proposed alternative processes and when the system has been developed, to monitor the business processes so that continuous improvement can occur.

A Role for Simulation?

At an early stage in the project, simulation modeling of processes is particularly useful for workflow systems. This can enable:

▶ Choice between alternative processes

▶ Assessment of the effectiveness and optimization of an improved process

▶ Reduced disruption during implementation

▶ Reduced cost compared to building and evaluating alternatives

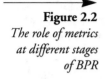

Figure 2.2
*The role of metrics
at different stages
of BPR*

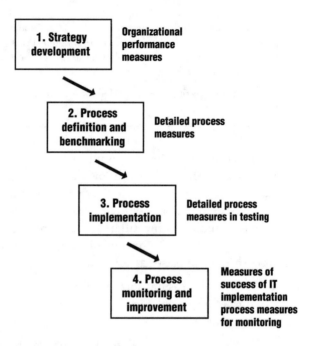

Simulation for workflow systems using products such as Metasoftware's Workflow Analyzer are covered further in Chapter 7.

High Level Measures—Critical Success Factors

Critical success factors (CSFs) are frequently used by companies to ensure that their key processes are delivering the objectives of the strategic business plan. A CSF will usually have an associated key indicator which allows it to be measured. Typical CSFs based on key performance indicators could include:

▶ Improve customer satisfaction index by 50%

▶ Reduce errors by 80%

▶ Reduce process management overheads by 100%

▶ Increase business unit profits by 10%

Table 2.1 is an example of how a real estate agency identified qualitative CSFs which were related to key business processes and how functions of a workflow system were specified to help achieve the CSFs. In this way CSFs can provide a straightforward method for ensuring that your collaborative system is linked to your strategic objectives.

Table 2.1 *Critical Success Factors for a real estate business and how revised business processes are achieved through a workflow system (Chaffey, 1996)*

CSF	Achieve through	Workflow system to assist through	Business process
Achieve inspections (viewings)	Attracting vendor for valuation of property	Illustrating efficiency of business (workflow, status indicators). Larger number of applicants will see property	Obtain listing
Market property to ensure offers received and accepted	Attracting applicant to branch, viewing properties	Workflow component to prompt negotiators to perform marketing activities and update vendors according to status	Market property
Achieve completion revenue	Controlling progress to completion	Workflow component to prompt negotiators to check with all parties involved in sale	Facilitate sale
Improve perfor-mance of sales staff	Personal characteristics	System to be used as a sales tool and promote collaboration between staff	All above processes
Managers to ensure that CSFs are achieved	Business and management skills	Monitoring of staff workflow Monitoring of branch performance by reports	Manage process

Benchmarking

Benchmarking is used to compare a company's process performance with others in its field of operation, typically compared with "best of breed." Benchmarking can work at two levels. First, it can be used to compare processes which are common to similar companies. Thus a tourism services company can compare how it selects the best holiday deal for a customer. Benchmarking uses metrics such as customer service levels, productivity and cycle times to compare processes. Lessons can then be learned by developing best practices through considering how processes are performed differently in the higher achieving company.

Second, benchmarking can be used to compare the performance of the information systems and also how they are developed and supported. Companies can best compare collaborative systems in terms of their speed of processing customer-related tasks such as dealing with a complaint.

Detailed Process Metrics

Metrics are important within BPR since only through these can we establish whether the hoped for improvements have been achieved and monitor how future improvements occur through time. They are significant within the context of this book since metrics can be usefully built into collaborative software to reduce the cost of their collection. This has the added benefit that they will then also have a high visibility with end users and managers using them to support their daily activities and measure their own performance. More detailed measures reflect the detailed performance of business processes and the "actors"—the people doing the work, the software and hardware. With workflow software these are often transaction based, for example:

▶ the number of bank customers handled per hour by an operator in a call center

▶ the number of seconds it takes to retrieve their personal details

▶ total time taken to complete a case

Such detail is obviously of importance in improving customer service. When using workflow systems another common metric is the length of the workflow queue of outstanding tasks. In my experience staff react positively to this and like to try clear the queue as far as possible by the end of the day.

There are no well established classifications of the types of business metrics used in reengineering—various terms are used. Table 2.2 summarizes some of the terms for different types of metrics that are found. Measures can occur at the company or process level and may be internal to the process or external if they describe its outputs—there are often overlaps between the types of metrics shown in the table.

Table 2.2 *Different types of metrics*

Metric	Notes	Examples
Organizational performance measures	These are "external" metrics which measure the outputs of businesses processes often using financial measures	Turnover, profitability, market share and customer satisfaction
Process performance measures	May include organizational measures at process level. These will include "internal" or diagnostic measures to monitor the process itself	Lead-time, profitability of process

Table 2.2 *Different types of metrics (continued)*

Metric	Notes	Examples
Critical Success Factors	Refer to organizational measures or processes	Customer service index and Employee satisfaction
Defect based metrics	Number of failures in a set period of time. Transactions between customers and suppliers can be measured as successful (on time) or unsuccessful (late). Through reengineering and continuous improvement the proportion of defects can be reduced.	Customer complaints or number of cases that are not processed within the target time
Project based metrics	Measure success of project through indicating whether the project is delivered on time or within budget	% of budget % of time
Quality metrics	These are based on Quality programs	Quality gap—SERVPERF SPC control charts Quality Function Deployment (relate customer quality to engineering factors)
Integrated metrics	See section below	Balanced scorecards

Balanced Scorecards

Many companies have metric collection programs separately covering the key dimensions of cost, time, quality and customer satisfaction. Integrated metrics such as the balanced scorecard have only become widely used recently.

The balanced scorecard, popularized in a *Harvard Business Review* article by Kaplan and Norton (1992) is intended to translate a reengineering vision and strategy into specific objectives. They use financial data, operational measures such as customer satisfaction, performance of internal processes and also the organization's innovation and improvement activities (indicators of future financial performance). The scorecard is structured in four main areas:

▶ **Customer concerns.** These include time (lead time, time to quote, etc.), quality, performance, service and cost.

▶ **Internal measures** (time, volume). Internal measures should stem from the business processes that have the greatest impact on customer satisfaction: cycle time, quality, employee skills and productivity. Companies should also identify critical core competencies and try to guarantee market leadership.

▶ **Financial measures**

▶ **Learning and growth: Innovation.** Innovation can be measured by change in value through time (employee value, shareholder value, percentage and value of sales from products less than x years old).

Workflow systems are particularly good at capturing metrics in the first two areas.

Collecting SMART Metrics

Many companies do not include metrics collection other than basic financial measures as part of their business operation before reengineering. With reengineering and total quality management programs a culture of metrics is usually fostered. However, with newly adopted metrics programs many problems can develop. Jeff Hiatt of the ProSci consultancy and Nick Obolensky suggest the widely used mnemonic SMART to advise clients on developing metrics, i.e. metrics must be:

⇨ Specific
  ⇨ Measurable
    ⇨ Actionable
      ⇨ Relevant
        ⇨ Timely

They advise starting with external measures initially, such as customer satisfaction, and then moving to detailed internal diagnostic measures.

Using SMART metrics avoids the following types of problems:

1. Developing metrics for which you cannot collect accurate or complete data.

2. Developing metrics that measure the right thing, but cause people to act in a way contrary to the best interest of the business to simply "make their numbers."

3. Developing so many metrics that you create excessive overhead and red tape.

4. Developing metrics that are complex and difficult to explain to others.

Web reference: http://www.prosci.com. Contains detailed resources on methods of BPR.

Metrics and Collaborative Systems

Metrics should be considered carefully when analyzing and designing collaborative systems since they provide an automated way of collection. If metrics are collected manually this can be disruptive and time-consuming. Metrics that are collected in this way are sometimes known as "virtual metrics." The following types of metrics can all be generated from a workflow system or can be used earlier to compare candidate processes.

▶ Time—cycle time

▶ Volume—throughput, materials usage

▶ Cost—derived from volume measures

▶ Complexity (based on process definitions)

▶ Number of sub-processes

▶ Number of alternative routes and number of hand-offs

▶ Length of shortest route

▶ Quality

The types of information metrics monitored by collaborative systems is well illustrated by the output available from the metrics module of the workflow product Staffware. This module groups metrics in the following types of areas:

1. What is our staff working on?

This shows the number of tasks each staff member is working on (number of outstanding or aged items on work queue).

2. What has been achieved?

This shows for each worker or type of worker how far the cases on the workflow have progressed—the proportion that have been started, been released to another worker or withdrawn.

3. Are we meeting our service levels?

Length of time to achieve certain stages in the overall process. This is illustrated in Figure 2.3.

4. What happened to this case?

This shows the time taken for each of the sub-processes.

As well as internal metrics looking at how well the workflow assisted processes are performing, external metrics are also required. A customer

Figure 2.3
Customer service level metrics for complaints handling in a workflow application using Staffware

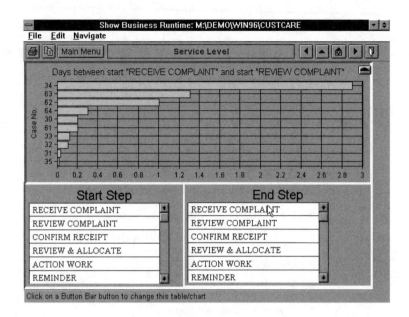

satisfaction index indicating their perceived level of service can be recorded regularly through conducting regular interviews or questionnaires with customers. Open questions asking about the process may highlight where the customer is experiencing delays or is not getting the information they need. The employees should not be neglected either. The effect of the system on their motivation and morale should be established to help make future improvements. These types of metrics cannot be directly recorded by collaborative systems, but could be input to a workflow system to be used alongside the other metrics.

Some Problems of Reengineering— Why Do 70% of Implementations Fail?

Despite the potential benefits of BPR, there are many problems that can and often do occur which may cause the reengineering effort to fail. Reasons for failure include:

▶ Lack of support from the top and an inability of senior management to maintain commitment

▶ Selecting the wrong scope for reengineering such as reengineering everything without piloting less critical processes first or reengineering non-critical, adequate processes

▶ Failure of implementation due to poor project management, insufficient resources or change management skills

▶ Failure of implementation due to technical difficulties such as failure to integrate systems, lack of methodology, inadequate performance or insufficient testing

While some of the best known reasons for failure are lack of management commitment or poor project management, technical problems are also important. The remaining chapters look at the technical decisions which must be made at different stages of the project and attempt to ensure that these type of mistakes are guarded against. The next section introduces these chapters.

Since many managers are wary of the returns IT can bring, there are also examples of IT being underused in BPR programs or the IT department being excluded from the redesign team because they are not directly involved in any of the processes. Given this and the high failure rate of BPR programs these guidelines for implementation from Davenport (1993) are useful:

▶ Recognize that IT is only part of the solution: it allows managers to collect, store, analyze, communicate and distribute information better.

▶ Cut and paste the IT tools needed, i.e. don't use tools from a single vendor, but use "best of breed."

▶ Bring in internal or external IT experts: their knowledge, skills, acumen and experience are invaluable.

▶ After implementation, continually monitor IT performance and keep up with new IT developments.

Stages in Developing Collaborative Systems

The major activities involved in developing a typical collaborative system are similar to any software development project. These well known stages from inception through analysis and design to build are shown in Figure 2.4.

Of course, in the real world the picture is a lot more complicated than this since when requirements change, which is sure to happen as feedback on prototypes occurs, we will need to start again at the top of the waterfall and repeat the analysis, design and build (code, test and review). This iteration occurs as initial prototypes are built for different functions or modules of the system, then reviewed, and redesigned and reimplemented in line with the new requirements of the end users.

Figure 2.4
*The waterfall
model of systems
development*

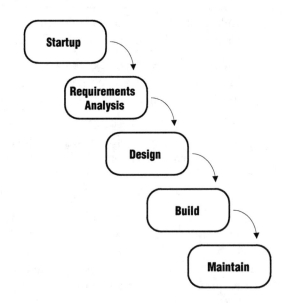

Figure 2.5 gives an idea of what really happens on a project. Here, following initial analysis, a framework for the overall application will be built into which the different modules of the system can be plugged as they are developed. The application framework and each of the modules will go through several iterations of prototyping in the analysis-design-code-review cycle.

Figure 2.5
*What really
happens—an
iterative software
development model*

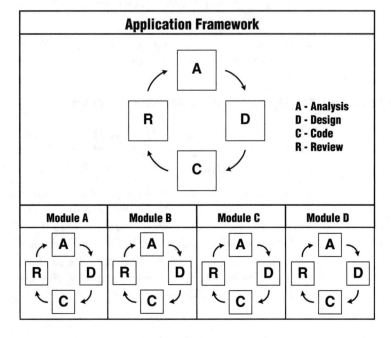

Chapter 9 gives further details on how prototyping is used in rapid applications development (RAD). Following testing and review, the cycle will be started again until the component is complete. Early versions of each module may be reviewed separately, but as they evolve they will need to be tested for integration with other parts of the system. Given that each of the modules is probably being developed independently by a different programmer or team, this makes synchronization of intermediate builds difficult, so clear objectives must be stated for each module, namely the target date for the integration build and which features must be completed for this build. For a workflow system typical modules or activities that might be developed separately but would need to be available together for a user review are:

▶ process definition module

▶ work management module—activity completion screen

▶ administration module

▶ workflow engine

A similar view of software development is given by the spiral model proposed by Barry Boehm in 1988. This is a risk based model where each cycle in the spiral addresses the stages of analysis, design, code and review for the different modules of the product. Each cycle in the spiral involves the identification of objectives, constraints and risk factors and methods of how to minimize them. At each stage there is a review to ensure that all parties are committed to the next phase.

Despite the complex nature of development, the activities of each stage of the waterfall do all still occur and provide a sensible framework for looking and the methods and pitfalls for developing collaborative software. Chapter 6 looks at important decisions in the early stages of the project such as do we build a new system or do we use a pre-existing tool, and if so which one do we choose? Chapter 7 concentrates on how to perform process analysis for workflow systems. Chapter 8 considers design issues such as security and the user interface. Finally, Chapter 9 looks at development and deployment.

The aim is not to provide comprehensive coverage of what needs to happen at each stage in the development project, that is the role of a book on project management. Rather, it is to highlight which issues are important to the development of groupware and workflow systems.

3

Groupware Functions and Applications

Groupware is software for teamwork. Groupware works because it aids communication in a company and helps staff work together on joint tasks. It also equips them with the information needed to complete their work and can help decision making. Groupware has grown to cover a vast range of potential applications. This growth has occurred with the availability of lower cost networks such as intranets within and between businesses providing the infrastructure for improved communication.

Groupware assists teams of people to work together because it provides key group functions; the "three Cs" of communication, collaboration and coordination:

▶ **Communication** is the core groupware feature which allows information to be shared or sent to others using electronic mail. Groupware for conferencing is sometimes known as *computer mediated communication* (CMC) software.

▶ **Collaboration** is the act of joint co-operation in solving a business problem, or undertaking a task. Groupware may reduce some of the problems of traditional meetings such as: finding a place and a time to meet, a lack of available information or even dominance by one forceful individual in a meeting. Groupware improves the efficiency of decision making and its effectiveness by encouraging contributions from all group members.

▶ **Coordination** is the act of making sure that a team is working effectively and meeting its goals. This includes distributing tasks to team members, reviewing their performance or perhaps steering an electronic meeting.

So groupware helps communication, collaboration and coordination within a business, but which specific functions can it be used for? The key groupware functions of Table 3.1 are usually present in groupware applications to help teams collaborate. Functions 1 through 6 are considered in this chapter. Functions 7 and 8 are considered in Chapter 4.

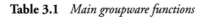

Table 3.1 *Main groupware functions*

Groupware function	Application	Notes
1. E-mail and messaging	E-mail, electronic forms processing	Original groupware function
2. Document management and information sharing	Improved information dissemination	Main use of company intranets currently
3. Collaborative authoring	Team development of documents	Annotation, revision marking and version control are key
4. Conferencing	Text conferencing, video-conferencing, whiteboarding	Relates to electronic meeting support functions
5. Time management	Calendar and group scheduling	
6. Groupware management and decision support	Remote and distributed access facilities including replication and access control	Functions used for managing other functions. Covered in Chapter 8
7. Ad hoc workflow	Loosely coupled collaboration	Covered in Chapter 4
8. Structured workflow	Structured management of tasks	Covered in Chapter 4

In This Chapter

Chapter 3 introduces different uses of groupware in business and looks at the different categories of groupware and the functions provided. The different types of groupware in Table 3.1 are reviewed in turn. The standards which are needed to help integrate different software within a business are also covered. This chapter is supplemented by Chapter 6 in which important factors in selection of groupware tools are considered. In Chapter 6 the features of alternative e-mail and groupware packages such as Lotus Notes, Microsoft Exchange and Novell Groupwise are compared.

The Standards Game

To help people work together, standards are vital since different people in different parts of a company, or in different companies, are often using different groupware packages. To build systems which interoperate, systems integrators are continually chasing new standards as they are proposed. To help understand how the messaging standards fit together is crucial when selecting and building systems, and these are described in reasonable (but not tedious) detail in this chapter. The importance of standards is indicated by the more recent rapid adoption of group functions through intranets which has been enabled by the Internet standards.

Types of Groupware Applications

Although the functions of Table 3.1 are available in specific groupware packages such as Lotus Notes and Microsoft Exchange, increasingly general applications such as word processors and spreadsheets have added groupware features. As explained in Chapter 1, applications were traditionally centered around a single user until the early 1990s. With maturity, however, the sophistication of such software has increased and it has become rich in functions for teamwork.

A good example of this is the once humble word processor which was limited to use by single authors. Today the latest offerings from Microsoft, Lotus and Corel all have facilities for teams of people to jointly review and annotate documents, e-mail integration and web access. Table 3.2 shows the way group working functions are incorporated into different types of software. Some groupware applications just provide one function such as e-mail or conferencing, whereas others, such as Lotus Notes, aim to provide a range of functions.

Table 3.2 *Groupware functions in different types of software*

Type of software	Functions available	Examples
1. Single function groupware application	E-mail applications, Text based conferencing, Document sharing	BeyondMail, Eudora, FirstClass, Telefinder
2. Multifunction groupware application	All of above	Lotus Notes Microsoft Exchange Novell Groupwise
3. General applications software, "Office" applications	Word processors, spreadsheets with e-mail and collaborative authoring features	Microsoft Word, Excel, Lotus WordPro, Corel WordPerfect
4. Web browser software	E-mail, news conferencing, as standard (with plug-ins and Java applets for other functions)	Netscape Navigator, Microsoft Explorer and Net Meeting
5. Operating System	Bundled applications or incorporated into O/S	Windows 98 and Outlook

The diversity of groupware functions and applications leads to the partly academic problem of where you draw the boundary of groupware—where does groupware end and other types of software begin? Increasingly, the answer is that there is no boundary as applications from word processors to web browsers to vertical market applications such as manufacturing systems are providing group functions.

Classifications of Groupware

A commonly applied division of groupware is based on where, when and how it is used. The "where" can either be defined as in the same location (effectively in the same workgroup) or alternatively, a different location in another office, whether on the same company site or the other side of the world. The "when" refers to groupware assisting communication either on a real time basis (synchronous) or when events are more protracted with coworkers responding to messages at a later time (asynchronous).

Figure 3.1 shows a classification of groupware in time and space. Here, the four quadrants are a common starting point for describing how groupware can be used and we talk of same time, different place for video-conferencing and different time, different place for e-mail software. Examples of synchronous or same time use of groupware include electronic meeting software such as a whiteboarding tool for recording the main ideas and actions of a meeting.

Figure 3.1
Groupware support for different business situations

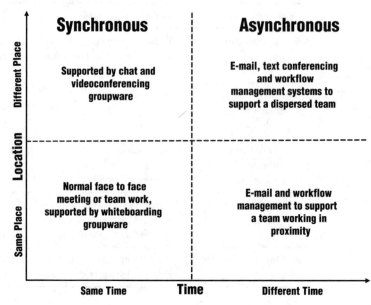

Conversely, e-mail software or discussion threads are typically asynchronous, with a response to a query being dispatched at a later time. By providing a range of options in time and space for communication and collaboration, groupware has been effective in giving businesses a new capability—it enables a team to function when people are not available to meet at the same time and place. Many of the functions of groupware such as replication and access control features are important in making updated information available and secure on distributed servers in different locations in an organization.

An alternative way of looking at groupware is to consider *how* groupware is used. When using groupware, users may be working directly on a *common task* such as reviewing a document or they may perform a *different task*. An example of groupware being used to perform different tasks as part of a larger task is authorizing a purchase requisition. The overall goal of purchasing a new item in the company is similar, but the detailed task such as specifying the item, authorizing it or arranging the purchase is accomplished by different people.

A further way of describing types of groupware is whether the environment is shared by coworkers. This would be the case with real time conferencing software such as a whiteboard, but would not be the case with an e-mail package.

Perhaps because of the wide range of the applications it can support, groupware suffers from many different names. These sometimes originate from an academic setting, and although accurate, this is only achieved at the expense of brevity! Such terms include *Computer Mediated Communications* (CMC) and *Computer Supported Cooperative Work* (CSCW). Since you probably agree that these are quite a mouthful, my preference, which is used throughout the book, is for *collaborative software* or *groupware*.

Groupware Function: E-mail

In many ways electronic mail is the most successful of the groupware tools, certainly in terms of volume—it is currently used by 75 million world wide. In fact, one of the main reasons for the introduction of the corporate networks which have enabled group working was to get everyone connected with e-mail. Electronic mail has become so prevalent that you may say it really needs no introduction. However, there are degrees of sophistication in which e-mail can be used, and many potential problems with its implementation, that are worth guarding against. We focus on these during this coverage.

E-mail works well in offices because it is a more rapid replacement for a well established way of passing memos and messages between staff. Like voice mail it doesn't rely on the person you need to talk to being available. It offers a number of advantages over traditional mail: it is faster to send and faster to receive; collections are instantaneous, not twice daily. It is also faster to review and then reply. These advantages of speed in decision making translate to cost savings for companies using e-mail.

E-mail Features and Functions

E-mail shares many terms with traditional mail and this is one reason for its widespread use. We talk about in- and out-boxes, post offices, collection and delivery. As with postal mail we must have features available to create, compose, address, send and receive mail. In the client application the user has an in-box giving a list of mail received from others with details of who sent it and when, a priority and a summary of the contents. Messages sent can also be reviewed in the out-box to see who has not replied. Figure 1.1 is an example of a typical mail client which features three panes. On the left is a tree of folders containing messages, on the right a list of the messages in each folder and below the contents of the highlighted message. Both messages received and sent can be deleted, when they have been acted on. To send e-mail, a form is available where the user composes their own message and can assign a priority and add attachments. Attachments are a handy feature of mail which enable users to send documents or data to other users to work on. So a sales manager might ask a sales team to submit their weekly sales figures as data typed into a spreadsheet template or an electronic form. How easy this feature is to use is important in selecting an e-mail package. It should be possible to view mail received in a number of ways according to different attributes of the mail, such as by date, person, size or category.

Addressing

The mail address of the recipient is normally selectable from an address book. In some basic packages, such as those included with web browsers, individual users will have to set these up manually. However, for corporate packages it is important that an address list for all members of the company is automatically available.

Dealing with Old Messages—Archive, Archive, Archive!

It is good practice to save mail for reference to different *folders* such as marketing, finance or personal. Most packages now provide this feature. Saving e-mail permanently is also important if you want traceability of company information down the line. I know of one business who had a "million-dollar e-mail" which had to be traced to resolve a dispute with a vendor. Increasingly, information contained in e-mail is used to obtain legal redress. In the UK, in 1997 a court found against finance company Norwich Union when a competitor's financial performance was devalued in an internal staff e-mail. The award for damages was over $700,000.

Given that e-mail may well need to be traced in the future it is important that e-mail be archived by system administrators and cannot be removed from company systems by end users. The move to Internet based e-mail using POP3 clients (see below for a definition) is a dangerous trend here. POP3 clients such as those provided with web browsers can be configured to remove messages stored on the POP3 mail server. The message may then reside on the user's hard drive or it could be deleted from here also.

The distinction should be drawn between deleting messages, when they will no longer be available (unless restored from an earlier backup) or archiving, when they will be accessible. Sometimes so-called archived mail is stored as text files created by the user on the hard drive. Better systems have a structured means of reviewing the archived messages to aid retrieval.

There are two approaches to deleting e-mail. One is the "I'm an important person, I have the most messages in the company displayed" and the other is "I'm real efficient and only have messages from the last day displayed." Users in the first category should be educated to act more promptly on messages and archive them to reduce the build-up of messages on the server, which can be a major problem of e-mail usage for the mail administrator. Similarly, traditionalists who insist on printing out every message to justify their actions should also be trained in the use of the archiving facilities.

Guidelines for implementation and maintenance of a mail system are given in Chapter 9. This also examines the "flame-mail phenomenon" where the ease of criticizing others causes problems since people write what they wouldn't dare say face-to-face.

E-mail Features for Power Users

Since e-mail is a deceptively easy tool to understand, users are often not trained in its use. This is unfortunate since there are a number of less accessible features available to the user to increase the efficiency of their work and the company.

▶ **Document attachments** are used routinely, but a lot of documents are still transferred by post or on disk because this feature is unknown or difficult to find, or because the e-mail client does not handle standards for attachments such as Multipurpose Internet Mail Extension (MIME) (see the later section on standards).

▶ **Notification** is a very useful, but rarely used option. This indicates whether a message you sent has been received or opened after it is sent. This allows the power user to use e-mail more effectively—they will know if an e-mail message has been opened, but not acted upon. In this case they can send a follow up e-mail to chase the action or even use the phone! This feature is easier to implement on local area networks using a single mail package. It is not usually possible when using Internet mail between different types of mail systems.

▶ **Group broadcasting** can be used to quickly mail a group of people such as a project team. It should be straightforward to set up groups of other users who you commonly send e-mail to. Using this technique it is possible to "broadcast" a message to all members of a team such as a weekly progress report. This tool is a neat solution to help increase information flow within a company; managers can mail all staff in the department or whole company regularly with company news. It is of course necessary to be able to re-use these groups to avoid having to multiply address each mail each time.

▶ **Security.** If the security of a message is important, some systems such as Notes mail have facilities to encrypt mail and also to provide a digital signature or key. Messages encoded in this way may only be read by people who possess the correct keys. Pretty Good Privacy (PGP) is a freely available program developed by Phil Zimmerman which offers encryption and digital signatures using the private and public key technique. This can be integrated with other mail packages such as Eudora.

Web reference: http://web.mit.edu/network/pgp.html

▶ **Agents.** Agents, wizards or rules give the power user tools to automate administration tasks and save time. For example, Beyond Mail has a rules based feature called Message Minder which places incoming messages in a particular folder. In the example shown in Figure 3.2, when a new request form such as a purchase requisition arrives, it is automatically placed in the request folder to help the user manage the many messages they receive. Other applications could include the following:

• You can route e-mails to different in-boxes or category folders such as sales, or finance according to the sender's address or keywords contained within the message

• Similarly an agent could automatically detect and delete junk e-mail from a particular address or containing a certain phrase

• Delete or archive e-mail after it has been on the system for a length of time

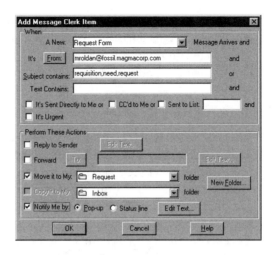

Figure 3.2
Beyond Mail rule based dialog to automatically place a request form message in a request folder

What Types of E-mail Packages Are Available and Who Is Using Them?

In the beginning, e-mail was available in standalone packages with no other group functionality. The most popular standalone packages used were cc:Mail from Lotus and Microsoft mail on the PC and standard mail tools for Macintosh, UNIX and mainframe users. Enterprise systems running on a mainframe may use SNA Distributed Services or PROFS, the IBM Professional Office System. VAXmail is still used in the DEC environment.

Today e-mail is often integrated as a feature of the operating system (Windows 98) or part of a groupware package such as Microsoft Exchange and Outlook or Lotus Notes. The publication of e-mail APIs has also made it straightforward to build e-mail into other applications such as spreadsheets. This does not mean that the standalone e-mail package is dead. Today, Lotus estimates that there are more than 13 million cc:Mail users, making it the most popular e-mail package on the market.

The standalone e-mail packages have also evolved such that they support filling in of forms such as a purchase requisition. This has extended their use to simple office automation tasks. There are now many forms packages with this type of functionality such as Beyond Mail from Banyan Systems. These applications may have standard forms to perhaps record a phone message or submit hours worked each week on different accounts. If your needs are not met by standard forms you should check the ability to tailor forms. This will usually require simple programming skills.

With the rise in popularity of Web browsers such as Netscape Navigator and Explorer, e-mail has also become available through these clients. Netscape claimed in late 1996 that their package had 12 million e-mail users, making it one of the most popular on the planet.

E-mail Infrastructure Requirements

So what is involved in setting up e-mail? E-mail works within the standard client/server framework detailed in Chapter 8. The way in which the services are partitioned between the client and the server is shown in Figure 3.3. Mail transport is controlled from the server with a post-office module managing the dispatch and receipt of e-mail. The server will also have a directory service giving a list of potential e-mail recipients within the organization. E-mail may be sent over the internal company network or may be sent to other companies via the Internet or leased lines. A list of all incoming and outgoing messages is also stored on the server. The client application has facilities for reading the mail received and sent by an individual and also composing messages to other users which are then sent via the post office. Services available on the server can be summarized as follows:

► Directory services provide a lookup table to allow routing of e-mail to the correct address.

► Different transport service standards such as X.400.

► A message store contains all messages currently available on the system, both read and unread together with their attachments.

The client/server infrastructure is based on the *Open Systems Interconnection* (OSI) model. This defines a layered model which enables servers to communicate with other servers and clients. The seven layers of the OSI model are:

► **Application.** Directory services and message handling services are included at this level.

► **Presentation.** These protocols are usually part of the operating system.

► **Session.** This includes data transfer protocols such as SMTP and FTP.

► **Transport.** This layer ensures the integrity of data transmitted. Examples include the Internet Transmission Control Protocol and Novell SPX.

► **Network.** Defines protocols for opening and maintaining links between servers. The best known are the Internet IP protocol and Novell IPX.

► **Data-link.** Defines the rules for sending and receiving information.

► **Physical layer.** Low level description of physical transmission methods.

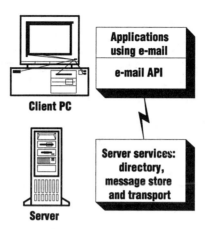

Figure 3.3
*A client/server
e-mail architecture*

Together these layers form a "protocol stack." Before messages are sent as packets around a network, information related to each layer is added to the packet. The e-mail standards described in the next section usually relate to the higher levels in the protocol stack.

Messaging Methods

E-mail and messaging are similar in that they operate with an asynchronous, "store and forward" method. Store and forward is used since when a message is received by the server, the packets may not be in sequence. As they arrive they are placed in order—stored, and then forwarded. A different form of storage and forwarding may also occur if the communications links are not continuously available, as in the example of a company that distributes Internet mail from its post office twice daily.

Integrating Mail Systems—The Importance of Standards

With enterprise e-mail there will often be different mail systems in different offices in different countries. Since each e-mail system has its own standards for addressing, format of message and transport method, tools and standards are required to allow the mail messages to be read transparently by different mail systems. Understanding these Internet based standards and knowing what is available in different products is clearly important when selecting products.

We will look at the different types of mail standard that are important using the categorization used by the *Internet Mail Consortium* (IMC). This is useful to provide a framework for the large number of standards in this area. "Host" in the following descriptions is analogous to "mail-server."

Web reference: http://www.img.org. Internet Mail Consortium (IMC)

Web reference: http://www.ips.id.ethz.ch/~parish/standard.html. This reference gives a source page for all important communications standards.

Directory Services

Directories act as an index of user names and devices accessible on networks. As such they are critical to a company to ensure that different users can be contacted easily using an electronic "white pages." Addresses of other network resources such as printers and servers are also listed in the directory service.

Domain Name System (DNS)

An important directory standard on the Internet and local TCP/IP networks is the Domain Name System or service referred to as DNS. A DNS is used to map the TCP/IP network address of a server such as 207.68.156.58 to a better known form such as www.microsoft.com. The DNS is hierarchical as follows:

1. Top level domain. These are sometimes referred to as "Generic TLDs" or GTLDs. The most widely used top level domain is .com. It is registered by over a million companies. It indicates a commercial organization, particularly one based in the US. Other categories include .gov, .org and .edu. Elsewhere, the top level domain indicates the country name such as .ca for Canada, or .co.uk for a British company.

2. Second level domain. This refers to the company name and is sometimes referred to as the enterprise name, for example ibm.com or novell.com.

3. Third level or sub-enterprise domain. The third level domain name can be used to refer to an individual server in an organization such as support.novell.com.

The lookup system for locating servers in the DNS is usually stored on a location server, but a local hosts file can be used for lookups on the client.

The DNS naming convention is used for Internet web and e-mail addresses which are in this well known form:

Name@hostname.organization(.com, .org, .edu, etc.) e.g. Dave.Chaffey@company.com

Netware Directory Service (NDS)

The tens of millions of Novell Netware users may use the Netware Directory Services (NDS) version of DNS. This is likely to be replaced in the future by the two X.500 based directories described next.

Active Directory Service (ADS)

Active Directory in Microsoft Windows NT version 5.0 will compete with NDS. This includes support for Internet based Domain Name Services such as the lightweight directory access protocol (LDAP) that is described below. It will give a single point of administration for a range of resources such as files, peripheral devices, host connections, databases and not least users.

X.500

This directory service is promoted by the CCITT (Consultative Committee for International Telegraph and Telephone) to operate with X.400 and other MHS. X.500 provides a lookup of names and addresses through the DIB or Directory Information Base. Each object stored in the DIB is organized into a hierarchy with user or common name objects nested within organization unit objects such as the finance department, which are in turn nested in organization objects (Figure 3.4). Individuals include both people and resources such as shared printers or storage devices. Although the hierarchy was intended to be easy to use by end users with familiar, recognizable objects, this has not been achieved because the naming convention is not easy to grasp. Another problem with X.500 is that the directory access protocol (DAP) used on the client was quite cumbersome. This led to the suggestion of LDAP by the University of Michigan.

Figure 3.4
Structure of X.500 hierarchy

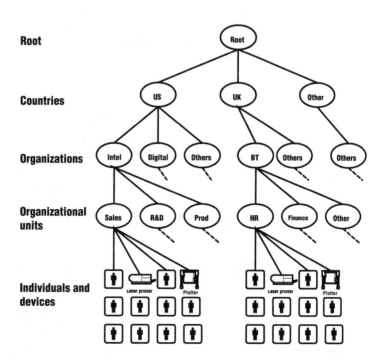

LDAP (Lightweight Directory Access Protocol)

LDAP is an Internet based method for locating users and resources on your network. It integrates with similar X.500 directory services. It is based on a similar hierarchy, but is implemented as a simpler and faster client protocol. It loses some features compared to X.500, thus the somewhat derogatory term lightweight.

It has the benefit that unlike X.500 directory entries it can be translated to the familiar address form of <name>@<host>.<domain-type>. LDAP was actively promoted by Netscape and has since been adopted by the major messaging vendors referred to in Chapter 6. Such a "white pages" directory is particularly important for large companies with users across several sites.

Web reference: http://home.netscape.com/newsref/ref/ldap.html
(a detailed description of LDAP)

Client-to-Host Communication (POP3 and IMAP4)

POP3 (Post Office Protocol) and IMAP4 (Internet Message Access Protocol) both define methods for e-mail clients to retrieve messages from a server on a TCP/IP network. POP is the earlier method, still widely used, which downloads messages from the mail server when connected. Management of these messages is then performed by the client end. Here, the burden tends to be on end users to manage their messages, rather than this being a central process. A further problem with this model is that a mobile or home user operating via a modem has to download whole messages, attachments, etc. to find out whether the information is worth downloading. Being able to query the headers, or MIME contents only, would be more efficient.

The more recent IMAP4 standard offers a server querying model more like that of the proprietary packages such as cc:mail or MS Mail. It can also operate in an offline mode similar to POP. IMAP has a further advantage over POP in that it is designed to assist sharing of mail and Usenet news articles. This is achieved by setting up shared mailboxes on the server and client. The profile of IMAP is set to increase, as it is a strand of Netscape Open Network Environment strategy and is supported in Netscape Mail server and newer versions of Groupwise, Exchange and Notes.

Host-to-Host Mail Transfer

SMTP (The Internet Simple Mail Transfer Protocol)

SMTP is the Internet e-mail standard used to enable delivery of a message between servers connected to the Internet. This could allow, for example, interoperability between a wide range of systems such as Windows NT or a

Netware based PC server and a UNIX server or a mainframe. All that is required is that the server is connected to the Internet and that it has a suitable SMTP gateway product to convert from the host mail system such as cc:Mail to the SMTP standard.

The SMTP protocol involves an SMTP server establishing a two-way transmission channel with a receiving server. The receiver may be either the ultimate destination or can be an intermediate server. Once the transmission channel is established, the SMTP sender sends a MAIL command indicating the sender of the mail. If the receiver can accept mail it responds with an OK reply. The SMTP sender then sends a RCPT command identifying the recipient of the mail. If accepted, the sender sends the mail data.

Basic Message Format and Encoding

An example header produced for an SMTP based mail messages is as follows:

From: "M MMAN <mmann@bmt.waiariki.ac.nz>

Organization: Waiariki Polytechnic Rotorua N.Z.

To: Sal Brockbank <sal.brockbank@zetnet.co.uk>

Date: Fri, 24 Jan 1997 07:55:25 GMT+1300

MIME-Version: 1.0

Content-type: text/plain; charset>US-ASCII

Content-transfer-encoding: 7BIT

Subject: Re: Tourism and Developing Countries: editorial queries batch 1

Reply-to: MMANN@bmt.waiariki.ac.nz

Priority: normal

X-mailer: Pegasus Mail for Windows (v2.42a)

Message-ID: <193BF763348@bmt.waiariki.ac.nz>

Standards for Embedded Documents—MIME and UUE

Within an SMTP message header the type of coding used for text and any embedded documents will be specified. The two most common standards for transferring attached documents or multimedia are the multipurpose Internet mail extension known as MIME and UU encoding. These are now supported by most e-mail systems, as well as standard document filters for different word processor formats.

Message Encryption and Authentication (S/MIME)

As well as PGP a more recent development is a proposed extension to MIME known as S/MIME which has a new security model including digital certificates. Details can be obtained from RSA, one of the promoters of this standard.

Web reference: http://www.rsa.com.

Gateways to Non-Internet Mail

Gateway Standards and Message Handling Services

There are two basic options for integration of different mail systems within a company. The first is the gateway approach. Here an e-mail gateway product is purchased and installed on a server to enable two-way translation of formats from one e-mail standard to another.

This approach is widely used, but can be unwieldy if several different e-mail products are involved as each will require a different gateway product. However, an alternative approach is available—that of switch based backbone. This is a more flexible distributed model. The backbone consists of several interlinked servers which are typically linked by X.400. Each switch then performs the conversions.

Netware Global Message Handling Service (GMHS)

This gateway standard is based on the established Message Handling Service (MHS) for Novell based LANs. It can operate on a dedicated server or as a Netware Loadable Module (NLM). MHS supports a *Standard Message Format* (SMF). MHS can also be used for applications other than e-mail such as *Electronic Data Interchange* (EDI) and Fax. It uses a "store and forward" model.

X.400

X.400 was defined by the CCITT (now the ITU's Telecommunications Standardization Sector, ITU-TSS). This MHS provides a standard for a range of platforms. Services defined in this standard include:

▶ a directory service for looking up user names and addresses

▶ a message transfer agent (MTA)

▶ a message store for messages that cannot be delivered directly because they are offline

▶ a "user agent" for client services such as compose and read—this will usually be provided by a standard application such as Unix Mail

To allow the enterprise to operate e-mail, *middleware* standards are important in several areas.

Middleware

Middleware is a specialized type of software important in the implementation of these standards. It acts as an intermediary software layer between different applications, often on different platforms. Through programming APIs this layer is used to achieve translation of data or messages that are in an incompatible format. The relation between the programming API and the connectivity standard to the user applications in two different companies is shown in Figure 3.5.

In this example Company 1 mainly uses Lotus products, for example a word processor from which an end user wants to send a proposal to Company 2. When they select Send from within their word processor it will use the Lotus sponsored VIM middleware standard to communicate across the internal network to a server running cc:Mail. This server will identify the e-mail as one to be sent externally and will then pass it on to the other company via a gateway middleware product to convert to the X.400 based network that links the two companies. After conversion, the message will be received at the e-mail server of Company 2 after retranslation using the gateway. The e-mail server will then place the mail message in the in-box of the end user. Note that middleware is a general term and describes a range of methods of glueing together different software applications and messaging systems. The examples given here are only a subset of the wide variety of middleware.

Figure 3.5
How e-mail standards are used to join companies with different products

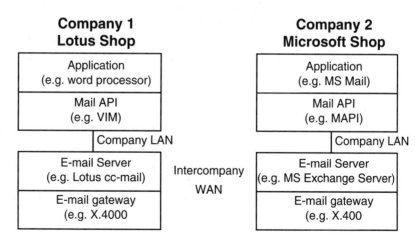

E-mail APIs for Applications Development

Many applications vendors incorporate e-mail functionality within an application. For example, facilities can be built to route a document straight from a word processor to its intended recipient. To enable this type of interaction, programmers call functions from a standard dynamic link library which supports one of the two common mail APIs (Application Program Interface). These are:

▶ MAPI—Mail API promoted by Microsoft

▶ VIM—Vendor Independent Messaging Service originally promoted by Lotus and supported by a range of vendors

Managing E-mail—System Management Problems

There are a number of issues involved with the management of mail systems. After backup and archiving, possibly the most important issue is the anticipated volume of usage. Sufficient server space should be allocated for each user to have thousands of messages with attachments. One of the major causes of failure of mail systems is when insufficient space remains. It will be necessary to set up an archiving system to remove messages from the server once they pass a certain age. If you are part of a company with multiple locations you will have to assess the frequency of connections to other servers as mail is distributed.

Linking different e-mail systems can cause problems, as discussed in the section on standards, so the correct gateway products have to be installed. This is particularly true when file attachments need to be received from other mail systems. Transmission rates have to be monitored to ensure delivery rates are satisfactory. Finally, the impact of network instability leading to poor availability should not be underestimated. Although not directly related to e-mail systems, downtime in company networks can cause severe problems if a company becomes reliant on e-mail for its operations, which is often the case given the success of e-mail.

Voice Mail

Voice mail shares many of the benefits of e-mail. It also has the advantage that it is clearer to understand the content of the message—you know your boss is angry when you have to hold the phone piece at arm's length. It works by converting the spoken message you record at your phone as a digital message, stored on a server. The recipient is then notified usually by a light/LCD on their phone that they have messages.

It suffers from the disadvantage that unlike e-mail there is not usually a priority system or a header summarizing what the message is about, or where it is from. Caller line identification can provide the latter. It is a lot quicker to scan through 10 e-mail messages than 10 voice mail messages. These disadvantages should reduce as voice mail is better integrated with the PC through CTI techniques. Voice messages are accessible from the in-box of Groupwise and this feature will likely be incorporated into similar packages.

In the Unified Messenger from Octel, voice messages and e-mail messages are also in a single location. The user simply clicks on a message to hear it or read it. This product has text-to-speech capabilities which converts e-mail messages to speech so that your e-mail messages can be read over the telephone.

Web reference: http://www.octel.com

Groupware Function: Conferencing

Different forms of conferencing can be used for shared discussions about particular topics. Conferencing's advantage over e-mail is that it allows many people to become involved, while e-mail is usually restricted to a small number of people receiving the message. In a business context, the discussion often revolves around proposals to solve a particular problem such as "which markets should we target to maximize revenue?" or for hosting support for electronic meetings. Computer based conferencing is an increasingly popular business application as it enables the distributed or virtual business to operate when decision makers are geographically separated. Additionally, the discussion does not have to occur as real time video-conferencing—if people are unavailable then asynchronous text based conferencing can occur. We look at the alternatives for conferencing by the media that are used.

Text Based Conferencing

Text based conferencing is usually asynchronous when used in the business world. Better choices are available for real time conferencing, such as phone or video-conferencing. Synchronous text conferencing is only really an option for 120 wpm typists—Internet Relay Chat is available for those who can make the grade. Despite lacking the immediacy of real time conferencing, asynchronous conferencing has the benefit that it gives participants the opportunity to reflect on their answers or find the information they need to contribute. A disadvantage of asynchronous text conferencing is that the user

Figure 3.6
Conferencing using Lotus Domino— window on the right shows detail of discussion thread on left

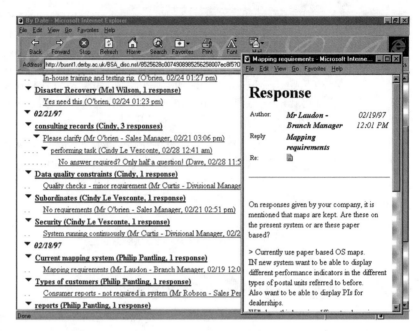

often has to proactively open the application for viewing the discussion to see whether there are any new postings. So, some education of users is necessary to overcome this or the conferencing system can be integrated with a mail system to notify users of new postings.

Text based conferences are based around the concept of a *discussion thread* where different participants discuss a particular topic (Figure 3.6). Products vary in how they implement the view of all contributions. A thread consists of grouped postings from different participants indented to show replies to an original comment. Within each thread supplementary questions may develop which are indented further. Usually, clicking on the header of the posting will give the contents of the posting. Good tools will allow export of a transcript of all comments for incorporation into a word processing document. The main options available in text conferencing software are:

▶ create new topic or thread—an area is available to type in the text of the posting

▶ respond or reply to an existing thread

▶ review list of existing topics and responses together with their authors and time/date of creation

▶ search topics for a text string

Good tools allow export of a transcript of all comments for incorporation into a word processing document. A moderator or administrator of the discussion will have the option to delete any inappropriate message.

Setting Up a Text Based Conference

To set up a text based conference does not usually require the large investment in hardware and networking that may be the case with video-conferencing. Existing network servers can be used to host the conferencing server software which will store the messages and hold the details of users of the conference. The client application can run on an entry level PC or Macintosh. Many vendors are migrating their systems to web based conferencing which offers cheaper conferencing with a familiar client.

Web reference: http://freenet.msp.mn.us/~drwool/webconf.html Conferencing on the World Wide Web, an index of over 60 tools and applications maintained by David R. Woolley who created one of the first computer conferencing systems, PLATO Notes.

A range of conferencing software is discussed in Chapter 6. Lotus Notes and the Domino web enabled package and Microsoft Exchange both support conferencing with independent packages such as Telefinder and FirstClass also available. Conferencing can be set up as public with open access or private with user name and password restricting participants.

Groupware Function: Video-Conferencing

Video-conferencing is not a new technology. In the early days, video-conferencing was the sole preserve of large multinationals with tailor made video suites, costing tens of thousands of dollars.

Within the last few years, video-conferencing from the desktop has become accessible to smaller companies at a fraction of the cost. This growth is being accelerated by the benefits of using the Internet, namely the lower cost of entry and usage charges.

Alternative video-conferencing products are compared in Chapter 6. Figure 3.7 shows CU-SeeMe software video-conferencing software which offers other facilities such as chat and whiteboarding. Organizations such as the World Bank are using CU-SeeMe from White Pine Software to expand their usage of video-conferencing beyond the board-room.

For large company or small, the reasons for using video-conferencing are clear. It reduces travel time and costs and offers the opportunity to arrange a meeting at relatively short notice. Unlike text based conferencing methods,

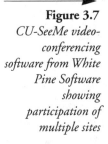

Figure 3.7
CU-SeeMe video-conferencing software from White Pine Software showing participation of multiple sites

video-conferencing offers an interactive virtual meeting very similar to the real thing. Above and beyond other conferencing methods, this technique offers physical expression to be conveyed, enabling a more effective meeting. The visual element also enables discussion of physical objects such as products, diagrams or charts to occur. Sharing of diagrams and applications is also helped by the whiteboard facilities which are included in packages such as CU-SeeMe (see separate section on whiteboarding).

Video-Conferencing Decisions

When deciding on a video-conferencing system there are a number of choices to be made. These are often a trade-off between quality and expenditure:

1. Do you want limited conferencing within the company on the LAN or the more common need of going beyond the local offices using leased lines or the Internet?

2. Do you go for desktop video-conferencing (DVC) between PCs and workstations or a more expensive video-suite?

3. Do you want point-to-point conferencing between two locations or multi-point conferencing involving several participants (Figure 3.7)?

4. The big question is what do you want as your quality in frames per second? This will be governed by what bandwidth you can afford and the techniques supported by the products you use to reduce bandwidth requirements. Bandwidth reduction techniques are described below. One of the methods to achieve this is multicast (see explanation below).

5. What integration with other types of groupware function such as whiteboard or application sharing is required?

Bandwidth Requirements

Video-conferencing was hyped at the start of the 1990s, but demonstrations of jerky, disembodied faces caused by dropped frames and a low number of frames per second permitted by the transmission capacity have been a key reason for the lack of popularity. Even with the compression techniques described below, there is no substitute for bandwidth. A suitable bandwidth for high end video-conferencing is between 350 to 400 Kbps, so good quality is not possible across phone lines even if using ISDN. So quality video-conferencing is not really a practical proposition for home use, even with modems running at 56 Kbps. The quality of image is, of course, also governed by your requirements for resolution and color. Color does not add much to the message content, so black and white suffices for most, while a resolution of windows of 200 by 100 pixels is a good compromise since full screen does not add much beyond the talking head.

For lower end use, White Pine support recommends a bandwidth of around 100 Kbps for "fluid motion." They illustrate the problems by showing that there are 75 Kbits in 120 × 160 pixel frame, which is equivalent to 45 Kbits/frame compressed. For 15 frames per second for fluid motion (with every frame being different) 675 Kbits/sec would be required. Fortunately, this is not required since only parts of the frame differ.

Techniques for Reducing Bandwidth Requirements

The vendors of video-conferencing solutions use a number of techniques to reduce the amount of bandwidth required to transmit the video-stream. Here we explore some of the key ones in more depth. All involve reducing the data-stream, but achieve this in a variety of different ways.

Image Quality

Reducing the number of frames per second will obviously reduce the data transmission requirements, but will result in poor quality. Thirty frames per second is necessary for excellent quality conferencing, but over a modem, less than 10 will be used. Video-conferencing servers such as White Pine

MeetingPoint can automatically detect the transmission achievable to any site and reduce the amount of data transmitted accordingly.

This is known as bandwidth pruning and offers a controlled way of reducing the number of frames per second rather than randomly dropped frames. Bandwidth needs can also be substantially reduced by going from color to black and white images. Since color does not add significantly to the message and can degrade the number of frames per second, it is only used when the highest speed links such as 10Mbps are available.

Compression

The video *codec* standard used is of vital importance in reducing the volume of data to be transmitted. The codec is used to *co*de and *dec*ode the signals from the analog video signal to the digital stream of bits that is transmitted across the network. This stream is then decoded at the receiving end to be displayed as a sequence of frames. As well as the conversion from analog to digital, a compression-decompression also occurs before and after transmission to reduce the number of bits that need to be transmitted.

Depending on the trade-off between quality and performance, lossy techniques may be used. In these the compression technique will cause a reduction in quality where some bits are discarded to give a greater reduction in the number of packets that need to be transmitted. Fractal based compression is a lossy method used for example by Iterated Systems. Non-lossy methods available include run length encoding (RLE) and pulse code modulation. Run length encoding is not "lossy" since repeating bits are stored in a more efficient form and reconstituted when decompressed. The delta technique involves only transmitting pixels varying from frame to frame. This technique works well for video-conferencing since when "talking heads" are involved the delta between frames is usually limited to changes in expressions and movement.

Local Replication

This involves using different servers at different sites to intelligently balance the amount of data that is transmitted across the slowest WAN link. Imagine a situation where four delegates are located in a headquarters and are holding a conference with a single delegate in a foreign sales office. Without replication, all data packets from the different participants at the headquarters are sent to the overseas location. With local replication this is not necessary since the server at headquarters intelligently routes all information in a single stream.

Multicasting

With simple broadcasting of video-conferencing data streams, each node on the network receives a separate data-stream regardless of whether they want to receive or not. This duplication places a severe drain on network resources. The multicast method is significant since it produces a single data stream, which is only routed to those users who request it. The multicast protocol uses a destination address to identify a multicast packet which allows a single packet of video to be sent to several destinations on the wire at the same time, i.e., its main benefit is that it is a *one to many* service rather than *one to one*.

With multicast techniques it is possible to deliver a range of business video content such as company-wide meetings, management and financial briefings, training programs and news bulletins. The H.323 standard referred to below is significant since it offers support for IP-multicasting which should improve the performance of video-conferencing across intranets and the Internet.

Video-Conferencing Standards

As with mail systems, these are important to allow interoperability between products from different vendors. The important standards are managed by the International Telecomms Union and supported by members of the International Multimedia Teleconferencing Consortium. The important emerging standard at the moment is H.323 which is supported by key players such as Intel and Pic-tureTel. Products from these companies are described in Chapter 6.

H.323 is an audio- and video-conferencing standard supporting point to point and multicasting over IP based networks such as intranets and the Internet. It has evolved from the H.320 standard which addresses video-conferencing across ISDN and other switched networks. A further standard is H.324 for use on dial-up video-conferencing across modems using analog lines. The best known methods for video playback are Video for Windows-Indeo from Microsoft/Intel, Quicktime from Apple and MPEG.

Web reference: http://www.imtc.org. The International Multimedia Tele-conferencing Consortium supports all key videoconferencing standards referred to above.

Web reference: http://www.itu.ch. The ITU manages many of the video-conferencing standards.

Why Has Video-Conferencing Not Happened Yet?

Despite years of hype, video-conferencing has not yet reached the mainstream of commodity software and hardware. According to Telespan Publishing the number of desktop video-conferencing units shipped in 1996 was just 300,000 worldwide. Although it is often said that teleconferencing has not taken off because of technical difficulties of dropped frames and jerky images, the business reason is probably that clear tangible benefits have not been delivered.

Of course, cost is another barrier to entry. Costs for video-conferencing are high, since as well as renting high speed links, additional hardware is required for hosting servers or reflectors, video-cards in the PCs and monitor-mounted cameras and microphones. The software tends to have quite a high cost per seat in order for the software vendors to try to recover their investment. This is a minimum cost per seat of $200 to $1000 dollars depending on the quality required.

The customer's viewpoint appeared recently in *PC Week*. Quoting George Bateman of American Express in Phoenix, Arizona, as saying "We look for technology to aid us in our business and if it doesn't aid in that or bring value, it carries a low priority for us. Desktop video-conferencing will come, I'm sure, but we have higher priorities now." Instead, American Express continues to use their boardroom video-conferencing systems while the cost of desktop video-conferencing is seen as too high by Bateman. "The cost for LAN based video-conferencing could climb up to $5,000 to $7,000 per desktop," he says.

Studies have shown that the introduction of teleconferencing has had only a marginal impact on travel costs in companies. However, it can promote new ways of working, for example, joint product development between remote sites in which more staff can participate, thus reducing development costs and increasing quality.

The creation of the H.323 standard will help the spread of video-conferencing to LAN environments, but it is difficult to see the technology becoming widespread in the near future. While it is a "nice to have" technology, the business imperative is just not there yet. Effective communications can occur via voice and e-mail—the marginal benefit of video-conferencing, of the talking head, is just not large enough for a lot of small and medium companies.

Other Varieties of Conferencing

Video-conferencing and text based conferencing are well known and widely used. There are also a number of other tools, many of which are Internet based, which are used widely for recreational use, but not by industry. A brief review of these is given here since these approaches may offer a low tech, low cost solution to businesses.

Usenet

Usenet text based discussion groups are available via the Internet through the *network news transfer protocol* (NNTP). Usenet is best known as a public method of conferencing in areas such as rec. for hobbies and games or comp. for discussions about computing related matters such as the Usenet group comp.groupware. It is also possible to set up a private company newsgroup on a news server and limit access to company users, but it is more usual to use web based conferencing because of ease of use.

In the beginning, Usenet newsgroups were accessed from newsreader applications. Increasingly they are integrated into the web browser as is the case with the Netscape newsreader. Some services such as DejaNews (www.dejanews.com) allow messages to be reviewed and posted from the browser itself.

Web reference: http://www.dejanews.com. This is useful for searching newsgroups and posting messages from a web browser.

E-mail Based Discussion

List servers such as UNIX *listserv* use e-mail to provide *e-mail based discussion* across the Internet. These function by each participant subscribing to the discussion and all messages posted by other users to the list server are then automatically sent as e-mail to all subscribers. This conferencing has the benefit that it is easy to set up and uses your existing e-mail package. It has the disadvantage that it can be difficult to follow the thread of a discussion since all other messages in your in-box will interfere unless you set up a rule to route listserv messages into a separate folder. Proprietary and web based discussion packages have the great advantage that threads can be easily reviewed.

A more primitive form of conferencing can be set up in an e-mail package by sending a message to a group of people and any person replying selects "reply to all." This has the disadvantage that each user has to remember to choose "reply to all" and again suffers from the messages being intermingled with other messages. Search facilities will not usually be available either.

Internet Relay Chat and Bulletin Boards

Internet relay chat (IRC), is a low cost Internet tool which provides a real time system that is used more for recreational than business use. It functions by the host you are connected to broadcasting what you type to all users around the world who are "tuned in" to a particular channel. It is not secure and the threads may be difficult to distinguish as several discussions may occur simultaneously.

The Internet talk utility or a secure private channel can be used for chat between two people. Telnet based bulletin boards are another alternative for conferencing which have been used in the past for product support and user groups. IChat has tried to carve a niche in the business-oriented chat market. Its iChat paging server runs on Solaris and Windows NT and offers the facilities of:

▶ Rooms—a standard chat facility for teams

▶ Paging System—for "instant" transmission and display of important messages in a global enterprise where e-mail is not sufficiently rapid since users have to proactively access their in-boxes

▶ Message boards—similar to traditional bulletin boards

Web reference: http://www.ichat.com

Phone Teleconferencing

As well as conferencing using analog or digital phones, there are now a number of options for using the Internet to promote phone conferencing. This is supported through Netscape cool talk and vendors of Internet phone facilities.

Groupware Function: Electronic Meetings Software

Supporting Meetings Through Electronic Meetings Software

Given that some managers can spend more than half their working lives in meetings, there are big savings available in efficiency if meetings can be made more productive. Consider these statistics from David Coleman's book on groupware applications:

▶ Middle managers spend 14 hours per week in meetings

▶ Senior managers spend as many as 23 hours per week in meetings

▶ Planning for the average meeting costs $55 per attendee

▶ The average cost of a one hour meeting of eight attendees is $692

Electronic meetings software can also reduce some of the problems of traditional business meetings such as: a lack of information, dominance by one forceful individual and the boredom and frustration of diversion onto irrelevant matters. Additionally, psychological studies have shown that decisions made through electronic meetings produce improved decisions which are more radical and polarized than those achieved face-to-face, possibly through greater equality and less inhibition of team members.

Electronic meetings software or systems (EMS) can also help with more mundane aspects of meetings through ensuring that an agenda is available, action points are noted and distributed to participants. This software is also commonly known as *group decision support* (GDS), although this term is somewhat dated now and EMS usually is used instead. Chapter 9 gives more insight into the psychology of group working, which should be considered by all embarking on the introduction of a new system. The paper by Nunamaker et al. (1991) offers a good introduction to the features and benefits of EMS.

The Functions of Electronic Meetings Software

McGrath (1984) considers a range of modes in which a group can operate, not all of which may occur in any single piece of group activity. These modes may be supported by different types of groupware, but in particular must be provided by electronic meetings software. All groups go through the stages of:

▶ **Inception (Mode I).** Group members are selected, roles are defined and relationships established. Problems are identified perhaps through brainstorming and plans produced by which the groups can solve them.

▶ **Decision making (Mode II).** Here technical problems are solved through decision making.

▶ **Conflict resolution (Mode III).** Problems are resolved through conflict resolution as the parties negotiate to achieve a satisfactory outcome.

▶ **Execution (Mode IV).** This is where the group functions effectively through performing the tasks.

Group interactions are only one part of the sequence of group functioning. Other aspects such as group forming and problem resolution also need to be built into software for group working. Additionally, group members are often not working on a single project, but several projects and groups are dynamic—software needs to be responsive to this. When a group is looking to take decisions and generate tasks to implement the ideas, the sequence of functions that must be supported are:

▶ arrange meeting (group scheduling software)

▶ generate alternatives (idea synthesis)

▶ choose alternatives (prioritization)

▶ negotiate (decision)

▶ execute (implementation—generate tasks)

Using a Facilitator

An additional function is that of *facilitation* of a meeting. The role of the facilitator in aiding conventional meetings is well known, but there is a danger of not bothering to appoint such a person when using *computer mediated communications* (CMC). Research has shown that the role of the facilitator or moderator in CMC is as important as in face-to-face group work. The facilitator is important to encourage participation, steer the course of the debate, resolve conflicts as necessary and ensure that clear conclusions are reached from which actions can be taken. Jay (1976) describes the role of the facilitator in down to earth terms; his suggestions for running a meeting are to:

▶ control the garrulous

▶ draw out the silent

▶ protect the weak

▶ make sure suggestions aren't squashed

▶ encourage the clash of ideas, but discourage the clash of individuals

We see that electronic meetings support can assist in this and reduce the risk of one of his colorful types of meeting occurring: "multi-headed beast; feuding factions; dominant species; recycling syndrome and sleeping monster."

Valacich et al. (1991) describe an early example of group decision support software and demonstrate that in a corporate environment both efficiency and effectiveness were improved in comparison with a conventional meeting. Decisions were reached more rapidly with a better quality of decision with more ideas generated than in face-to-face meetings. Questionnaires indicated that over three-quarters of participants rated electronic meetings more effective.

Support for team members in group decision support is sometimes considered as being of three types according to the level of access to the technology. With f-groupware there is a single workstation for the *facilitator* of the meeting. With k-groupware there is a *keypad* where members can make decisions through voting. Finally, the norm today is w-groupware, where *workstations* are used by each member to view information and contribute ideas. Electronic meeting support is a common application of GDS (*Group Decision Support* systems). The facilities provided by these systems are categorized according to the capabilities that are available.

▶ **Level 1** facilities for sharing opinions and information in a structured way, but on its own this is usually not sufficient for running meetings. Text conferencing software, software to follow an agenda, and write up minutes to help brainstorming and whiteboarding software would also fall into this category.

▶ **At Level 2,** additional tools are available for evaluation of proposals using statistical or decision-tree techniques, voting and viewing the relationships between ideas. Groupware that is specifically for Electronic Meeting Support will fall into this latter category.

▶ **Level 3** tools are largely experimental and allow for the automation of group communication and decisions through the use of rules and artificial intelligence.

An example of Level 1 or 2 meeting support software is VisionQuest from Collaborative Technologies Inc. This product is based on the idea of goal directed dialogs in which meetings focus on desired outcomes and work toward an agreement through structuring the collaboration within an agenda framework and providing documentation on idea generation, evaluation and prioritization during the group decision process. The product is well based in theory allowing for anonymous contributions as ideas are generated and prioritized and providing tools to solve well known problems of meetings. These tools include:

▶ brainwriting (a shared chat space)

▶ commenting for sharing opinions on agenda topics

▶ categorizing, for synthesizing views

▶ ranking and rating different solutions

▶ voting (Yes, No or Abstain to a proposal)

When "ranking and rating" individuals give their suggested rank or score to a proposal and the group averages are computed. "Reducing" is used to select a limited number of alternatives—say the top three choices to exclude unpopular alternatives. This system is not prescriptive in that people attending the meeting can roam around the agenda, although guided by the facilitator.

Web reference: http://www.netsites.net/~one/vision.htm (OneNet Inc is a reseller for VisionQuest which is principally used in government and education.)

GroupSystems, a tool originating from the University of Arizona, provides Level 2 and 3 facilities to analyze ideas by outlining and then establishing relationships between them in a matrix. Figure 3.8 shows the alternative analysis module which is used here to compare alternative employees according to differently weighted criteria shown in the columns. This can then give an objective group decision when comparing a number of alternatives.

Web reference: http://www.ventana-east.com/ and www.ventana.com/index.html—the primary site for Group Systems from Ventana.

Figure 3.8
*Alternative analysis
tool from Group
Systems*

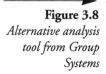

Two list, Employment Candidates [Alternative Analysis]						
Primary List	DOS(1.40)	Network(1.30)	Hardware(1.20)	Certification(1.00)	Total	Mean
Weight	1.40	1.30	1.20			
1 Stephanie Richard	6.33	2.33	6.67	5.33	79.00	7.18
2 Brad Lemsky	6.00	3.33	6.67	7.33	72.00	6.55
3 Michael Lopez	8.00	7.67	7.67	3.67	66.67	6.06
4 LaKeisha Williams	5.00	3.67	5.67	5.33	68.33	6.21
5 Sally Fong	4.67	3.67	5.67	7.67	78.00	7.09
6 Richard Puccio	4.33	3.33	5.00	5.33	68.67	6.24
7 Michelle Walters	7.67	5.33	8.33	6.67	83.33	7.58
Total	42.00	29.33	45.67	41.33		
Mean	6.00	4.19	6.52	5.90		

Through using GroupSystems its creators claim the following are possible:

► increase meeting preparedness and participation

► reduce the length and number of meetings by up to 50 percent

► improve the quality and quantity of creative ideas

► focus on the issues and energize the process

► quantify and compare opinions on subjective issues

► provide an electronic forum for managing ongoing communications

► encourage innovation, trust, and commitment to organizational goals

► document meeting proceedings, capture ideas and record the outcomes

Real Time Multimedia Group Conferencing Software

Multimedia conferencing software for business meetings uses a range of different media:

► video-conferencing

► whiteboard conferencing

► document conferencing

► data conferencing

This category of software is now sometimes referred to as Teamware. This is slightly confusing since there is a groupware product from ICL called TeamWare.

Whiteboard Software

Whiteboard software is a real time technology which is usually accompanied by other real time applications. It is used for brainstorming and summarizing decisions just as with standard whiteboards. Most commonly it is an option of a video-conferencing package such as CU-SeeMe, Picture Tel Liveshare Plus or Intel Proshare. Figure 3.9 illustrates the whiteboard feature from Microsoft Netmeeting. In such products a separate window is dedicated to a shared whiteboard which is drawn on using a stylus and then the annotation replicated to all others viewing this virtual whiteboard.

The whiteboard is a graphical bit-mapped environment like the Paintbrush program. It should be possible to zoom, type text, draw lines, import images, highlight and of course erase using the mouse or a pen type of pointer. Another approach involves the use of a physical whiteboard which detects the motion of a pen and transmits the image to screens. Importing images from other screen windows that are not shared is useful, if for example, discussing a prototype of a new program. The other facilities that real time conferencing packages include are:

▶ **real time chat** between delegates—often unnecessary if video-conferencing is available

▶ **shared applications** (or remote access)—an effective way of reviewing prototypes, what-if business simulations or multiple authoring of compound documents (document sharing)

▶ **file transfer**—file transfer may allow financial spreadsheet data to be easily transferred between users using a similar model to e-mail with a file attachment being sent to delegates or using File Transfer Protocol

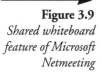

Figure 3.9
Shared whiteboard feature of Microsoft Netmeeting

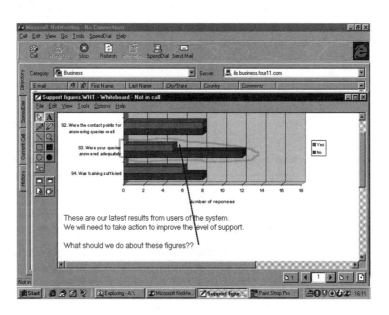

Document Conferencing

Document conferencing is another form of collaborating on documents, but in real time. A primitive form of document conferencing is to capture a bitmap image of a word processed page or a spreadsheet and then annotations can be made using the whiteboard software described above. It is now possible to perform interactive document conferencing where it is the document source itself that is modified rather than a passive bitmap image of the source. This method, although more complex, has the advantage that it is only the commands to modify the document that are passed down the line rather than a modified bitmap. Similar techniques are used for shared applications.

Data Conferencing

Data conferencing is an alternative term for conferencing which includes the transmission of digitized audio or voice together with numeric data such as financial information. T.120 is the ITU data conferencing standard. This specifies standards for file transfer, whiteboards and application sharing.

Groupware Function: Collaborative Authoring and Document Sharing

The functionality to enable coauthors to work together on documents is now a mainstream feature of most word processors such as Lotus WordPro or Microsoft Word. This group working facility enables a document to be reviewed and changes suggested according to two different models.

First, it is possible for each author to insert annotations at different points in the document while retaining its original structure. In Word, annotations are shown as a separate pane at the foot of the screen with the choice of viewing all reviewers annotations, or selecting a particular coauthor.

The second method enables different authors to make revisions to the structure and content of the original document which are highlighted in particular colors or styles. Each author can be allotted a particular color and different types of revisions will be shown differently. For example, deletions as strike-through, insertions as underline. An example of a document being modified is shown in Figure 3.10. To review changes there is an option to review revisions in turn and either accept or reject them. Facilities also exist to compare separate documents and merge different versions.

When using these facilities it is important to limit access only to the authors either by using permissions assigned by the network administrator or by using password protection on the document through the authoring package.

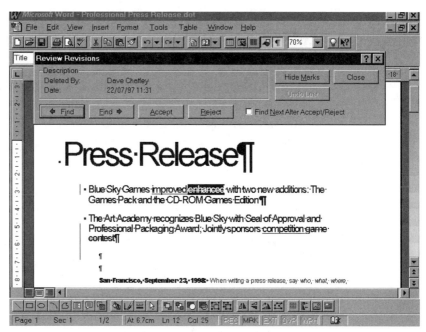

Figure 3.10
*Use of revision
marks and annota-
tions in Microsoft
Word*

The adoption of these features is limited in many companies as authors prefer to review and mark up a paper copy and the use of these features needs some training. However, all that is necessary to view revisions in a Word document shared by several authors is to choose the Revisions option from the Tools menu and select "show revisions when editing." Another difficulty is that it is necessary to decide on a strategy for managing the editing process. The choices are similar to those for paper documents.

One alternative is that the common or master document can be mounted on a shared network drive and then reminders sent out by e-mail to make modifications to the document. This has the disadvantage that if multiple users wish to access the file there may be conflicts in revision. If the word processor is integrated with the mail system such as Microsoft Mail or Exchange, documents then can be routed easily to coauthors. This can be done sequentially with each author receiving the document in turn or more commonly the document is routed to all workers simultaneously and then a copy of the document returned after the individual has made the changes. The latter has the advantage that more time is available for review, but has the disadvantage that all the modifications must be reviewed and merged separately. The routing of documents is a straightforward example of workflow.

Groupware Function: Electronic Document Management Software (EDMS)

While a standard word processor can be used to manage production of documents in a workgroup, more powerful software is needed to enable large documents sets to be created, reviewed, edited and approved and subsequently accessed throughout an organization. This process is known as the document lifecycle and consists of the stages of:

▶ author

▶ review and annotate

▶ modify

▶ publish

▶ distribute

▶ modify and repeat the cycle

An example of a package that is used to help in this lifecycle is shown in Figure 3.11. *Document management software* (DMS) or electronic publishing software is used to enable people to collaborate in the production of such documents and also provide tools for the distribution and sharing of documents through the enterprise. Three of the best known companies providing document management software are Interleaf, Documentum and Filenet/ Saros Mezzanine. All are in the process of introducing web browser based access for their products. Many startups are also beginning to introduce similar tools for intranets as described in Chapter 5.

Figure 3.11
Interleaf document publishing used for larger document sets such as company procedures

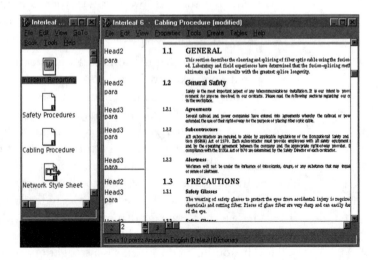

Typical EDMS tools, for example from Interleaf are for:

▶ creation of compound documents with check-in, check-out version management of updates (Interleaf product)

▶ document management (WorldView and RDB product)

▶ document access using Internet tools across an intranet or the Internet (Intellecte/Business Web)

▶ document conversion and scanning

▶ database publishing (DBLink) for example of catalogs, directories and price lists

Web reference: http://www.filenet.com (includes information on Saros Mezzanine product).

Web reference: http://www.interleaf.com

Web reference: http://www.documentum.com

Web reference: http://www.keyfile.com

Such tools are necessary to manage the thousands of documents which exist in a large company to define processes, products and customer information. For example, the CERA bank in Belgium uses Interleaf to manage 18,000 pages containing commercial, legal and fiscal information of which 150 have to be updated each week and distributed to branches. In the UK, the Abbey National Bank may send out up to 300 changes a month to its two million pages of product information, procedures and manuals. Intereaf WorldView is used by 15,000 users to access this documentation across the company WAN.

When supporting documentation is important in product development, document management software can help reduce production times and reduce the risk of specification and design errors. Glaxo Wellcome, the multinational pharmaceutical company uses Documentum to manage their new drug development while Boeing uses a DMS to manage product information and 70,000 pages of standards that define key business processes. The sources of savings at Boeing identified by IDC are illuminating: 31% of savings are through time saved in accessing the documents with only 6% through removing the paper distribution of documents. Significantly 63% of savings come through reduction in the amount of rework caused by out-of-date documents.

As the industry matures, EDMS are increasingly being linked to workflow systems. This is reflected by the company activity. For example Eastman-Kodak with a focus on imaging has taken over document management functions from Wang and workflow vendor Filenet has bought document management specialist

Saros. Today an EDMS may provide the following functions, of which workflow functions are covered in more detail in the next chapter.

► Document management

► Imaging

► Workflow

► Computer Output to Laser Disk (COLD)

Groupware Function: Scheduling and Calendaring Software

The final category of groupware considered in this chapter is that used for diary or calendar management within an organization. When justifying groupware to managers who are unfamiliar with the technology, this is perhaps the easiest function to explain since the problems of arranging times for meetings will be known to all, and an electronic solution will have obvious appeal. The functions of these packages include calendaring (the process of entering names and times onto calendars) and scheduling (arranging a convenient time for a meeting).

These packages provide a shared diary available via the network for employees to arrange meetings quickly without clashes. Sophisticated group scheduling products automatically seek the optimum time for a given list of participants and confirm the meeting time and agenda using e-mail. Products available to provide these functions are available in a range of categories, according to the scale at which they are deployed:

1. Workgroup based applications

2. Department based applications

3. Whole enterprise applications.

Workgroup based applications are often based on Personal Information Managers. Early versions of Lotus Organizer provide an example of such a product. These products tend to focus more on individual information management rather than group features. They may not scale well to larger numbers of users. For larger numbers of users, integration with the company e-mail and directory services are required. This may be achieved though integrating products such as Lotus Organizer with Lotus cc:Mail or Notes.

An alternative approach from Lotus was to provide a special document template in Notes for calendar management. Although functional, this was quite primitive compared with more specialized solutions from other vendors.

Crosswind Technologies introduced a client/server solution in 1992 for the enterprise market and other competitors have entered the market since this time. Enterprise solutions can also be deployed using the prevalent groupware packages—Exchange, Notes and Groupwise.

One of the biggest problems of implementing a cross-enterprise solution is the popularity of this type of package. Different departments and subsidiaries and even individuals are likely already using a variety of different packages which are often incompatible. In this case, a high-level decision to standardize on a single product may be the only way to achieve a solution for the enterprise. Standards such as ICAP (see next page) are being developed to help improve interoperation between different products. If and when this standard becomes widely accepted it will greatly improve intra-enterprise scheduling and could open the door to interenterprise scheduling. Increasingly, the client parts of calendaring and scheduling functions are being built into the operating system. At the same time, there is a trend to using TCP/IP based networks, including the Internet as the means for transporting the information.

Web reference: http://www3.lotus.com/organize

A specialized type of group-scheduling software is that used for project management such as Microsoft Project. This software was originally used by the project manager as a standalone application, but group availability of the schedule is now common to many of these packages.

Figure 3.12
*Group-scheduling
software—
Organizer
from Lotus*

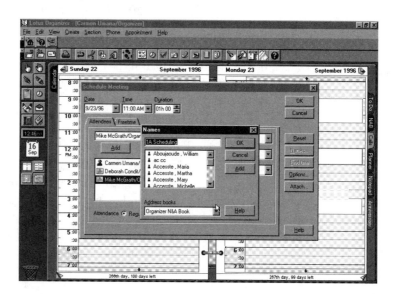

Calendar Standards

Previous attempts at developing a single calendaring standard have been well supported, but not translated into delivered products. The XAPIA Calendaring and Scheduling API (CSA) of 1994 was one result which was not widely adopted, possibly due to its complexity. The emergence of the Internet as a medium for scheduling has resulted in further efforts to produce a standard.

The Internet Calendar Access Protocol (ICAP) has been sanctioned by the Internet Engineering Task Force under the moniker Internet calendaring and scheduling core object specification. This very likely represents the future of calendaring. It allows group schedulers, Personal Information Managers and Contact Managers to share information. The protocol has the following features which are closely linked to the IMAP4 standard referred to under e-mail standards:

1. Selective retrieval of calendar information based on date ranges. This is to minimize network traffic.

2. Permit users to browse other users' calendars, subject to access control limits. This allows a user to find free times during which to schedule meetings with other users.

3. Posting of new schedule items in another user's calendar.

4. Creating, deleting and renaming of multiple calendar stores per user. A user may want to separate their personal calendar information from their work calendar.

> *Web reference*: http://www..ietf.org/home.html or
> http://www.ietf.cnri.reston.va.us/

A closely related standard is the vCalendar format from the Versit consortium which is supported by the Internet Mail consortium. This is not a protocol, but defines the format of the data normally stored within a calendaring or scheduling application, and allows the cross platform exchange of information about items such as events and to-do items. It is probable that the two standards will be integrated in the majority of scheduling products.

> *Web reference*: http://www.imc.org (Internet Mail consortium)

If this happens, and it is a big if, the adoption of these standards will be a big breakthrough since different calendar products do not interoperate in the way that e-mail programs do currently. Different products will be able for the first time to check with other calendar programs for the availability of participants. This will be most useful for very large organizations with different calendar systems and when different companies need to collaborate. The standard is designed to function across time zones, so this is also advantageous for the global company.

4

Workflow Management Systems

Introduction—What Is Workflow?

Workflow Management Systems (WFMS) are specialized types of software systems used to assist in computer supported collaborative work. WFMS are often referred to as workflow automation since they can automate the tasks or activities undertaken by both people and computer resources of an organization. WFMS are often introduced since they support new ways of working as businesses reengineer. They are used in mission critical areas such as in financial services for issuing loans and for common administrative functions such as processing purchase orders.

The Workflow Management Coalition (WfMC) describes workflow as:

"The computerized facilitation or automation of a business process in whole or part."

and a Workflow Management System as:

"A system that defines, creates and manages the execution of workflows through the use of software, running on one or more workflow engines, which is able to interpret the process definition, interact with workflow participants and, where required, invoke the use of IT tools and applications."

As an example of a workflow application, let's return to the clerk investigating a claim on a car insurance policy. The clerk will have to follow a series of steps over days or weeks in deciding whether to settle the claim. Over this period he or she will be dealing with many other similar claims and the documentation associated with them. A workflow system will assist by providing a checklist of tasks to be conducted each day and providing information on the customer and other insurers. The system will permit collaboration by enabling other clerks to share the same case if necessary or provide a manager doing the final authorization with the information they need to approve the claim. The workflow system will also provide an overview of the status of the process, such as how many claims are completed each day, how long do they take on average and what are the bottlenecks? This management information can then be used to improve the process further.

In This Chapter

In this chapter we start by considering the different types of workflow systems and typical applications such as document image processing. The components that make up these systems and the concepts on which they are based are then reviewed. This forms the basis for a more detailed consideration in Chapters 7 and 8 on how analysis and design for workflow systems is performed. The work of the Workflow Management Coalition industry association and other standards groupings are described as a means of achieving interoperability between products.

Why Workflow?

Workflow can make big differences to the operational efficiency of processes occurring in a business. It can do this both by assisting managers in coordinating tasks undertaken by staff and providing information to staff to help them perform tasks. The bottom-line business benefits of implementing a workflow system are that completion time and cost of existing business processes can be reduced.

For example, a bank in the UK used a workflow system to reduce the average time to approve a house loan to a customer from 21 to nine days. Additionally, with customer service ever more important to the success of a business, workflow can improve the quality of processes and increase customer satisfaction. Improved quality of customer service is also possible through standardizing the approach to dealing with a claim. In this way everyone is treated the same and no corners are cut regardless of which employee or which branch deals with the case.

Workflow can achieve these benefits since some roles performed by staff can be replaced by the system and work can be performed faster. Workflow has changed office based "blue-collar" work, in the way that Just-in-Time manufacturing techniques and automation of production lines has transformed the manufacture of many consumer products.

The delivery of information to the person performing the process can also be improved through workflow automation. Rather than having to repeatedly walk across the office while retrieving information from a filing cabinet the user can access customer or case information simply by selecting the work item or typing their name or reference number. All correspondence, customer and policy details are available within an electronic customer file. To achieve this, workflow systems are often hooked into a Document Image Processing system (DIP). This permits all customer letters to be scanned in and then stored as digital images for later retrieval and display when the customer case is next opened.

Examples of Structured Workflow Applications

An example of a large financial services company leveraging workflow and imaging technology to improve business performance is the Prudential—the UK's largest insurance company. This company is looking to achieve cost savings from a major reduction in paper handling, allowing the redeployment of staff to customer service functions together with faster customer response times. The Prudential estimates that a 30% increase in productivity will save $7.5 million each year for an initial $9 million investment. As with many implementations, the company has developed a heterogeneous system from multiple suppliers, FileNet for document image storage, retrieval and routing, Sybase for database storage of case and work item details and Hewlett Packard for optical storage using SureStore juke boxes. Up to 55,000 documents are scanned and stored daily.

Workflow technologies are not only restricted to banking and financial applications, however. Federal Express uses workflow technology in a number of its business areas. In its core function it has a mission critical system to track its parcels as they are routed around the world. The workflow information is available by the Internet to customers who wish to track their packages. The interface for this product is shown in Figure 4.1.

Figure 4.1
Federal Express workflow tracking for parcel delivery

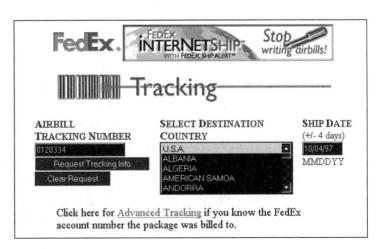

Federal Express also use a workflow system within their Human Resources Management function. For a large company such as FedEx with over 93,000 employees in 1994 when the system was introduced, managing job applications, contracts and training records is a major undertaking. PRISM, a workflow system with imaging has been used since 1991 to scan up to 10,000 images a day. Workflow is used to automate the process of hiring and also to build in checks. If a manager decides to hire, the system checks the candidate has not worked in any other offices previously, then checks that the position is budgeted, assigns an employee identification number and finally transfers information from the applicant tracking database to an employee database.

This automation does not usually involve human intervention—no onscreen forms need to be filled in and not a single piece of paper is generated. Workflow is used in a range of Human Resources Management packages to assist in administrative functions and performance management with packages such as PeopleSoft's PeopleTools HRMS, Dun & Bradstreet HR Stream, Humanic Design and the Oracle HRM module.

Managing a Team Through Workflow

Workflow enables managers to manage their team better since the workflow system can be used to automatically assign tasks, such as a particular customer case for an insurance claim, to an individual team member. This assignment is usually achieved by the use of a prioritized workflow queue which will assign the most important case to the next available person who has the correct profile to complete it. Workflow also assists managers by improving the monitoring of staff performance. For example, the average time it takes a person to deal with a case can be easily displayed by the computer.

The performance of the team as a whole can also be viewed from the number of outstanding tasks on the workflow queue. Problems can be identified more easily and earlier action taken to solve them. The overall effect of this is that the manager needs to spend less time communicating to individuals either to give them work to do or discuss problems. This gives more time for both managers and workers to concentrate on their key roles.

In addition to the specific benefits described above, workflow systems also act as a catalyst to process change. Through their adoption existing processes will be examined and redesigned to be more efficient. Hammer and Champy in *Reengineering the Corporation* identified document image processing and workflow as key IT enablers of Business Process Re-Engineering. To summarize, the benefits of a workflow system include:

1. **Process efficiency increased.** Processes are made more efficient giving lower time for task completion and reduced costs as fewer staff are needed or throughput increased.

2. **Process standardization achieved.** The automation of process improves the quality of service by giving a standard approach to each customer and again through the reduced time to provide the service, for example a response to a customer enquiry about the status of their loan.

3. **Information availability improved.** Direct electronic delivery of case information to a user's desktop rather than from a filing cabinet or from another person's out tray.

4. **Automatic assignment of tasks to staff.** Tasks are assigned from a workflow queue.

5. **Process monitoring automated.** This is made possible by monitoring tools and tables and charts of metrics showing performance of the team or individuals.

How Do Workflow and Groupware Relate?

To digress for a while, we need to tackle the thorny issue of how workflow relates to groupware. I would argue that both workflow and groupware are categories of collaborative systems, but are quite different from them in some respects. As with other groupware applications, workflow can help teams of coworkers to cooperate, communicate, share information and complete tasks. For this reason workflow is sometimes considered to be a sub-category of groupware or a function available in a particular type of groupware.

So, for example, Lotus claims that the Notes product supports workflow. However, workflow management software does not usually have the full range of groupware facilities for conferencing, shared authoring, e-mail and calendar management, although some workflow products have some of these.

Some authors state that workflow is quite different from groupware because it does not necessarily have to be used for collaboration and that it is process centric rather than group centric. This distinction is made since at a given point in time, when using workflow software, a worker will not be working directly with others as tasks are often performed sequentially by individuals as part of an overall process.

However, in reality, a business process enacted in a workflow system always involves at least two people—someone performing the work and a supervisor or customer—and often a task is routed from one worker to the next. Indeed, when computer supported cooperative work was originally defined by Irene Greif and Paul Cashman in the 1980s they stated that it referred to both direct collaboration and indirect collaboration.

What Defines a Workflow? Key Concepts in Workflow Management Systems

A workflow can be thought of as being made up of a series of *activities* such as "assess credit-worthiness" and "check identity" which together form a *business process* such as "issue a loan" (Figure 4.2). The figure shows how an activity is broken down further into an individual *work item* that needs to be completed. Each of these work items is performed by a *resource*, either the software, hardware or a person who must have the correct responsibility to perform it. The items to be completed are presented in a *workflow queue* which is a worklist of all tasks to be completed by an individual or those in a team.

The order in which work items and activities take place is governed by business rules which describe the sequence of activities or dependencies between tasks. The formal statement of these rules is a *process definition*. Thus an activity of a clerk confirming a loan to a customer in writing must be preceded by authorization by a senior manager. How to model workflow and processes is considered in detail in Chapter 7 where the alternative methods for defining processes and workflows are considered. For now we will introduce some of the key workflow concepts.

Figure 4.2
The relationship between key work elements in a workflow system

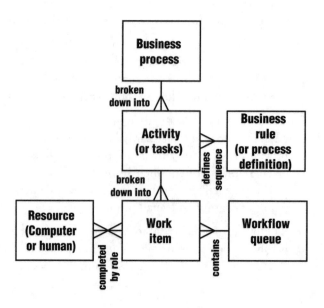

1. Process Elements (Work Activities and Tasks)

These are the individual units of work which make up the workflow. The terminology used varies between authors and product vendors. Most commonly, these are referred to as *tasks* or *activities*. An activity might be to "check identity" or "check credit history" in a home loan application. These activities can usually be further decomposed to sub-tasks creating a hierarchy of tasks.

The WFMC standard adopts a hierarchical approach by identifying *activities* which together make up a *process*, with the activities being further divided into *work items* performed by end users. As activities are completed, object state transitions will occur which need to be recorded by the system. These represent progression in completion of the case. In the example of a house sale the property object may change from "under offer" to "sold."

A *process instance* refers to one particular activity or task such as "approve the loan for customer Smith." When the process instance is first created this is called instantiation.

2. Resources and Their Roles

These are the human and computer resources that perform the activities that make up the business processes. Users or computer resources known as *workflow participants* are given one or several roles which will determine whether they can perform a particular task. Roles might include:

▶ clerk

▶ administrator

▶ branch manager

▶ senior manager

In the example of a loan application, only the senior manger would be able to authorize loans above a certain value. So a manager such as "Karen," would be given a role of "Approver." It is important that these roles are easy to assign dynamically while the system is operational. Proxies can be set up for other workers to assist with tasks, for example when a worker is on vacation.

The use of roles rather than individuals is important as it makes it easy for the responsibilities of one person to be transferred to someone else with the same role. This may be necessary if someone is absent sick, or away on vacation. This facility is known as using a proxy or sometimes, delegation.

In some situations it is necessary to specify that a task is escalated to a different role. For example, if the approval is not made after one day it is routed to the supervisor.

3. Dependencies and Business Rules

Dependencies describe how the different activities relate to each other. These are defined by the *business rules* which make up the workflow. For example, the activity of authorization by a manager must occur before a clerk can grant a home loan to a customer. The sequence of activities may be governed by pre- or post-conditions that need to be fulfilled before initiation or completion of an activity. These conditions may specify that a number of activities need to be completed (AND condition) or one of several alternatives (OR condition).

The dependencies specify how material is routed from one workflow participant to the next. Business rules include not only dependencies but also the prioritization of tasks and the roles or authority of staff who are permitted to perform tasks. These dependencies are sometimes known as routing primitives. These are discussed in more detail in Chapter 7 on process definition. They include:

1. **Sequential.** Task A is followed by Task B followed by Task C.

2. **Parallel.** After Task A, Tasks B and C can occur simultaneously.

3. **Splits.** After Task A, Tasks B and C must occur.

4. **Joins.** Before Task D can start both tasks B and C must be complete.

5. **Iteration.** An item is routed to an earlier stage if a condition is not met.

4. Workflow Queue

Workflow systems usually employ a workflow queue which is used to assign tasks to individuals. A workflow queue will contain a list of tasks or activities that need to be performed in a priority order. The item at the head of the queue will be automatically assigned to the next worker who becomes available who has the correct role to complete the work.

5. Case Management

Since workflow applications often deal with information relating to an individual such as a customer looking to take out a loan or insurance policy, a patient, or an employee, the use of a case or folder metaphor is common to workflow systems. A case will consist of a single instance of the principal object subject to workflow; the customer. Each case can be thought of as a folder from a filing cabinet which has all information related to that individual such as application forms and letters to and from the person. For each case a number of activities will need to be performed. The case folder will be created when a workflow is first instantiated in relation to a particular person. A folder metaphor is often used within the user interface of workflow products to relate to a particular case.

An example of such a case management oriented software application is shown in Figure 4.3. This shows the history associated with a particular case—Mr. P. Taylor. This provides an audit trail of all activities associated with this customer. If the customer calls, it will be easy to tell them the current status of the case. As the case progresses there may be checklists of tasks such as providing identity as documents are added to the case.

These checklists are, of course, useful for monitoring the status of each case. Most customer centered workflow systems adopt the case approach, but not all workflow systems involve case management. For example, middleware workflow transaction managers operate at a transaction level without consideration of a whole case. Methods of designing case ownership are given in the final case study in Chapter 8.

6. Messaging

Additional messages may be sent between coworkers when exceptional events occur which prevent the smooth running of the system. For example, if a worker has to query a possible case of fraud on a loan they may need to notify a manager to check this. The system may use the standard company mail system or the workflow system will allow a notification to be issued or can permit re-routing of a task or its retraction. Alternatively, the case would be paused or suspended in this case so that no further work items were produced.

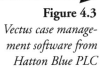

Figure 4.3
Vectus case management software from Hatton Blue PLC

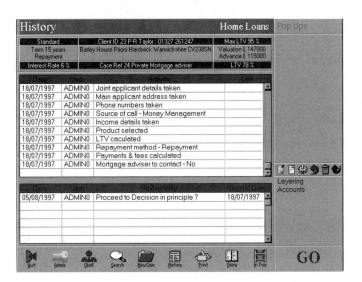

Types of Workflow Systems

Two broad divisions of workflow are commonly recognized. These are ad hoc workflows and more structured workflows known as production and administrative. These different types of workflow can be broadly classified according to their degree of structure and the amount of collaboration that is required. This is illustrated in Figure 4.4.

Ad hoc workflows are those most commonly addressed by simple groupware products. They usually involve one-off tasks which are not conducted in a pre-defined order. For example, when preparing a sales proposal or a product design which involves collaboration and decisions coordinated not through automation, but via human intervention. They often involve routing of documents to people. Traditional groupware such as Lotus Notes or Microsoft Exchange is often used in this way. Task instructions can be viewed in the Microsoft Outlook groupware client.

Since traditional groupware products are commonly used for this type of workflow these are sometimes referred to as *collaborative workflow* software. Intranet document management systems such as Webflow often assist in this type of workflow (Chapter 5).

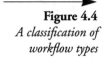

Figure 4.4
A classification of workflow types

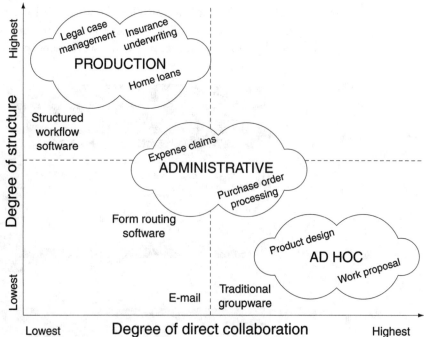

Structured workflows are defined, repeatable tasks which can be specified according to business rules. For example an insurance company may use an insurance claims processing workflow system to manage the process of paying insurance damages to a customer. This would usually be enacted in a WFMS such as Visual Workflo which might first instruct the business user to check validity of the existing policy, then check identity, correspond with other insurers and so on. This category of workflow is usually implemented in a specific workflow package.

Structured workflows are divided further into *administrative workflows* which are usually forms based applications for company administrative procedures such as purchase ordering, applying for vacation or travel claims and *transaction or production workflows* which are highly structured, usually mission critical systems often built on a relational database.

Administrative Workflow Systems

These are commonly forms based workflow systems using electronic forms linked to e-mail. Administrative applications cover routine tasks such as vacation approval or purchase order processing. Although routine, this can offer big savings to companies. The amount spent on paper forms is staggering.

The Gartner Group estimate that 83% of all business documents in the US are forms with an annual purchase cost of $6–8 billion and a processing cost of up to $360 billion. These paper forms are even the target of a 1995 Paperwork Reduction Act.

So, major benefits can occur through automating forms based processes. The process can be turned round more quickly using electronic forms and costs reduced through reduced cost of forms purchase and the shorter cycle time. One of the greatest cost savings is in the coordination of processing the form which is now handled by the business logic built into the application.

In a forms based workflow such as JetForm Corp's JetForm or Caere's Omniform, a user fills in a typical business form such as a purchase requisition on screen and it will then be automatically routed to the person who will authorize it and the purchasing department. Pre-defined routes will be created by an administrator.

Routing is usually achieved by attaching the contents of the form to an e-mail and then using the rules facilities in the groupware to forward it to the relevant person. Tracking of the progress of forms and reporting the efficiency of the process are important features in administrative systems. Examples of products in this category are given in Chapter 6.

Production Workflow Systems

Production systems are the most highly structured workflow systems with clearly defined business rules and precedence. These are required because of the commercial risk involved if prescribed stages are not followed in undertaking mission critical business activities. These systems will be highly automated, with often little collaboration between team members. There will also be links with other organizational information systems such as transaction processing systems.

Transaction Workflow Managers (TWM) are highly automated systems. An example of the application of such a TWM might often involve middleware which is used to manage transactions in a transaction processing system such as credit authorization.

The middleware TWM achieves this through defining routing between separate clients and servers for which it acts as a request broker, often in association with a Transaction Processing Monitor (TP Monitor). Further details on TP monitors, which are the workhorses of many mission critical production workflow systems, are given in Chapter 8.

Push and Pull Workflows

Two other terms which are often used to describe workflow are "push" and "pull" workflows. In the push model the user is fed tasks automatically by the software, usually from a workflow queue. With the pull model the onus is on the end user to select tasks from an available pool of tasks and perform them in the order they see fit. It will be apparent that the "pull" model corresponds more closely to ad hoc workflows and the "push" model to structured workflows.

Within Lotus Notes, the corresponding terms that are used are the Send model and the Share model. In the first case, a workflow is set up to route information in a document from one person to the next. In the share model, the onus is on the user to be proactive and see whether any documents in the shared database warrant their attention.

Object Oriented Workflow Systems

These are increasingly being used to solve business problems. Relatively few commercial examples of true object oriented systems exist, but in the future they will become increasingly common. They are considered in Chapter 10 on the future shape of collaboration. The best known example of an object oriented workflow product is InConcert, which originated from Xerox Parc.

Where Does Document Image Processing Fit In?

Document Image Processing (DIP) or Document Imaging Systems formed the initial impetus for the development of workflow software. DIP provides capture, storage and retrieval for managing digital images of documents. Workflow was then introduced to manage the automation of the initial stages of processing from initial capture through scanning, to indexing and association with a customer or case. It then became apparent that the role of workflow could be extended to managing the whole business process. Note that DIP does not have to involve workflow and workflow does not necessarily include imaging. Most production workflow will include document imaging.

Digital images are useful in many production workflow applications since they are used for easy access to and storage of supporting documentation such as letters from customers or other companies. Often the images are displayed using a separate image viewer applet. Figure 4.5 shows a Staffware form containing case data and a separate image viewer window.

DIP is now a major industry, worth nearly $3 billion in the UK by the end of the decade according to Wharton Information Systems research. When DIP was first conceived it arrived with much fanfare, heralding "the paperless office." Its development was based on the premise that much time in offices was wasted through searching for paper information stored in filing cabinets or vast vaults of deeds and documents. Delivering information to the desktop through a document retrieval system could save time both searching through these vaults or filing cabinets and returning to the desk.

Figure 4.5
Integrated image viewer and case data in a Staffware form

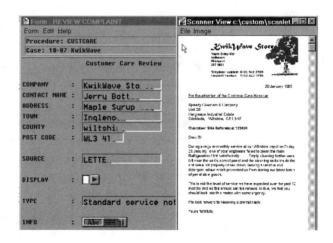

The type of architecture needed for a DIP system is illustrated in Figure 4.6. A scanner PC or workstation is used to operate the scanner and, if appropriate, associate the digital images with a particular case or customer. Following scanning, the image is indexed by the document management software which is running on the image or index server and the image is stored on a high capacity storage device such as an optical jukebox.

These can store a large quantity of information. For example, the Hewlett Packard SureStore is based on individual 2.6Gb capacity magneto-optical (MO) disks giving a maximum storage of 618Gb. This gives up to 628,000 pages of text at 4.1Kb/page or 43,000 pages at 60Kb/page of compressed raster image. Optical storage is usually used since the images are stored as a compressed raster image which occupies much more space than a word processed text document with similar content. Read/write access to the disk is not required since, once scanned, images do not need to be modified.

Since images are retrieved infrequently, the poorer performance of optical compared to magnetic media is not a significant problem. The document management software (DMS) is usually integrated with a standard RDBMS system to store other information related to the image such as customer information. In many implementations the RDBMS is stored on magnetic media for faster read/write access and will also contain the image index.

When a DIP system such as that in Figure 4.6 is set up, the document management software may simply provide a query and retrieval facility to

Figure 4.6
Architecture of a Document Image Processing System

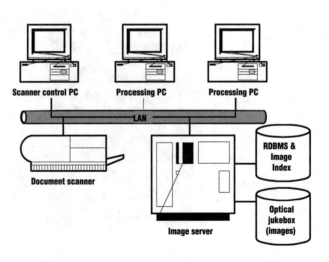

access images on demand. However the power and ease of use of such systems can be increased dramatically if workflow facilities are built in to manage the processing of the documents once they are scanned. This is the way in which the early workflow systems evolved. Once images are scanned, staff need reminders to act on the documents according to their priority and the rules of the business.

What are the benefits of all this technology? Firstly, retrieval times in searching for and bringing a document to a desk are greatly reduced compared to a paper document in a filing cabinet or warehouse. With a single paper document, processing must proceed in a serial fashion with lengthy pauses as the document is passed on from one person to the next, and it lies in their in tray waiting their attention. With the document available to all workers via a network tasks can be performed in parallel if practical and even when working sequentially large gains in speed are possible since the next stage in processing can potentially be completed immediately since transportation from one desk to the next is no longer necessary.

When workflow and DIP processing systems are combined they may also be termed *electronic document management systems* (EDMS). This is a general term that does not necessarily imply the presence of either DIP or workflow, but describes electronic document management facilities such as OCR, indexing, revision control and search and retrieval methods (such systems are described at the end of Chapter 3).

For applications involving processing customer loans through brokers, workflow and DIP technology can be augmented by video-conferencing. In 1996 *Datamation* magazine reported on the case of Flagstar, a loan company who use Intel Proshare video-conferencing to link over 500 brokers and their customers around the United States. This is reported to have reduced the time for loan approval from several weeks to a week. Problems with the loan application can be discussed and resolved rapidly through conferencing and on-line access to case details and documents that have been scanned into the workflow system.

COLD

Computer Output to Laser Disk (COLD) systems are a technology related to DIP. They also use optical, read-only storage for large volumes of information. They differ in that rather than the contents being scanned, they are output from legacy or transaction based systems for auditing and accountability purposes. This might include billing or transaction records which would previously have been stored on paper or magnetic tape and would be difficult to access.

Workflow Products

A range of workflow products for both administrative and production work-flow are compared in Chapter 6 and intranet based products are discussed in Chapter 5.

Workflow System Components

The typical components of a WFMS are identified by the WfMC in their Standard Reference Model (Figure 4.7). This illustrates the components of a generic WFMS. At the core of the system is the *workflow engine or scheduler* which assigns tasks to people according to the availability of staff and the priority for each task. The tasks are notified to end users through a *workflow client* which provides other tools and information for staff to enable them to complete their work. The programming interface between each component (interfaces 1–5) is defined by the Workflow Application Programming Interface (WAPI).

Ancillary tools are also important: *process definition tools* map out the business rules which will be enacted in the WFMS; *monitoring tools* simulate the volume and routing of workflow and measure the performance of the staff and system producing metrics to assist managers. Process definition tools are used to define the existing business processes and the improved or reengineered business processes and these requirements may then be translated into a working system.

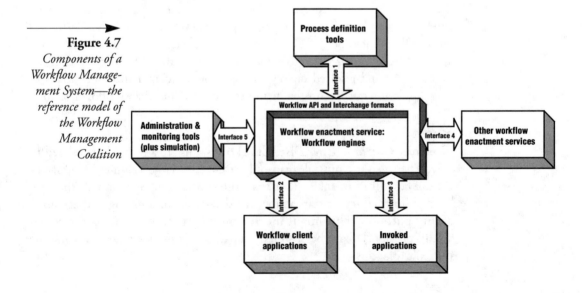

Figure 4.7
Components of a Workflow Management System—the reference model of the Workflow Management Coalition

Workflow Engine

The workflow engine is the most important runtime component of a workflow system. It will usually run as a process or service on a server and will be instructed by other workflow components to perform certain tasks. Its main role is the scheduling of tasks through prioritizing and then assigning them to individuals. Before it can do this though, it must interpret the business rules from the process definition. The main functions of the workflow engine are:

▶ Read the process definition (this may be updated while the engine is running)

▶ Read active participants (may be updated also)

▶ Read other data relevant to workflow

▶ Create work items which comprise the activity and process instances

▶ Schedule work items and assign them to participants

▶ Perform administration tasks such as suspend or terminating a problem task

Types of Data Used in a Workflow System

The workflow engine reads a range of different data types which have been categorized by the WfMC according to how or whether the workflow engine uses the data in its operation.

▶ **Workflow relevant data** are used to control the state transitions and scheduling within the engine. This information is often based on business rules contained in the process definition. For example, if we are dealing with a large invoice for payment which must be dealt with promptly for a discount, then this will be given a high priority. The workflow engine may also act as a broker to pass information to other workflow components via WAPI.

▶ **Workflow control data** is internal data on the status of objects that is used by the engine during its operation, but is not required by other components of the WFMS through WAPI.

▶ **Workflow application data** is information relating to a particular case which is *not* required by the workflow engine for scheduling, but may be used within the client application to give information about the case to the end user. An example of this is the customer's personal details or a document image of a loan application form from the customer. This is often also referred to as case data.

Figure 4.8 shows how the different types of data are used by the workflow engine and the client application.

Process Definition Tool

The process definition tool provide a method for defining processes, activities and work items and who the participants should be. This is normally possible through a graphical interface. An example of such a product is the Action workflow process definition tool from which an example definition is shown in Figure 7.8. The Action process definition model involves setting up a contract type arrangement between a customer and performer for each task and then linking these tasks together. Further details and alternative methods of performing process analysis and definition are described in Chapter 7 on process analysis and modeling.

Process definition tools may be part of the workflow product toolset as is the case with the Action workflow definer or it may be part of another class of product such as a CASE tool, BPR or simulation modeling tool. Available tools are considered further in Chapter 6. The WfMC WAPI interface 1 enables you to mix and match your preferred tool with your workflow engine.

Figure 4.8
Workflow interactions between different software modules, data types and users

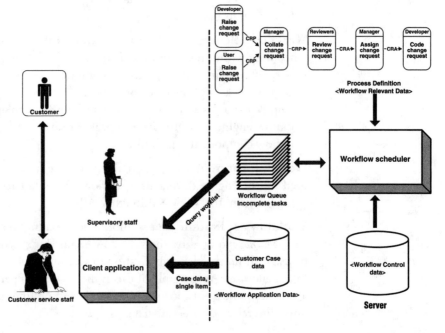

Workflow Client

The client software is used by workflow participants to interact with the workflow engine. This allows the user to perform the following types of function:

▶ **Login.** This identifies the participant and their role such as supervisor or clerk and then connects to the workflow engine.

▶ **Create new process instances.** For example when a new customer case is added to the system.

▶ **Request or select new tasks.** Depends on whether the workflow engine is operating under a push or pull model.

▶ **Access case data necessary to complete the task.** Here the client application will use queries to access information on the case from a relational database. Case information may include the personal details of the customer and document images detailing the nature of their transaction. This information may be retrieved through WAPI using the invoked application interface 3 or it may use proprietary queries

▶ **Mark tasks as complete.** Options are available to mark individual work items in a checklist as complete or alternately suspend or reroute them to some other workflow participant if there is a problem with the application

▶ **Review tasks status.** This may be used by end users or supervisors to see which tasks are not completed.

▶ **Change process definition.** This may be possible for a customizable workflow through the client. For example a new process type could be created or the role necessary for completion could be changed.

The workflow client will often include functions for both workers and supervisors with the functions available controlled by the role of the user identified when they log-in to the system. The main functions of the system such as identifying, reviewing and completing tasks will be accessible via the worklist handler. This will give a list of tasks of different types from the workflow queue with their due dates with buttons available for marking the selected work item as complete.

A typical worklist handler is shown in Figure 4.9. The Staffware Queue Manager illustrated shows an administrator's view of queues for different staff. The worklist can be configured to show different information. It will usually display the task name and its deadline, the most urgent items being at the top of the list. The example shown involves a series of support problems which do not involve any dependencies. This type of simple workflow application is sometimes referred to as queue based workflow.

Figure 4.9
Worklist handler
from Staffware

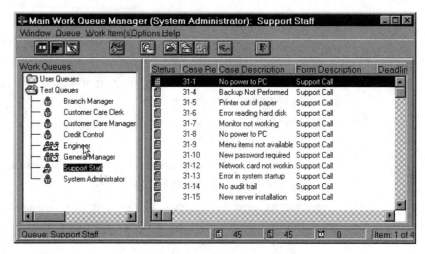

How are Workflow Systems Implemented?

Workflow systems are normally implemented as either of the following alternatives:

1. Relational Database based. The majority of transaction and production workflow applications will be based on RDBMS, either proprietary to the workflow system or more often based on a commercial product such as Oracle or Sybase. Database tables contain information defining the key components of the workflow such as users and their roles, activities and work items, business rules on sequencing and priorities and the workflow queue. The server runs processes for executing the business rules through a workflow engine or through stored procedures based on triggers which are activated by inserts and updates to database tables. Each client application operated by the end users will make SQL requests to query the next item on the workflow queue or to update the status of a task to complete. Messages are not usually transmitted to users as part of the mail system in these implementations.

2. Messaging or mail based. This method is more typical for ad hoc and administrative systems which are often based on e-mail or forms enabled e-mail. In a forms enabled application new work items are normally notified to workers or routed from one worker to the next by e-mail messages. With the e-mail approach more of the processing and business rules are likely to be implemented through the client application than on the "back-end" server.

It is apparent that the basis of the two approaches is quite different, although it can be argued that these two architectures are not dissimilar in that mail systems are based on a database-like table of messages which are queried or polled from a mail client. The RDBMS solution is more appropriate where large numbers of transactions occur. Built-in database facilities, which are lacking in the mail based solutions, are vital for production workflow and include:

▶ Security—Restricting access to certain information in table

▶ Rollback and recovery from failed transactions

▶ Optimization of data queries

Mail based systems tend to be lower cost and simple rules are easier to configure. More complex rules may not be possible. Monitoring facilities of process performance are often absent.

Can Standards Help? Workflow Standards and APIs

Workflow Management Coalition (WfMC)

One of the main industry bodies that is attempting to define standards for workflow is the Workflow Management Coalition (WfMC). Founded in 1993 as a non-profit making organization of vendors, analysts and users, it is supported by all the main vendors and has been active in the development and promotion of workflow standards to achieve interoperability between the different components of workflow reference model.

The definition work of the WfMC is supported by Edinburgh University consortium Workflow Ontology project. The standards produced to date include a glossary to promote a common terminology and specifications for interoperability between the different modules of the reference model shown in Figure 4.7. These API and data interchange standards are known as WAPI (Workflow API and Interchange standards). Each of the five interfaces provides an API between the workflow enactment service, more usually referred to as a workflow engine and another component of the workflow management system as follows:

▶ **Interface 1—Process definition tools.** Enables the workflow definition to be updated in real time and the engine adjusts accordingly.

▶ **Interface 2—Workflow client applications.** Possibly the most important API since it governs how the end user application interacts with the workflow engine. It specifies how tasks are completed and reviewed through the worklist handler. One API call, for example, will return a list of all outstanding work items for a participant.

▶ **Interface 3—Invoked applications.** Other programs can be invoked by Remote Procedure Call and other methods.

▶ **Interface 4—Other workflow engines.**

▶ **Interface 5—Administration and monitoring tools.** Used by administrators of the system to assess performance of the overall system and individual participants. This interface can also be used to perform simulation to predict the behavior of a workflow system before it becomes live.

Note that there is some overlap within the API so function calls may be used in two or more interface definitions.

Web reference: http://www.ed.ac.uk/WfMC

At the first demonstration in June 1996, the WfMC demonstrated interoperability between software from: DEC, Staffware, IBM, CSE Systems, Wang and ICL. These were the first combined demonstrations of an attempt at an industry-wide workflow standard.

Performance Monitoring and Process Metrics

Metrics produced by the WFMS are used to monitor the daily performance of the human and computer resources of the workflow system. They also are used at a macro scale when aggregated to derive business benefits such as as hoped for improvements achieved in the total cost and time of processing a case. Metrics were considered in detail in Chapter 2.

Real time metrics can be obtained through WAPI Interface 5 between the workflow engine and administration tools from events such as the creation, suspension and completion of process instances. Additional metrics can be obtained through WAPI Interface 2 which can give a time integrated view on the number of events to yield metrics such as the number of tasks completed over a certain period of time.

Workflow and Reengineering Industry Association (WARIA)

Workflow and Reengineering Industry Association (WARIA) is another significant industry body which again has good industry support and is active in promoting conferences and sharing of experience and documentation. It has been less active in promoting standards.

Web reference: http://www.waria.com

The MAPI Workflow Framework

The MAPI workflow framework was originally proposed in the mid 1990s by Microsoft in collaboration with Wang Software (now Eastman Software). It does not now appear to be positioned as a major Microsoft initiative and is also separate from the WfMC initiative. When first touted, this appeared a significant venture, partly because Microsoft is such a major player, but also because the concept and focus of the framework was quite different from that of the WfMC.

This framework is based on messaging using the Microsoft Mail API rather than an interprocess communication type client/server API specified by the WfMC. The use of MAPI lends itself to message based workflow across the Internet and this is how Microsoft/Wang are positioning it. The vendor support for this standard is limited compared to the WfMC, which has established momentum.

MAPI workflow will probably become the main method of supporting administrative or even production workflow within Microsoft Exchange. Exchange will act as the client for viewing workflow queues within its in-box. Additional applications in Visual Basic or C++ will provide additional facilities included with production workflow products such as Staffware or Flowmark. Given the installed base of this product, this will certainly make this standard important in the future.

Technical Details of the Standard

The MAPI Workflow Framework is based around the components of:

▶ **Workitems.** A workitem is a message containing a task and supporting documentation delivered by the mail system. A workitem is defined as a class having standard properties such as a type and attachments for related documentation. The framework is based on Internet messaging standards with SMTP being used for workitem creation and IMAP4 for querying or updating workitems and MIME used to encode the contents of the message.

▶ **Queues.** Workflow queues are collections of messages stored in folders. Through setting up access control, folders can be shared or private. Viewing the workflow queue can then be achieved by selecting different criteria of messages such as creation or target completion date. IMAP4 is used for the management of these queues providing functions such as create, delete and rename item and list all items.

▶ **Routing.** Any message can be routed using mail rules in the ways necessary for workflow, i.e. sequential, parallel and conditional.

▶ **Command messages.** These messages are equivalent to the WfMC interface 4 for interoperability. This specifies interprocess control features such as Start, Stop, Suspend and Resume which are again sent by mail messages.

Web reference: http://www.eastmansoftware.com (Wang workflow now relocated to this site)

How Do the WfMC Standards Relate to the MAPI Framework?

Recent developments have seen some convergence of standards, with the WfMC publicizing the use of a similar mail based binding for its Interface 4 standard for interoperability between workflow engines. This is based on Internet mail for transport, and content is encoded within the Multipurpose Internet Mail Extension (MIME) based attachments.

The WfMC Interface 4 MIME binding was demonstrated at three major workflow conferences in 1996 and 1997. Vendors demonstrating integration included: IBM FlowMark, WANG OPEN/workflow, Staffware, DEC, CSE Workflow, Computron Workflow, ICL RoleModel, DST Systems, DOMUS Software. Other vendors who have declared the intent to support the MIME binding are: Business Review International, Computron, FABA—Fallmann & Bauernfeind, FileNet Corporation, Hitachi Ltd., IA Corporation, InConcert, Meta Software, Open Text Corporation, SAP AG, Sema Group and Siemens Nixdorf. With the majority of the major vendors supporting this standard the WfMC looks to be the forerunner in the workflow standards battle.

Document Management Standards

There are also standards bodies associated with document management systems. The best supported are those associated with AIIM, The Association of Information and Image Management. The Document Management Alliance (DMA) is a task force created by AIIM in April 1995 attempting to create a uniform approach to the design, implementation and management of enterprise-wide DMS. The DMA specifications define APIs between the different applications vendors. Version 1.0 was published in January 1997. Fewer vendors support these standards than those of the WfMC and it is a stated aim of the DMA to encourage interoperability with the WfMC standards. This will probably be the future pattern of standards development in this area.

Web reference: http://www.aiim.org

Also under the umbrella of AIIM is the ODMA (Open Document Management API). This is supported by key imaging/DMS vendors such as Documentum, Eastman Kodak, Interleaf and Wang Labs and some combined Workflow/DIP vendors such as Filenet Corporation and Staffware. The API provides applications such as workflow applications with a consistent method to integrate with clients from DMS. For example a FileNet imaging application could be integrated with a workflow system based on Oracle. There is also an ODMA Extension for Workflow.

It is apparent from the range of standards that there are conflicts that will arise although the work of the WfMC is widely supported. This will be compounded since the Object Management Group (Chapter 10) is seeking approval for an object workflow standard since it believes that existing standards are not transferable to the object model.

Web reference: http://www.omg.org

5

Intranet and Internet Based Groupware and Workflow

The growth of intranets and the Internet as a means of deploying applications represents one of the most dramatic changes in the history of computing. The market for services in this area has grown from zero to over $1 billion in a few years, according to research by Zona Research, Redwood City, CA. Web browsers make a great platform for sharing documents and managing tasks. They give familiarity, ease of use and simplicity. They also bring clear benefits. A 1997 survey by the Meta Group of 55 companies, mainly taken from the top 200 Fortune companies, showed that intranets were delivering average Return on Investment of 38%. This figure was higher when companies had developed intranets which went beyond information publishing to collaborative or interactive applications.

This combination, plus their low cost and the ease of deploying applications surely represents the future for all groupware and workflow applications. All major collaborative software players have, or are actively enabling their applications to integrate with the Internet.

Although the Internet has many tools to navigate and transfer files between servers, it is really the increase in use of web browsers to access information on web servers which has caused this change in groupware. Browsers such as Netscape Navigator and Microsoft Explorer provide an easy method of accessing and viewing web documents stored on different servers.

Intranets arose because companies who experimented with using Internet tools to share company information realised intranets offered several benefits over traditional information systems. Intranets use the tested standards and tools of the Internet, but access is limited to employees within an organization. Of course, security becomes important to stop unauthorized access to company data. Early adopters found that intranets can be:

▶ quick to set up

▶ cheap to maintain

▶ easy to use and so popular with users

▶ easily deployed across different operating systems and environments

Note that I have used the phrase "can be" since the more you want your applications to do, the less clear these advantages become.

Extranets are intranets that are extended outside a company for access by trusted third parties such as suppliers and customers. They are now used by companies such as Cisco and Boeing to receive online orders for components. Customers can also track the availability and delivery of these components. With functions such as this, extranets are difficult to set up and maintain. The electronics supplier Racal spent over $1 million setting up its extranet.

In This Chapter

In this chapter we examine the reasons for the increased use of intranets and consider the range of benefits available to a company looking to set up group enabled applications on an intranet or on the Internet. We also look at the stages involved in setting up an intranet for groupware. I highlight the pitfalls in areas such as security, performance and usability created by the newness of the technology. We also review the progress of the major vendors to date and look at other newer products that have been developed for the market.

Because of the newness of the Net and the speed at which it is changing, terms used to describe it are often used interchangeably. We start by defining these terms to provide a common reference. These are very well known so you may well want to skip forward to the section on collaborative software for intranets.

Key Terms

The Internet

The Internet refers to the physical network that links computers across the globe. It consists of the infrastructure of servers and communication links between them which is used to hold and transport the vast amount of information on the Internet. The history and origin of the Internet is now well known. It started life around 1969 as the ARPAnet network in the United States which linked servers used by key military and academic collaborators at the time of the cold war. In this coverage we take the existence of this network as a given, and ask what we can do with the tools that are available now.

Intranet

While the Internet is a well established term the intranet as a concept only came into existence in the early to mid 1990s. An intranet is a network within a single company which enables access to company information through the familiar tools of the Internet such as web browsers. An example of the type of project related company information that can be shared is shown in Figure 5.1.

Intranets have experienced a surge in popularity since they have proved relatively cheap and rapid to set up and deliver benefits soon providing a good return on investment. They use the tested standards of the Internet such as TCP/IP and Local Area Network topologies.

Extranet

An extranet can be formed by extending an intranet beyond a company to different partners such as customers, suppliers, collaborators or even competitors. Of course information is not available to everyone with an Internet connection—access is restricted to trusted partners using usernames and passwords or certain IP addresses. Extranets are sometimes known as virtual intranets.

The World Wide Web

The Internet has many tools based on different protocols such as ftp, gopher and telnet which can be used to navigate and transfer files between servers. The *World Wide Web* (WWW) is another access method which has become very popular and responsible for the growth in the use of the Internet as a

Figure 5.1
Example of an Open Text Livelink intranet page used to display product information for a product design and marketing team

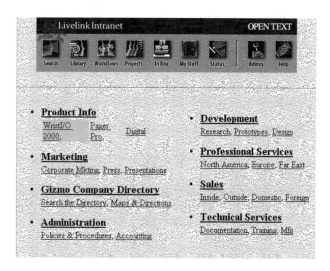

serious business tool. The World Wide Web or web is a medium for publishing information on the Internet in an easy to use form which also supports interactive applications. The medium is based on a document format known as *Hypertext Markup Language* (HTML), and is similar to a word processing format. It is significant since it offers hyperlinks which allow users to move from one document to another—the process known as surfing. HTML pages are served using the http protocol which is described in the section on web standards.

Web Browsers

Browsers such as Netscape Navigator or Microsoft Explorer provide an easy method of accessing and viewing information stored as web documents on different servers. The web pages stored as HTML files on the servers are accessed through a particular standard supported by the web browsers. This is the *hypertext transfer protocol* (http), that you will always see preceding the web address of a company. For example http://www.microsoft.com is well known.

Web Addresses (Uniform Resource Locators—URLs)

Web addresses refer to particular pages on the WWW which are hosted by a company or organization. The technical name for these is *Uniform Resource Locators* (URLs). They are usually prefixed by http://www. to denote the web protocol and then are broken down as follows:

http://www.domain-name.extension/filename.html

Web Standards

Web standards are considered briefly here since they are again well known. The World Wide Web is based on the two key standards and the underlying TCP/IP network protocol.

Hypertext Markup Language (HTML)

A standard markup language known as Hypertext Markup Language (HTML) is used as the format of documents displayed on the web browsers such as Netscape Navigator. These browsers interpret the HTML codes to display different hyperlinks, text styles and graphics. Because HTML is a rapidly evolving standard it is necessary to use a recent browser that supports the most recent standard (currently 4.0). Indeed many of the browser vendors have their own language extensions which only they will support while they lobby for incorporation into the next revision of the standard.

Dynamic HTML (DHTML) is an extension to the original standard incorporated in the latest browsers from Microsoft and Netscape. This offers the opportunity to update page styles more rapidly, but more importantly, improved interactivity is built in with developers able to respond more effectively to user mouse and keyboard events. This will improve the usability of collaborative applications used from within web browsers.

A further recent development is *Extensible Markup Language* (XML). This is a significant standard in that it provides more flexibility than HTML to tailor specialist applications and content. This should lead to better document management facilities for indexing, searching and retrieval of documents.

Hypertext Transport Communications Protocol (HTTP)

The Hypertext transport communications protocol is always referred to in the shorthand form of HTTP. HTTP is used to provide connections between the servers and the clients which access them. The protocol involves a request for information specified by the address (URL) of the document and a response which is different packets comprising the whole document. This protocol is stateless (connectionless) meaning that after downloading a series of packets or a page, there is no link maintained between the server and the client. The transport of these packets is mediated by the underlying TCP/IP protocol. The stateless connection is significant since it reduces the bandwidth requirements for effective operation of the network. It also means a difference in the way the web works to existing groupware applications.

Common Gateway Interface (CGI)

In its early days the web was mainly used as a passive way of publishing information such as marketing information about company products. For a company with many products though, this is limiting since the user has to use hyperlinks to scroll through many screens of information for the product they want. However, the *Common Gateway Interface* (CGI) was at hand to offer a way of providing interactivity to the web. CGI provides extensions to the web server which allow scripts to be run which process information submitted through web based forms. With a form built into the HTML document a user can supply the name of the type of product they are interested in and a query can be performed returning the details of the product. With this facility the web is transformed from a passive document publisher into an interactive tool which can be used to write groupware applications which update, query and share databases and make commercial transactions possible. The scripting language Perl is commonly used for processing information generated by CGI interactions.

Other Standards for Dynamic Content: Javascript, Java and ActiveX

When browsers were first introduced, they consisted of static web pages of text and graphics. These could not be used to implement the interactive functions of groupware applications. CGI was an early method of enabling user interaction through on-screen forms. There are now a range of competing methods which can be used to implement features such as command buttons, menus and drop-down lists, and execute control flow of a program according to the events generated by these controls.

The best known of these emerging standards is Java—a programming language in which full function applications such as the word processor and spreadsheet in the Lotus eSuite (formerly Kona) package have been written. Microsoft has also extended its Object Linking and Embedding technology into ActiveX which will also enable functionality such as a spreadsheet engine to be embedded into the web browser and then used as part of the application. A more limited scripting language to extend the interactivity of pages is JavaScript and *dynamic HTML* (DHTML). All of these new methods are now being used to develop the next generation of groupware and workflow products.

Why Intranets?

Intranets have become popular for exactly the same reasons that groupware has been used—they are good for helping collaboration and communication in a business. In particular, intranets are very good for sharing information between staff. Plus they have two benefits that traditionally groupware has not had—intranets are quick and cheap to set up! Through intranet enabled groupware these familiar applications are possible:

▶ Publishing information

▶ E-mail

▶ Shared document authoring

▶ Text and video-conferencing

▶ Electronic meetings

▶ Workflow

Intranet based workflow to date has mainly focused on administrative workflow such as ordering internal supplies, booking holidays or travel claims. Vendors of production workflow systems such as Staffware have also produced web browser based clients for their workflow engines.

Many companies start to use intranets as a means of increasing the availability of information, while at the same time reducing the cost of producing it and managing it. Opportunities for sharing information include:

▶ Staff directories and organization charts

▶ Company standards and working procedures such as performing customer care

▶ Personnel information such as staff handbooks

▶ Company financial performance reporting traditionally handled by Executive Information Systems and communications/news from management to staff

▶ Marketing information—customer information and sales information including access to data warehouses and datamarts

▶ Product information, e.g. price catalogs, technical sheets

In fact, anything which is already held as a document or as part of a database can be accessed via an intranet and web browser. British Telecom has recently introduced an intranet to 65,000 of its employees worldwide. It is estimated by the company that putting the price catalog online has saved $1.25 million in direct costs of paper and media. Indirect savings in staff time to search and update the list are ten times greater!

As well as providing these applications to support the business, intranet groupware offers further benefits which it shares with the web:

1. It is relatively quick to author web content in comparison with developing traditional business applications. Simple web publishing can be accomplished by anyone who can use a word processor.

2. Web browsers provide an easy to use graphical environment popular with users. Web pages support graphic images and interaction, making it an attractive and visual medium. It is easy to use since navigation between documents can happen by clicking on hyperlinks or images. This is a very intuitive way of navigation which is similar across all web sites and applications.

3. Browsers provide a cross platform medium for delivering applications, which is important for large corporations who may need to support a

range of web clients on Windows PCs, Macintoshes and Unix work-stations to access the same information or run the same application.

4. Lower support and ownership costs exist for a company since browsers are relatively easy to configure and administer compared to other client/server applications each with a proprietary client. Purchase costs have been driven lower too since much Internet software is also available at low cost currently due to promotions trying to increase market and mind share.

5. Reduced hardware purchase costs can occur since lower hardware specifications are needed if intranet applications are designed so more processing occurs on the server. This is the premise behind *Network Computers* (NCs).

6. There are a large and growing number of people using the web. The number of users connected to the web is estimated to be 152 million by the year 2000 (Table 5.1). The numbers of businesses using it make it good for cross company collaboration.

Table 5.1 *IT users worldwide. Source: IDC Oct 1996; Morgan Stanley, Feb 1996.*

Millions	*1995*	*1996*	*1997*	*1998*	*1999*	*2000*
PC users	144	167	184	204	217	225
E-mail	35	60	80	130	180	200
Net/Web	9	23	46	81	122	152
On-line	8	13	18	23	27	30

Collaborative Software for the Intranet

With the growth in popularity of the Internet and intranet all major groupware and workflow vendors have had to take notice as their markets are threatened by new upstarts. Microsoft, Lotus, Novell and relative newcomers such as Oracle, Corel and Action Technologies have been compelled to update their proprietary client systems. The turnaround has been rapid with companies such as Lotus rebranding their product and integrating existing Notes technology with a web server to release Domino within a short period (Figure 3.6 illustrates a Domino based discussion).

Two approaches to embracing the web have been used. Companies such as Lotus started by developing new web enabled groupware clients. These support traditional groupware functions such as e-mail and forms based applications while also enabling web access. Other companies such as Oracle and Radnet have made all functionality available from a standard web browser by making changes to integrate their server software with the web server.

The second approach has the benefits of being cheaper and users can type in e-mail messages or contribute to a conference direct from their familiar browser without the need to learn client software such as Lotus Notes or Microsoft Exchange. This will probably be the most common situation once the market has stabilized since users will demand all the features available in the most up to date browsers. Lotus and Microsoft have also made modifications to the groupware server to enable co-existence with web servers.

Intranet Architectures

The architecture used for web based groupware is still based on the client/server model as described for standard groupware applications. Most applications are currently configured as two tier client server (Chapter 8). As is to be expected, additional software is required on both server and client to host web based groupware and access it.

Setting up Intranet Access

Client Software

To set up intranet access for employees it is necessary to install each client PC or workstation with a web client and TCP/IP networking software to connect to company web servers. The client PC will need to be configured with drivers to access the Internet using a TCP/IP stack with Windows Sockets. One of the most popular Windows Sockets options is Trumpet Winsock. A web browser will need to be installed together with any plug-ins that are required for playing sound or video for example. Netscape Navigator and Microsoft Explorer are the two most common browsers in use today.

Server Software

To host a web site for an intranet then there are two choices. The most common option is to host the intranet within the safety of your firewall to give you local control and administration. Otherwise, you can distribute information via an *Independent Service Provider* (ISP) by renting space on their web server or co-locating a server on their premises. This model has been extended by Lotus with their TeamRoom initiative. In this users rent space on an external Domino server to provide access to e-mail, documents and Domino applications. Netscape has introduced its VirtualOffice which follows a similar model. This approach will reduce the administration workload since this is performed by the third party.

Server Hardware

Early web servers were frequently UNIX based and these are still common, but PC based Windows NT web servers are increasingly being used. A Pentium processor based PC with 32Mb or more of RAM is a typical entry level configuration for a site with a moderate number of visitors or hits. The preferred software for running a PC web server is Windows NT running Microsoft *Internet Information Server* (IIS). As well as the web server software the groupware server software such as Exchange or Domino will co-exist on the server although it could be placed on another server in large installations. These products will need significantly more RAM.

Gateways

To extend access from the intranet to the Internet a company gateway to the Internet must be installed. This could use a modem, but normally a dedicated server will be used as the gateway. By providing Internet access there are major issues of security which need to be guarded against and these are referred to below.

A connection to the intranet for the mobile or teleworker can be established using a modem and registering them as a user with an *Internet Service Provider* (ISP) such as AOL. This arrangement can also be used for the small business.

Securing the Intranet

If a small to medium company deploys a groupware intranet using their internal LAN facilities and they are on a single site they face few security worries other than setting up access control lists for their users to safeguard sensitive data. When a larger company is connected to other sites by a WAN and also using a web server to give customers access to promotional information the risk becomes much higher. Several approaches should be taken to reduce the risk of corporate information being accessed or deleted.

Access Controls

Internets and intranets can be setup so that no registration is required by the end user, but this will obviously create security problems. It is best to restrict access to users with accounts. This feature is provided with most of the new intranet groupware products referred to below. Through logging on the user is then identified as having a particular user name, e-mail address and role. However, using this as the only security method is notoriously unreliable since users lose and swap passwords.

External Hosting

A reduced risk of access to other company data is one of the benefits of the TeamRoom and Virtual Office approaches described above.

Firewalls

The Internet gateway provides a potential entry point to anyone with a malicious intent and this must obviously be guarded against. A strong, but not impenetrable line of defense which should be used by anyone running web based groupware across the WAN is the *firewall*.

A firewall is a general term used to describe any method of screening the internal network from unwanted visitors. It may vary from cheap software solutions to expensive integrated hardware and software solutions. Typically, a software firewall application is mounted on a separate server at the point the company is connected to the Internet. Firewalls may have the following types of facilities to monitor access requests to your site and take preventative action:

► Firewall software can be configured to only accept links from trusted domains representing other offices in the company. In fact, it is possible to configure a standard router to achieve this. However, *IP spoofing* or simulation of these other addresses can be used to gain access. For this reason, security measures are continually evolving. New standards such as the authentication of IP addresses in new IP standard version 6 for example should reduce the problem of IP spoofing.

► Encryption of data packets as they leave the site to other company offices and decrypting on arrival will become standard to make things more difficult for eavesdroppers.

► Specialized software for placing on proxy servers such as Webwall from Network Associates Inc. (formerly McAfee) or Novix from Firefox are software based solutions which also include anti-virus features. Novix costs a few thousand dollars to install.

► Hardware and software based "black-box solutions" such as Firewall-1 from Checkpoint for NT based networks can cost tens of thousands of dollars for a large organization. BorderWare Firewall server 4.0 can be used for NT and Unix based networks.

Web reference: http://www.securecomputing.com (information on Borderware)

Web reference: http://www.checkpoint.com (information on Firewall-1)

Web reference: http://www.nai.com (Information on WebWall)

Web reference: http://www.ftp.com (Nov*ix is now part of the Internet Gateway Suite for Netware)

Safeguarding Transactions

There are many evolving standards to protect company information while it is in transit on the intranet or in particular the Internet. These have mainly been developed to enable electronic commerce. The most widely supported methods for securing transactions are to encrypt outgoing packets with the *Secure Sockets Layer* (SSL) or *Secure HTTP* (SHTTP). The *Secure Electronic Transaction* (SET) standard is a new standard proposed by Visa and Master-card to secure credit card transactions.

Stages in Setting Up an Intranet

The stages that are involved in setting up an intranet unsurprisingly follow those of any groupware application as described in the following chapters. However, developing an intranet tends to follow a more organic, informal pattern than building a production workflow application. To make the intranet work, a more informal approach can help produce a more vibrant and responsive intranet which is more likely to become popular.

As always, user involvement is important and prototyping can help here. Setting up an outline structure or "web-map" for the site showing the type of information that will be available and how it will be arranged should be done early to help sell the project and start discussions about what should be included. Here is an outline of the types of decision that need to be made at each stage. There are five key stages.

Stage 1. Establish the Need

In making the business case for an intranet you will be well supported by surveys from research organizations such as the IDC that show return on investment of several hundred percent in several months and other figures showing an adoption rate for intranets of over 90% in Fortune 500 companies. This stage will involve talking to business users to find out their needs and getting buy-in from senior management. Prototyping will start at the beginning to demonstrate the type of benefits that can be delivered.

Key decisions: Whether to proceed with project or not! The scope of the project will also be established—is it initially trialled in one area such as in marketing or is more limited information for the whole company published? Which applications are targeted—is it static information and e-mail only or are conferencing and interactive forms also required? Over what timescales will these functions be phased in?

Stage 2. Design Applications and Plan Implementation

This involves structuring the information made available over the intranet and designing the capabilities of any specialized workflow features that are required. Often the main design focus will be integration with existing applications and how to access information stored in legacy databases for display over the intranet. Such design issues are described in Chapter 9.

Key decisions: An access policy will be set up stating who can access each application and what information is available. How will the intranet be produced? Through low level tools such as HTML editors and CGI or will groupware packages such as Lotus Domino be used to deliver the information? How will existing applications and the data they use be integrated? The platform architecture of the system will be defined, whether it is based on PC, workstation or thin clients such as NetPCs or NCs. The style of browser necessary to support your system will also be defined. Will the web server be hosted internally or externally? Will the intranet be accessed remotely from mobile users?

Stage 3. Setup Web Server and Clients

On the server the web server and groupware product are set up. User accounts will be created and security measures taken such as setting up an Internet firewall. On the client this stage is straightforward involving installation of web browser clients, plug-ins and setting up TCP/IP connectivity and testing effectiveness.

Stage 4. Develop Applications

Development will have occurred since stage 1 or 2 when early prototypes were produced. During this stage, development of the individual applications will occur and the full web content for the pages will be produced using authoring tools. Other activities such as user training, documentation and setting up change management procedures will occur at this stage.

Stage 5. Deploy Applications and Maintain

Rollout of the system should be straightforward after Stage 3 and 4 have been completed since clients will already be set up. It is often said that web sites are never finished so plan an efficient way of updating pages and applications and notifying users through a "What's New?" area. If the intranet content becomes "stale" it will not be used in a similar way to customers not revisting a boring web site. If it is not clear when information was last updated it rapidly loses its value.

A program of regular weekly and monthly updates giving new company information can assist in keeping momentum. Another method is too make individuals responsible for keeping pages up to date and to get them to mark when each page was last updated and its next planned update. Promotion of the intranet to users and creating a temporary help desk are good for getting users up and running when the system is first introduced. Note that lack of a maintenance plan is the biggest threat to the success of an intranet.

Difficult Choices When Implementing Intranet Based Groupware

With the rapid introduction of new products, awkward choices are faced by those considering the introduction of intranets. Here are some of them:

1. *Do we need a web-enabled groupware package to set up an intranet?*

The short answer is no. To publish static information on an intranet web server then this is possible without a groupware package and many companies have taken this route. If you are publishing documents then there are many HTML editors to achieve this or there are converters such as the Microsoft Internet Assistant, which converts word processed documents to HTML with little knowledge of the markup tags required. Although it is perfectly possible to publish company information in this way it is much more efficient to publish documents stored in a document database. Products such as Lotus Domino or Open Text Livelink make the management of updates easier and documents are less likely to become out of date.

Other groupware components such as e-mail and Usenet based conferencing can be set up on the server as e-mail and news servers again without the need for purchasing a groupware package. You will, however, be restricting your groupware applications by following this route.

Forms based applications for sales or purchasing purposes are possible using CGI and Perl scripts without groupware. But, again, they can be produced more rapidly using groupware with functions such as security easier to build in.

2. *We already use a groupware client. Should we swap to a web browser client?*

This question is faced by those companies who have deployed the millions of Exchange, Notes and Groupwise clients. In the short term it is probably not necessary to migrate to a web client because of the cost and disruption that will occur. No significant new group functionality will be available, indeed the functionality of a web client is usually more limited than that of a Notes or Exchange client currently. In the long term though it is likely that support for the original clients may become limited and some features will only be available in the web client. This will make migration inevitable. If the users are already using a browser to access the web then they will probably favor using a single browser client since this is a more productive way of working.

3. *Which browser should we adopt?*

The similarities between available products make this a relatively unimportant decision. The main precaution is to use a release of the browser that supports the latest standards of HTML, Javascript, and plug-ins and to be sure the browser will run embedded applets such as Java and Active-X. The browser choice comes down to the well established product Netscape Navigator or the relative newcomer Microsoft Internet Explorer. After playing catch up for a while, it is now generally recognized that Internet Explorer is the best in usability and performance although differences between products are limited as they leap frog each other in each release. With Explorer continuing to be available free, this may be the important factor for many corporates who may also wish to standardize on Microsoft products for the desktop. Netscape Navigator is now available with a range of messaging tools as part of the Communicator release, so this may make it attractive in comparison to Explorer although these facilities are available in Microsoft Netmeeting.

4. *Should we host our intranet externally?*

Here, a service such as Lotus TeamRoom or Netscape Virtual Office is used to hold the groupware application and its information third parties' server. With this approach there are clear cost advantages in that the administration overhead is outsourced. This is countered by the reduction in flexibility as it is a lot less easy, if not impossible to make specific modifications for your company as you will be using a standard service. So, most companies with installations large enough to need system administrators prefer to ensure they can remain responsive and keep administration internal by using a dedicated web server.

5. *Who owns the intranet?*

When applications development is conducted in-house, the IT group are usually the de facto owners of the development. Since intranets are relatively easy to set up they may originate in a marketing or HR group. If the initiative comes from one of these areas it is often best if ownership remains in these areas, but with IT providing support as required and providing input in infrastructure related areas such as development tools and security, but with the control of the business applications coming from the business group. With different groups independently developing intranets there is a risk that separate "information islands" will occur. The IT group also has a role in coordinating these developments so that it is easy to access information that needs to be shared across departments. A person should be nominated in each department to be responsible for updating the intranet pages.

6. *What bandwidth do I need?*

Existing LAN speeds will be sufficient for the intranet unless video-conferencing is introduced at the same time.

A Review of Collaborative Intranet Applications

Lotus Products—Notes, Internotes and Domino

Lotus have responded to the popularity in intranets by repositioning Notes to provide its familiar features in a web environment. This was achieved initially using Internotes web publisher which enabled any Notes document or database to be published to the web. With Domino this was taken a stage further by integration with a web server (now supporting integration with *Microsoft Information Server* [MIS]) and incorporating security mechanisms. Many existing Notes users have used these products to produce Internet and intranet sites, since if you already have material in a Notes database it is relatively simple to publish it.

Domino is a good solution for companies wanting to make secure information available across a wide-area network, however the security methods used cannot be as secure as when using the Notes client. With the Notes client an encrypted Notes ID is required on the user's machine. The same level of security is not available across the Internet. To provide additional security Lotus suggests a separate server is used for public Internet databases which is updated using the Notes replication feature from the secure company intranet database.

Domino has been divided into four separate products as follows:

▶ Domino.action is intended to be a simple "out-of-the-box" intranet solution. This version of Domino is currently bundled with IBM servers. It functions by providing templates for different aspects of an intranet such as marketing, finance and discussion.

▶ Domino.doc is a collaborative document management system available from within the web browser environment. Unlike some web based document management solutions it will scale well to a distributed network.

▶ Domino.merchant is for web enabled commerce from a catalog which supports secure payments via credit cards.

▶ Domino.broadcast is a push application for disseminating information in a company or distributing applications.

Web references: http://www.lotus.com and http://www.net.lotus.com (Domino applications).

Microsoft Exchange

Microsoft has rationalized the number of client products to correspond with the advent of the web. It now offers Outlook Web Access as a product which gives Exchange users access to e-mail, calendaring and Exchange public folder data through a web browser. This will help extend Exchange across platforms to unsupported UNIX environments. Details of other Exchange clients are given in Chapter 6.

This product now supports a wide range of standards: SMTP, POP3, IMAP4, LDAP, NNTP, MIME and S/MIME. Microsoft Netmeeting 2.0 is integrated with Explorer browser 4.0 and provides facilities for chat, video-conferencing and document sharing.

Web reference: http://www.microsoft.com

Novell Groupwise

Groupwise also has an Internet client version—Groupwise WebAccess. With this the Groupwise "universal mailbox" is available from a web browser. To access this the user's mail ID and password are entered through a form and then the mailbox is available. Not all facilities such as document management or forms routing are available at the time of writing, and some require additional gateways. The following are available:

▶ Calendaring—personal appointments, tasks and notes.

▶ Group scheduling—schedule meetings and track whether invitations to meetings are accepted or declined.

▶ Task management—assign tasks to other users and track their status View text files and other MIME attachments.

▶ Fax Gateway—send a message to any fax machine worldwide.

▶ Phone Access—listen to voice mail messages received in the Groupwise Universal In Box.

▶ Pager Gateway—send a message to a recipient with pager.

▶ Internet E-mail—available with an additional SMTP Gateway.

▶ Web Publisher—publishing documents on an intranet.

Web reference: http://www.novell.com/groupwise

Oracle InterOffice

Oracle InterOffice (Figure 5.2) is a significant web based technology for deploying groupware intranet applications. It differs from the products mentioned above in that it is developed from the ground up for the Internet. It shows how full groupware client functionality can be supplied in a web client. It seems to have failed to capture mindshare, but has great potential as an intranet application. Although it can be scaled for deployment across sites linked by the Internet, performance in early versions may dissuade some companies from doing this.

Figure 5.2
*Oracle InterOffice
e-mail in-box*

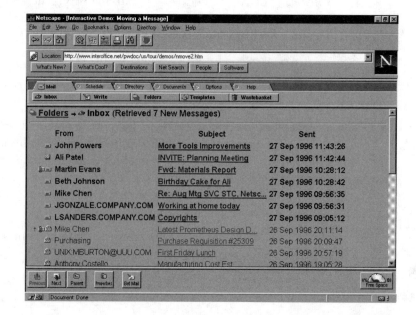

Web references: http://www.interoffice.net (At writing it is possible to test drive InterOffice at this site) and http://www.oracle.com

Netscape SuiteSpot

SuiteSpot is positioned by Netscape as an intranet based competitor for Microsoft Exchange and Lotus Notes. It offers messaging based features such as discussion groups, calendaring, web publishing, and content management and can be used for web based database applications. It can be purchased in a standard edition with these functions, or as enterprise edition, which also has replication and the additional administration facilities of "Mission Control" including certificate based security. Each feature is implemented as a function of a single server as follows:

▶ Messaging Server—an Internet mail server giving centralized administration of users through LDAP (see Chapter 2).

▶ Calendar Server—calendaring and scheduling of people, groups and resources.

▶ Collabra Server—a full-featured text discussion server developed from the successful product originally sold by Collabra.

▶ LiveWire Pro—Used for web hosted database accessing Oracle and Informix relational databases.

▶ Netscape Directory Server—global directory services for SuiteSpot.

▶ Catalog/Compass Server—automated search of intranet or Internet content including documents in a range of formats.

▶ Certificate Server—for the issue, signing and management of public-key certificates using Secure Sockets Layer (SSL) for secure, private communication over the Internet or an intranet.

▶ Proxy Server—a web server that provides replication and filtering of web content. Replication improves performance and reduces network traffic. This server is additional to the standard Netscape web server software.

▶ Pericles Server—a new product for document management that provides a workflow engine.

At the time of writing it is not clear what success this recently released suite of products will achieve. Netscape will be hoping that the frequent use of their web browser client and web server by corporations will lead to the adoption of the other components. In doing this, it will have to battle against the large installed based of its three main competitors.

Web reference: http://home.netscape.com

Radnet Webshare

This product is one of a new breed of collaborative web software for intranets which is designed from the ground up. It offers the Webshare Designer development environment for building form and table based applications and integration of Java and ActiveX components. Simple BASIC scripts based workflow is supported and SQL links to RDBMS are supported. Standard templates giving Starter Applications include a threaded discussion database, a problem tracking application and a document reference library. It includes replication for mobile users. Webshare Server can be configured for use with other HTTP servers such as Netscape SuiteSpot and Microsoft Internet Information Server.

Web reference: http://www.radnet.com

Specialized Groupware Applications for Intranets

This listing is a snapshot of groupware products that have migrated to the Internet/intranet. Many of the products mentioned in Chapter 6 which are not currently accessible via a web browser will be shortly.

Text Conferencing and Bulletin Boards

TeleFinder is a well established Macintosh system providing text conferencing, bulletin boards, e-mail and shared file areas. It has been integrated with a web server to provide access to these facilities from a web browser.

Web reference: http://www.spiderisland.com

Alta Vista Forum

Alta Vista Forum is a structured storage solution for office documents by team members which also gives annotations and discussions facilities. Forum 98 is the latest release. Each forum is a collection of related information resources. Forum types include discussion forums, document forums, news stands and calendars.

Web reference: http://altavista.software.digital.com/forum/products/overview/index.htm

Electronic Meetings Software and TeamWare

Although GroupSystems and VisionQuest are not currently offering web based access to their servers, new products are emerging in this area. These tend to be simpler in terms of facilities, offering chat, discussion, whiteboarding and video-conferencing without Level 2 facilitation facilities such as voting and brainstorming.

Databeam Meeting Tools

This product gives the facility to share live applications, brainstorm ideas, and deliver presentations and product demos to people in remote locations. The suite comprises the T.120 Conference Server software, whiteboarding and the Learning Server for remote delivery of training.

Web reference: http://www.databeam.com

Facilitate.com

Facilitate.com provides a range of tools for hosting virtual meetings over the Internet or your intranet. The meetings can be either synchronous or asynchronous. Tools include shared chat-rooms for brainstorming, facilitating and voting.

Web reference: http://www.facilitate.com

Netopia Virtual Office

This product, formerly from the Farallon Group gives real time Internet chat, screen sharing, remote control, file exchange and messaging. Virtual Office uses an office analogy with different doors for different participants and in and out baskets for leaving files and messages.

Web reference: http://www.netopia.com

Commander DecisionWeb

This product is a decision support tool giving multidimensional data views for web based decision support applications. It requires a Java enabled browser.

Web reference: http://decisionweb.comshare.com

Microsoft Netmeeting

Version 2 of this product looks set to bring group collaboration into the mainstream. Netmeeting provides text and video-conferencing, whiteboarding and Internet phone facilities.

Web reference: http://www.microsoft.com

Lotus Instant TeamRoom

This service is currently available from some ISPs and uses a meeting room metaphor to give collaboration tools for brainstorming, whiteboarding, discussion and voting. It runs using Lotus Domino as does a similar solution from Changepoint's involv Intranet.

Web reference: http://www.lotus.com and http://www.changepoint.com

Instinctive Technology Room

This is a new product which uses ActiveX and requires browser support for this. This provides better real time features than some of its competitors. It also provides support for file versioning and attachments.

Web reference: http://www.instinctive.com

Video-Conferencing

All the main suppliers of video-conferencing solutions mentioned in Chapter 6, namely CU-SeeMe, PictureTel and Intel now offer products which enable multicast video-conferencing across the Internet.

Calendaring and Scheduling

Open Text Livelink OnTime

OnTime is a well established enterprise product, now acquired by Open Text as part of their Livelink Suite, also available for Novell NetWare, Banyan VINES and Windows NT via a Windows client. There is now an intranet edition. OnTime is known as a scalable architecture run by many enterprises operating across multiple sites. It has the benefit that it offers up-to-the-minute scheduling since it does not work by periodic replication of its calendar database which is the method used by other products such as Notes. Instead a separate OnTime service runs on a server in every local workgroup and requests timing and delegate information from the other servers as required.

Web references: http://www.ontime.com and http://www.opentext.com

Crosswind Cyberscheduler

Synchronize from Crosswind Technologies is another enterprise level server which runs on many flavors of UNIX and on NT. The Internet client is known as CyberScheduler.

Web reference: http://www.crosswind.com

Webcal

This is a calendar system giving scheduling and different views of shared diaries. It is based on forms submission using CGI scripts. It is more appropriate for a small group of co-workers.

Web reference: http://www.webcal.com

Web Broadcasting and "Push" Technology

The "push" paradigm is changing the way content is provided and accessed on the web. Rather than users having to search the web to find what they want, users can subscribe to the services providing content they are interested in and this information is broadcast to them. This happens, much in a manner similar to conventional TV broadcast with a subscriber choosing from a number of channels. The content is hosted on a server acting as a transmitter which broadcasts information at intervals. Repeaters can be set up to repeat signals from the server and reduce bandwidth constraints. The information can enter a company through a specialized transmitter on a proxy server outside the company's firewall. Meanwhile a tuner residing on the client machine will poll for updated information at set intervals and then download when appropriate. Options are also available to personalize information to the individual.

The groupware applications of broadcast technology are not clear yet, but applications are likely to lie in the provision of information to teams—a team or a company may have a news channel to give them information about the team project. Figure 5.3 shows the PointCast client (which is now integrated in Microsoft Explorer 4.0) in action delivering technical news. An interesting example of the fusion of groupware with "push" is provided by Unilever Europe. Unilever have integrated Notes with Push technology using Point-Cast. A program has been written to extract key information from the many

Figure 5.3
PointCast web broadcasting client delivering news information

Notes databases used by the company and then broadcast it to staff, the aim being to improve information sharing across departments. Interactive applications of "push" seem less relevant, although it will also be possible to use this technology to deliver updates to groupware applications over the network.

Lotus released Domino.Broadcast in 1996 to provide a similar push facility as an add on to Notes. The other major players are Marimba with their Castanet product and BackWeb. Together with ten other vendors they have formed a partnership to produce standards for broadcast technology. The main outcome of this, to date, has been the *Application Distribution Protocol* (ADP). Emerging standards are the *Channel Definition Format* (CDF) which is used by Microsoft in Explorer 4.0 and the Netscape version of Push in Netscape Communicator 4.0. which uses the MCF definition (Meta Content File). Both of these have been proposed to the World Wide Web consortium (W3C).

Web references: http://www.pointcast.com and http://www.marimba.com

Document Management

All the main suppliers of EDMS software listed in Chapter 3 such as Interleaf, Documentum and Filenet now provide web based access to their documents. These facilities are mainly for review of documents currently rather than updating. As an example, the product from Interleaf is Interleaf Intellecte/Business Web. With this Cross-Repository Retrieval allows the corporate knowledge base to reside in separate systems, yet still function as one integrated resource.

Workgroups can manage their own documents locally, while documents are simultaneously available to the enterprise via web browsers. Workflow for documents allows users to route documents through the enterprise in a logical progression. Application templates are available for developers to quickly create document management web based applications. Developers can create custom applications to meet the needs of their organizations or vertical markets.

Web reference: http://www.interleaf.com

Web reference: http://www.filenet.com (includes information on Saros Mezzanine product)

Web reference: http://www.documentum.com

Web reference: http://www.keyfile.com

Workflow on the Internet/Intranet

Intranet and intranet based workflow uses web browsers to act as the client. The tasks are shown as a series of hyperlinks in a user's in-box which can be clicked on for additional information on the task. The browser is used for reviewing the list of workitems and individual tasks that need to be performed (Figure 5.7).

Internet based workflow uses Internet protocols to enable messaging between clients and servers as follows. The early approach was for CGI based forms to be provided for completing a work item, today more solutions are based on Java and ActiveX applets. Now IMAP4 can be used for querying worklists on the server.

The contents of a work item can be included as an attachment in MIME format. There is a new MIME standard proposed which will assist in encoding workitem contents. *(http://ds.internic.net/internet-drafts/draft-shakib-mime-prop-00.txt)*. The MAPI based workflow standards from Microsoft/Wang/Eastman software described in Chapter 4 will also be important for Internet messaging based workflow. We now consider the types of workflow available on the Internet using similar workflow categories to those defined in Chapter 4.

Simple Forms Based Routing

Simple forms based workflow applications are now available using a web browser. These have evolved from Windows based e-mail form applications such as Informs and JetForms. These products differ from the proprietary client interface versions in that they are usually more limited in their administrative and routing facilities. Forms based routing is also available in the major groupware packages Notes, Exchange and Groupwise, but currently it is less easy to develop and deliver applications than using the specific forms based products outlined below.

JetForm Corporation JetForm

JetForms Filler application can now be deployed over an intranet or the Internet using a plug-in, helper application or Java applet such as that shown in Figure 5.4. An applet such as this could be used to enable customers to initiate a workflow across the Internet by performing loan calculations with follow up by staff of the loan company. Since this is a Java applet it has the advantage that calculations can be performed locally, although this particular application has the disadvantage that the applet to be downloaded is over 300K.

Web reference: http//:www.jetform.com/

JetForm Corporation Formflow

A widely used package, previously distributed by Delrina and Symantec. It shares many features with JetForm. It remains to be seen how the two products will be integrated. Its forms can be displayed on the web, but in place editing is not currently possible.

Groupwise Informs

This currently cannot be accessed from Groupwise WebAccess, but access will be available in future versions.

Web reference: http://www.novell.com

Caere Omniform Internet Publisher

This product offers basic forms capabilities, but is more limited in areas of routing, security and tracking. Its strength is the handling of scanned paper based forms which are processed using OCR.

Web reference: http//:www.caere.com/

Netscape and JavaScript

Netscape have promoted the capability of performing ad hoc forms based workflow from within a browser. This development is code named Pericles and is available as a SuiteSpot module. This uses the scripting language Java-Script available with recent versions of browsers to implement simple forms based routing. There are few tools to support this currently and developers are probably better using a traditional forms enabled e-mail package such as Formflow or JetForms. Netscape have recently signed an agreement with Hewlett Packard to integrate with the HP workflow engine.

Administrative Workflow

Livelink Intranet Workflow from Open Text

Livelink Workflow can be used to graphically create serial, parallel, rendez-vous or conditional workflow processes. Livelink Workflow is a component of

Figure 5.4
JetForms Java applet for submitting forms across the Internet

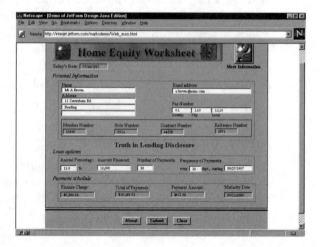

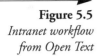

Figure 5.5
*Intranet workflow
from Open Text*

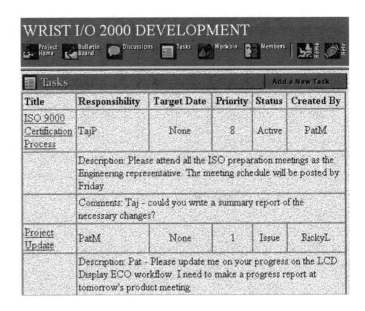

Livelink Intranet, which provides other collaborative features such as Search, Library (document manager) and Collaboration (discussion and ad hoc workflow based on project documents in other modules). A Workflow Painter tool is used for process definitions known as workflow maps. Workflow in progress can be assessed through the graphical workflow maps and detailed status obtained from the audit trail covering every event in the process. Work routed to users includes all the information they need to do their job—due dates, specific instructions, documents and an area for comments (Figure 5.5).

User administration features are also available with version control and check-in/check-out for documents and folders and the ability to set permissions for view, edit, add or delete for a user or group of users. With these features, Livelink workflow can be used for administrative or ad hoc workflows. A detailed tour of the product is available from:

Web reference: http//:www.OpenText.com/livelink

Action Metro from Action Technologies

Action is an established workflow company who were one of the first companies to migrate the client application of their workflow system to a browser. The result is their Metro product. This offers a front-end for administrative or ad hoc workflow. A frame based interface is used with the user who is logged on being given a choice of their personal to do list or different forms based applications (Figure 5.6).

Chapter 5

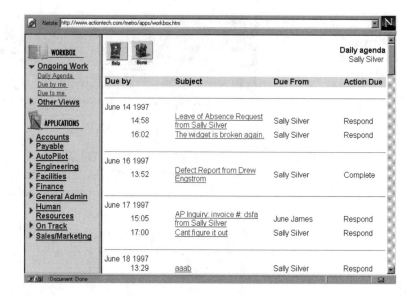

Figure 5.6
*Internet workflow
from Action Metro
product*

Forms based applications are administrative forms such as purchase requisitions or travel forms. Forms can be designed online using the Autopilot module. The product has a clear interface, but suffers from the general limitations imposed by web-browser based applications (see: Short-Term Limitations to Web Based Workflow and Groupware). The product is not suitable for production workflows where case data such as scanned documents and customer details all need to be rapidly available to the operator. Additional development would be required to achieve this.

Web reference: http//:www.actiontech.com/metro

Ultimus Webflow

Ultimus is marketed as a business workflow automation tool. It is comprised of a workflow engine and clients for process definition and an end user client for starting and completing tasks. It also has an interesting feature of an organization chart definer which is used to create roles for users which are then taken into account in the workflow. Standard desktop applications such as spreadsheets can be integrated with Webflow to enable standard tasks to be completed. This is the means by which case data would be displayed. This makes Ultimus more suitable for administrative workflow applications such as travel claims rather than production workflow. It does however have a more complex rules definition than many forms based products since is stores the rules necessary for structured workflow in an event action table.

Web reference: http://www.ultimus1.com

Production Workflow

Owing to the size and complexity of the products the production workflow systems have been the last to come to the intranet. It is difficult to develop web based versions of the administrative and process definition tools owing to the number of options that are supported and the graphical nature of the front end. While it is relatively easy to create a task list in a browser it is less easy to integrate other windows containing case data and images.

Staffware have developed a Java based client for managing the work queue in their Staffware Global product. Figure 5.7 shows a work queue view in Staffware Global. This product represents a glimpse into the future direction of production workflow.

Web reference: http://www.staffware.com

IBM has developed a similar access method for Flowmark work queues. This is the Internet Connection product for Flowmark.

Web reference: http://www.software.ibm.com/ad/flowmark

Applications of Internet Workflow

Currently, the main opportunities for Internet based workflow is on wide-area corporate intranets making use of the Internet. This is a good starting point since most workflow systems operate internally in this way at the moment. In the future the Internet offers opportunities for new ways of working. Web

Figure 5.7
Staffware global Java based workflow client (running from Microsoft Internet Explorer)

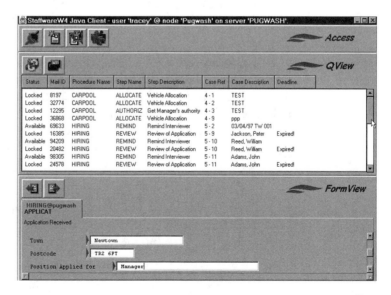

based workflow can be set up with suppliers as an extension of the way EDI operates currently. Web based workflow also can involve consumers and allows a way for cutting out the middleman in many commercial transactions such as insurance or loan brokering.

One of the main constraining factors in workflow involving customers, is the difficulty or speed of contacting customers by letter or phone. Internet based workflow offers a faster way of achieving this. A simple application of this is used today with electronic commerce. If you buy a CD or book over the Internet, a workflow function will automatically mail an order notification and can keep you updated or progress or ask for more information.

Short-term Limitations to Web Based Workflow and Groupware

Today, the three main limitations to web based workflow and groupware systems are the user interface capabilities, performance and security. These problems exist because the intranet is based on new technology. The technologies will certainly evolve to gradually reduce the extent of these problems

User Interface Limitations

User interface features are limited by existing versions of HTML and DHTML. User interface elements are currently limited to relatively simple non-scrolling HTML tables, forms and action buttons. These are quite primitive compared to proprietary workflow interfaces. This can add welcome simplicity though. Limitations such as this will be removed as new HTML standards are implemented. Navigation can be difficult between different views of data because of the speed of refreshing the data.

Limited forms features cause problems of validation. With a traditional workflow client validation of fields would normally occur locally on the client. With Web based workflow the form may have to be sent to the server for checking and then a separate form prompts what the problem is before the user returns to the original form. This is clunky in comparison with what is available now in proprietary workflow clients.

Active-X or Java controls or other add-ins offer the means of extensive interaction which is required with a process definer for example. As yet these have not been implemented, but some companies such as Novell do, however, offer a facility for viewing the process definition in the browser. Web based security standards on the Internet are also restricting the use of intercompany workflow currently. A further problem is the rapid pace of change in products with both Microsoft Explorer and Netscape Navigator requiring frequent upgrades to adopt changes to the latest HTML standard or plug-ins.

Performance

Performance is another key issue in web based workflow. Use any of the demonstration applications made accessible across the Internet by the suppliers above and you will find that performance is either poor or makes the applications unusable. Each new user interaction requires a new form or add-in to be loaded. Even the appearance of a simple dialog prompting a list of options may take seconds when it would be instantaneous using a traditional client/server application. New display forms will take many seconds across the Internet even with a high speed company connection. The delays encountered make use of Internet based workflow impractical for frequent users performing production workflow. We will have to wait for future generations of the Internet.

For users accessing the software less frequently, perhaps once or twice a day these delays are more acceptable. Performance becomes much less of an issue if running these applications across a higher speed company intranet. This is where the future of these products lies since the company networks do not slow the products down to the extent of that across the Internet.

Security

Many workflow and groupware systems contain mission critical or confidential data. Intranet based systems working within a company firewall on a local area network are as secure as other internal applications. Security becomes a bigger problem when connecting different offices or different companies. Although most systems provide user name and password access this is known as an unreliable form of security. If it is possible to restrict access to particular trusted domains or specific IP addresses this will improve security, but is not infallible. The use of leased lines used only by the company or *Virtual Private Networks* (VPNs) offers the best method of running these types of application in a secure wide area environment.

6

Selecting the Right Software

In This Chapter

This chapter answers the question "How do I choose the best solution for my needs?" Is it groupware, workflow, or neither? Which specific products should I choose? Is it best to implement as an intranet? How should I source the development of the system?

Our starting point is the completion of an initial feasibility study. We want to go ahead with the project and now need to match the business benefits we hope for against the features available in the software. For a large scale implementation a request for proposals is issued at this time.

We start by considering how to source the software—is an off-the-shelf solution best or will we need to do some development work? We then look in turn at each of the main categories of e-mail, groupware and workflow. Different methods and criteria for choosing between the many different competing collaborative products will be reviewed. A brief comparison of the main products in each category will also be made.

The details of how to select the right hardware infrastructure for collaborative systems are in Chapter 8 which looks at the features of client/server systems. In this chapter we make the assumption that the selection of the software tools is driven by the business requirements and hardware selection is delayed until software is finalized. This is a logical approach since you should not embark on specifying your hardware architecture until your software solution has been selected. Then you will know the recommended kit required to run the software. In reality, the decision on which hardware to choose is often made at the same time as the software selection, to ensure the kit is in place on time.

Summarizing Your System Requirements in an RFP

A feasibility study normally is completed before embarking on implementation of a groupware or workflow system. The feasibility study establishes whether the return on investment anticipated from the system will justify its development—we will not go into the details of this here. If we decide to go ahead the next stage for a major implementation will be to issue a tender document or a Request for Proposals—an RFP. The RFP is a specification drawn up to assist in selecting the supplier and software. A framework for this targeted at workflow systems for document management is shown in the box "Standard Request for Proposals for a Workflow System." The purchaser fills in the first four sections and vendors fill in the last two sections.

Standard Request for Proposals for a Workflow System

Summarized from AIIM International's Standard Recommended Practice for RFPs

Executive Summary—Company background, acquisition mission statement and timing, return on investment targets, preferred technology strategy.

Project Administration Information—Includes procurement timeline, shortlist requirements, proposal submission preparation guidelines, evaluation criteria checklist.

Business Case—Includes business benefit, description of current operations (portfolio analysis), expectations, critical success factors and key decisions.

Technical Case—This section gives a list of requirements which must be met for acceptance by the buyer. Includes system functional specs, workflow and queue-management functions, expected system response time, document management requirements, integration requirements, other integration requirements, exception handling, hardware requirements, software requirements, mass storage specifications, microfilm requirements, COLD (Computer Operated Laser Disk) requirements, communications requirements and required image-handling functions.

Project Management—Shortlist vendors complete. Includes system acceptance criteria; project management plan; site preparation plan; training plan and schedule; delivery and installation plan and schedule; system maintenance plan; documentation (description and pricing); qualification and experience (number of installations, etc.); customer references and financial report.

Agreement—Vendors' price breakdown, itemized by definitions, so vendors can be readily compared.

What Is the Right Acquisition Method?

At this early stage in the project we also need to take the "make or buy" decision. Our options are to:

▶ Go it alone and develop a new system in house either using the IT department and/or end users.

▶ Develop a new system "from scratch" using a software house for development.

▶ Buy an "off-the-shelf shrinkwrapped" package that runs out of the box.

▶ Buy a shrinkwrapped solution, but do the development to tailor it to your needs.

▶ Combine the other choices by purchasing the object components you need and then building a system using these.

Most software now gives the further option of runtime customization by end users after development is complete. This feature is particularly important for groupware in areas such as e-mail and workflow where agents can be set up to reduce the manual intervention required. Customization increasingly can go beyond the user interface.

The decision taken will vary according to the size of the company and the resources available to it. Table 6.1 attempts the impossible by comparing different options for the average company looking for the average groupware product. If you are a small company without a big development budget and no in-house developers, you will most likely be forced to choose an off-the-shelf solution. Even if you have the budget and the staff, the shrinkwrapped approach will often be the best option in terms of cost and time to deployment. Software for workgroup computing will often be marketed as being able to run out of the box, but in reality some tailoring or configuration to your company will be required. At the very least you will need to have an administrator to set up user accounts and maintain the server.

Table 6.1 *Alternatives for procurement of software*

Procurement option	Cost	Quality	Delivery time	Meet business needs?	Other comments
Customized in-house	Poor	Poor	Poor	Good	Quality and delivery can be poor if no contractual arrangement
Customized software house	Very poor	Medium	Good	Medium	Meets needs, but high costs and error rates
End User Development	Medium	Poor	Poor	Good	OK for small scale specialist applications
Tailored-off shelf	Good	Good	Good	Medium	Usually the best option!
Standard-off shelf	Very good	Very good	Very good	Poor	Cost and testing shared with others
Component assembly	Medium	Medium	Medium	Medium	Combination of other options

As a rule of thumb, tailored off-the-shelf or component assembly gives the best compromise of a relatively cheap, proven and rapid solution, but with modifications made to your needs. Customized development is still conducted frequently, but the incremental benefits you get over tailored off-the-shelf are limited.

The option of using "componentware" is increasingly used since this allows reuse of code which performs the common functions needed by most companies. This approach has become more popular with the advent of object-oriented development since this promotes the production of components. With the use of objects, it is easy to override the default behavior of the objects and so tailor the components to the peculiarities of your company. This option is similar to tailoring a single shrinkwrapped package except you are starting with more components so the approach is one of building and tailoring rather than just modification.

E-mail, Groupware or Workflow?

Selecting the right type of product for improving collaboration and communication in a company is not straightforward. Some groupware has been designed from the ground up for the intranet, other groupware has evolved from e-mail or document management products.

There are two basic approaches to selecting the type of software. First and most common, you decide on the type of product you want such as e-mail, groupware or workflow and then choose from the offerings in that category. Second you can assess the business benefits you are looking for and try a mix and match approach to find the components with the functions you need.

The route that many companies have selected has followed a natural progression. They start with e-mail and then upgrade to a groupware package before finally moving to workflow. This pragmatic approach is recommended since an evolutionary approach can then be taken to implementing groupware functions. For example, as the benefits of e-mail become apparent, the functionality may be extended to share company news or more structured ways of information exchange such as using forms software to submit travel claims.

It follows that you should determine from the outset how the initial package can be extended through integration with other packages or ideally with functions that are built into the initial package. For example, DaVinci SMTP mail does not support forms, so it may be a good short-term solution, but not in the medium to long term. We now look at the best route to meet your needs by reviewing the best fit for each category of software.

E-mail Only

E-mail is a good starting point if you want to start to achieve some of the benefits of workgroup software, but do not have the money or intent to make a further commitment. This is a good small company option. Companies deploying e-mail only are looking for a simple method of improving communication between staff, while reducing the cost compared to traditional methods of communication. Many companies following this approach opt for a product such as Lotus cc:Mail or Banyan Beyond Mail which provide sophisticated mail features at a relatively low cost per user. A strategic thinking purchaser would opt for a product such as Exchange, Groupwise or Notes which offers other groupware facilities such as calendaring, discussion and forms based workflow.

A further choice in this category is that of proprietary e-mail such as cc:Mail compared to Internet E-mail using POP3 or IMAP4. Internet based mail is possibly the best option in terms of cost and support if you are planning to set up an intranet. Surveys of adopters of IMAP4 have shown that it is simpler to administer than traditional e-mail systems and experiences less downtime. There are also fewer problems with the transmission of file attachments due to the use of the MIME standard.

Groupware Package Including E-mail

If you want more collaboration functions than are available through e-mail, the best option is to purchase a groupware package such as Lotus Notes, Novell Groupwise or Microsoft Exchange with built-in e-mail support. Some companies who have an investment in one product may even mix and match the products used. In the UK the Halifax bank has decided to standardize on Microsoft Exchange for e-mail and messaging while continuing to use Lotus Notes for other groupware applications.

The groupware package route is the best to follow if some simple office automation applications are envisaged. These might include administrative workflow such as processing purchase order forms. Here there is an overlap between workflow functions of groupware packages, forms based packages such as JetForms and the low end workflow systems. If forms routing is important to your company it makes sense to adopt Groupwise which offers in-built forms with Informs together with all the other groupware facilities.

Workflow System

If you are looking to automate a mission critical process such as customer service dealing with complex cases then a workflow management system is the obvious choice. A production workflow system will be selected for applications such as call center sales of financial products or processing insurance claims. For an administrative workflow use of an integrated system such as the Groupwise Informs module may represent the best choice.

Should We Use an Intranet?

Beyond the choice of e-mail, groupware or workflow there is a further option—whether to use a traditional groupware client or a web browser to perform group functions across an intranet. Starting with a clean sheet, or if you have a TCP/IP based network already, then this is the clear choice. This offers a cheaper approach than the proprietary groupware or e-mail client and the system likely will be easier to use by the end users and easier to administrate and set up the client machines. There are several major disadvantages to this approach which were covered in Chapter 5. Firstly, the functionality of intranet clients will not be suitable for applications currently where the required screen elements cannot be easily constructed in a web browser. This would include rules based e-mail or production workflow involving imaging which requires onscreen windows for task lists, case data and images. For production workflow, proprietary clients are still commonly used. So, on balance, an intranet based solution is probably best for e-mail or basic groupware functions including forms based administrative workflow. For production workflow it may be some time before the intranet gives the best solution. Chapter 5 is devoted to considering the growing number of collaborative products available for use over an intranet or the Internet.

Decision Points—Factors in the Selection of Collaborative Software

Cost is clearly an obvious constraint on any purchase, but since this is often a fixed constraint we will look here at the technical merits of products and how they vary. My ordered list for the importance of different factors and the questions to ask of vendors or system integrators is given in the box, "Eight Key Factors in Selecting Workgroup Software."

The importance attached to different features will of course vary according to the focus of the project and from company to company. The order of my list is based on the fact that ease of use, performance and even stability problems can usually be worked around, by training, tailoring or purchasing higher specification kit, or failing that, using a patched interim release of the product. There is not usually a workaround for that missing feature you need. We will now look at some of these factors in more detail with particular regard to workgroup computing.

Eight Key Factors in Selecting Workgroup Software

1. **Workgroup functionality.** Does software have the features described in Chapters 3, 4 and 5 to enable teams to work effectively together and support the identified business requirements?

2. **Ease of use.** This is for both end users and initial set up and administration.

3. **Performance.** For different functions such as data retrieval and screen display. If used in a customer facing situation, this will be a critical factor.

4. **Compatibility or interoperability.** How well does your solution integrate with other products? This includes what are you using now and what you will be using based on your strategic direction. If you are already using Lotus cc:Mail but you want to develop document sharing features, then the migration path to Lotus Notes rather than a Novell or Microsoft product is the obvious one. What are your future plans for operating systems? Some groupware will only be supported by Windows NT on the server for example; this makes a purchase decision a no-brainer if your business runs on UNIX.

5. **Security.** This includes how easy it is to set up access control for different users and the physical robustness of methods for restricting access to information. Some security issues are reviewed in Chapter 8, Design.

6. **Stability or reliability of product.** Early versions of products are often buggy and you will experience a lot of downtime and support calls hence the saying never buy one dot zero (Version 1.0.). Issues involved with database reliability are considered in Chapter 8, Design.

7. **Prospects for long-term support of product.** If the vendor company is small or likely to be taken over by a predator, will the product exist in three years' time? Is the company responsive in issuing patches and new features for the product? Is the company forming strategic alliances with other key vendors which will improve the product's features and interoperability?

8. **Extensibility.** Will the product grow? Are the features available to accommodate your future needs? Can an e-mail package be used in future as a method of routing information between decision makers using forms based software, or would a different package need to be selected? Are the features available in the initial purchase or will you have to integrate with software from another vendor? As a rule of thumb, it is best if you can single source software, or use as few vendors as possible as this system will have greater reliability than making different modules interoperate. Are application development tools available for extending functionality?

Workgroup Functionality

Look for functions in these three main areas:

Communication—How easy is it to contact another person in the workgroup, are address book and directory features available, and how easy is it to find their response? How are you notified of their response—is it clear from the user interface?

Collaboration—What are the facilities for sharing ideas and information? How readily available is information for sharing, are there searching facilities? How easy is it to contribute your opinions? Can access control be applied to the reviewing of this information? Can joint decisions be taken? What are the facilities for routing information from one person to the next? How easy is it to collaborate on document authoring?

Coordination—What are the group scheduling and time management features of the package? What features are available for the facilitator? How easy is it for the end decision maker(s) in the group to make the final decision and inform group member? In a workflow system what are the monitoring tools available to ensure team members are working effectively?

Interoperability

Check for compliance with standards supported by a range of products or de facto industry standards. For the rapidly evolving groupware market and the distributed nature of the products, this criterion is particularly important. Key standards detailed in Chapters 3 and 4 include:

▶ **E-mail.** MAPI and VIM API standards and transport standards allow interoperability between e-mail systems. Check for gateway products to SMTP and X.400 for example.

▶ **Video-conferencing.** H.323 and H.324.

▶ **Workflow application interoperability.** Workflow Management Coalition standards of interoperability (WAPI) in areas of integration between the workflow scheduler, process definition and process modeling tools. Support for document management standards of AIIM including the Document Management Alliance and *Open Document Management API* (ODMA).

▶ **Document compatibility.** Includes issues such as support for object embedding—support of OLE/ActiveX or OpenDoc or common formats such as Rich Text. Which import and export filters are supplied with the package?

▶ **Data access.** Does a workflow system support access to its database using SQL or ODBC?

▶ **Development standards.** Can any tailoring or scripting be conducted using your preferred in-house method such as Java, Visual Basic, ActiveX or Perl, or is there a less widely used scripting language your developers will need to become familiar with such as Lotus Script?

▶ **Internet support.** Such as http and ftp.

Ease of Use

Ease of use covers areas such as ease of initial learning and then ease of use once familiar with the product. Design of the interface of particular modules is covered in Chapter 8.

Performance and Scalability

Performance should be measured for a range of key features:

▶ Retrieval of information from message or transaction database

▶ Time for updates and inserts of new records or messages in message store

▶ Time for moving between different work areas (interface components) of the application such as the message entry and message view component of an e-mail package. How long do key dialogs or views of data take to appear on the machines you have specified for installation?

Scalability refers to the ability of a system to support a large number of users and transactions in the larger enterprise. When purchasing applications for the enterprise it is necessary to check with vendors and other adopters on the scale of their implementations—what are the maximum number of users and transactions that are supported? This is particularly true for groupware and messaging systems, since many products originally developed for the workgroup market may then evolve into enterprise offerings.

Benchmarking before selection and volume testing before implementation are particularly important when there are a large number of transactions such as a production workflow system. In one project to develop a call center CTI application I am aware of (not managed by me!), this key stage was omitted—testing was only conducted with tens of customers stored in the database. Realistic volumes were not used. When the trial system went live and the number of customers increased to the order of thousands there was an exponential degradation in performance which resulted in customers having to wait up to one minute for their details to be retrieved. This mistake is of course critical in any customer facing workflow system. Designing and configuring applications to optimize performance is covered in Chapter 8, Design.

Stability and Reliability

In addition to the obvious criteria of the number of bugs likely to exist in a new product, a particular feature to watch out for in collaborative software is the messaging reliability—what is the success rate of messages arriving? This may be down to the carrier system rather than client application, but still needs to be considered and benchmarking and testing performed prior to evaluation.

Cost

Returning briefly to cost, it is worth noting that there is a growing realization that the cost of ownership of a software or hardware product is potentially much higher than the purchase cost. This is mainly due to the cost of trouble-shooting software bugs and hardware faults, phone support, installing upgrades and paying for support and/or upgrades from the vendor. IDC figures show that the cost of ownership for a PC may be as high as $8000 per year reducing to $2000 per year for a thin client such as a Network Computer. The cost of ownership of your selected software/hardware combination should obviously also be factored in to your cost benefit analysis. The cost of training and education and documentation of staff should also be included with standard development costs of paying analysts and programmers.

Techniques for Making Product Comparisons

Three simple methods for making product decisions are given below:

1. **Feature checklist—first cut exclusion**. Use a tick list initially to exclude products that perhaps are missing a key function or do not support the operating system you use. The humble feature checklist is the most easily applied and useful tool. This is much abused by marketers who use it selectively, perhaps missing out on one of the main contenders or features for which their product does not rank well. You can use your own check-list or one drawn up for use by one of the industry magazines such as *Byte*, *Datamation* or *PC Magazine* which are good reliable guides. *Web references*: http://www.byte.com, www.datamation.com, www.pcmag.com

2. **Feature checklist—detailed ranking**. The main deficiency of check-lists is that they do not attach relative importance to features. To extend them, give each feature a weighting of say between 1 and 10 points, and then add up the scores for the different products. Having a numerical basis for the comparison certainly helps. I have used this technique for deciding on products costing tens of thousands of dollars and it certainly increased my confidence in justifying the investment to my boss.

3. **Final selection using benchmarking**. After you have narrowed down your selection of software using feature checklists to two or three contenders a number of possibilities are available to make the final decision.

These can be quite costly both for purchaser and supplier. First, it is possible to benchmark against other organizations who are performing similar tasks to you—what are their experiences, what performance is the software achieving, are they an independent reference site? Second, if it is a large order you can ask the suppliers to provide the software and test important functions using the example process scenarios from your company. For a groupware package these might include the functions given in Table 6.2. This table gives some example business scenarios which you can walk through to see how easily they can be achieved with the products you are considering. Even if it is not practical to perform these functions, test cases can be used in conjunction with the documentation to help select the product.

Table 6.2 *Example scenarios for selecting a groupware package*

Function to test	*Scenario*
1. Administration. Add new user.	How readily can a new user be added to system or personal details changed? How easy to set up client PC?
2. All staff or workgroup e-mail broadcast.	How easy is it to set up a list of all staff, or find the addresses of individuals and then re-use?
3. Create a new document using a structured form giving name of company, attendees, date of meeting and report of meeting.	A report database containing a summary of all meetings with key client needs to be updated by a salesperson. What is involved with finding the relevant database, entering information into a form, submitting and informing manager by e-mail of report?
4. Update a document and republish.	Perhaps a quality procedure needs updating. How easy is it to locate, update, review, publish and notify staff of the update?
5. Information query and retrieval.	You have all customer contacts stored in groupware system. A customer rings reporting a problem with their salesperson. How quick is it to find the customer, salesperson and retrieve information required?
6. Import document, read attachment.	Import word processor document into groupware package from three different formats, or try interpreting e-mail attachments.
7. Export and printing.	These are often awkward in group systems since designed to minimize printing. But what are reporting facilities? How easy is it to export unstructured text and alphanumeric data for import into a spreadsheet?

Table 6.2   *Example scenarios for selecting a groupware package (continued)*

Function to test	Scenario
8. Simple administrative workflow, document routing.	Process a customer complaint that is received by customer service then routed to manager in area responsible for problem as an action item on their task list. This will test customization and will likely need some programming or scripting.
9. Mobile and remote working.	How easy is it to connect and operate as a mobile user?
10. Conferencing.	How straightforward to set up and contribute to a discussion group about market opportunities?
11. Replication.	You have three offices connected by WAN. How long to replicate shared information on servers?

Choosing a General Purpose Groupware Package

Until recently, this choice was between Lotus Notes, Novell Groupwise and Microsoft Exchange. More recently, intranet based solutions such as Lotus Domino, Open Text Livelink intranet and Radnet Webshare are starting to become viable contenders. The features that should be present on a checklist for general groupware packages will be:

▶ Mail integration

▶ Replication

▶ Directories of staff and resource addresses

▶ Conferencing—text and video

▶ Document sharing

▶ Decision support

▶ Intranet integration

▶ Standards support

▶ Development tools and environment

Details on which features to look out for are given in the boxes "General groupware and server administration features" and "Replication."

We now consider the main integrated groupware alternatives.

General groupware and server administration features	
Feature	**Details**
1. Ease of installation and adding new users	How much hand configuration is required? Does an installation "wizard" guide you through installation? Can new users be added from a list in a file or do they have to be typed in manually?
2. Ease of learning	Usability and documentation support—manuals and on-line help and wizards.
3. Support for integration with other products/ adherence to standards	Does the mail product have gateway products to link to other mail products? Is Internet SMTP mail supported? Are POP3, IMAP4 and LDAP supported (see Chapter 3)?
4. What is limit on size of message store?	Many products have built in limits, e.g. originally 16Gb in MS Exchange Server. 4Gb in cc:Mail.
5. Is Server shutdown necessary in maintenance?	This was required in early versions of Lotus cc: Mail and caused disruption to users.
6. What is effect of the message store becoming full?	This results in severe degrading of performance or failure for some products.
7. Is a global address directory supported?	Can a directory list be set up for every one in the company, even across several sites? This is a very important feature to ensure wide use of a groupware system.
8. Access: On which platforms will the client run?	What are remote access facilities? This is a crucial factor for the large enterprise with mixed computing platforms. Is a separate add-on required for this?
9. What is Web support?	Can the message stored be accessed via a web browser? Can new information be submitted via a browser?
10. Security	What security model is used? Is it limited to access control? Is message encryption possible? Is it certificate based? Are electronic signatures or trusted relationships possible?
Replication	
Feature	**Details**
1. Is replication supported?	Can information in message store be replicated to other sites?
2. At what level does replication occur?	Field level replication is usually quicker than replicating complete records.
3. How is replication invoked?	Options include scheduling at set times, fixed interval, on demand or change triggered.

The Groupware Giants—
Notes, Exchange Server and Groupwise

Lotus Notes

IBM Lotus Notes is a well established groupware product that offers a range of group functionality. Sharing and distribution of information in the enterprise happens by users accessing a document database or built in mail. The Notes database differs significantly in concept and use from a relational database (Table 6.3), but there are a number of similarities. The key difference from a relational database is that unstructured text and documents can be easily stored and viewed in the Notes database as well as alphanumeric information. The hierarchical views such as that shown in Figure 6.1 are a powerful method of viewing company and project information.

Table 6.3 *Summary of differences between Notes and relational databases*

Notes	*Transaction oriented RDBMS*
Browse data using hierarchical views of tables	Browse data in tabular format
Limited, static computations of structured data	Robust computations and combinations of data
Full-text search and query formulas	More powerful search facilities via SQL
Good for unstructured data, including OLE objects, document links and rich text	Strong support for structured data, less good for unstructured data storage
Supports parent-child relationships between documents. Complex relationships difficult.	Supports one-many relationships between tables
Not optimized for transactions and rollback/recovery	Fast, reliable transactions
Built in replication, networking and security	Built in replication, network access and security common

Information is entered into Notes using *Forms* in the same way data would be entered into a traditional database via a form with fields available for different data types such as plain text, numeric and time/date. The data entered in each form is stored as a *document*, which is broadly equivalent to a record in a database. Each line in the Figure 6.1 is a document. Each document has header information in *fields* such as date, author and title with the body of the docu-

Figure 6.1
A Notes view show-ing hierarchical information

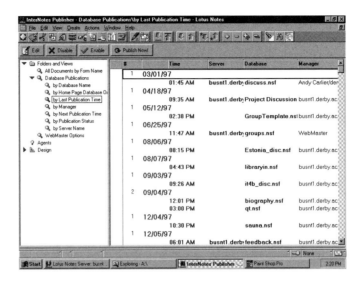

ment formatted Rich Text or other fields. It is easy to search documents using a *full-text search*. Data stored in the database can be queried and displayed in different ways by rapidly setting up different *views*. Within the Notes model, e-mail is made available as another database through which records are added through mail and memo forms. A discussion group for conferencing can be set up very rapidly through duplicating a discussion template. Notes provides advanced administration features to ensure documents remain secure within the company. This is achieved through setting up access control lists for different categories of users to restrict users to only reading or writing certain documents and using password access mediated by keys or certificates on each machine. Administration is conducted through the name and address book which contains all user details, plus details of other servers.

Notes is well suited for sharing information in a large organization which runs its operations through different offices. This is achieved through replication which is a scheduled process that duplicates the database contents to make them identical on all networked servers on which they are stored and synchronizes any updates or deletes that have been made by the users since replication last occurred. The replication feature makes Notes easy to use by mobile workers who can use Dial-up Notes to access e-mail and document databases while on the road. They can work offline and when they next connect to the server any changes made will be replicated to other users. Out of the box the following facilities are available:

▶ E-mail

▶ Text based discussions

- ▶ Forms based applications
- ▶ Collaborative authoring
- ▶ Group scheduling and calendaring
- ▶ Simple workflow facilities
- ▶ Replication of databases for use in different parts of an organization and remote access

Many of these facilities are provided through *templates* for specific document databases which can be used as the basis for other applications. There are many third-party templates available for a range of applications. Notes is sometimes criticized for being expensive to develop applications. This is less true today since many pre-existing templates exist for a range of business functions and will only require minor tailoring for your company. In earlier versions the Notes server was only available on OS/2 servers, but now Windows 95 and NT, AS/400 and UNIX environments such as RS/6000 and Solaris are supported. Clients are available for a range of Windows platforms.

For many years Notes was synonymous with groupware and it defined the term. This is becoming less true as a range of competing products arrive. An analysis by IDC of the groupware market in Q1 and Q2 in 1996 estimated that Lotus Notes captured approximately 1.6 million users, or 37 percent of the 4.3 million new groupware package users worldwide. This is more than twice as many new users as its nearest competitors, Groupwise and Exchange. Total global Notes users stand at 13 million.

There has been much industry discussion recently about whether the growth of the Internet and intranets spell the end for Notes. Some pundits see this as an opportunity for Notes to expand its market share whereas others point to more open solutions from other competitors becoming widespread. Whichever opinion is valid, Lotus has responded by first producing Internotes Web publisher for Notes version 4.0 and then producing a newly branded product "Domino" which combines Notes and Web server functionality. The features of these products are described in Chapter 5.

Web reference: http://www.lotus.com

Microsoft Exchange Server

Microsoft Exchange Server is another significant groupware product. It is different in focus from Lotus Notes in that it is promoted as a messaging system with facilities for document management and sharing. In contrast Notes can be thought of as a document management database which also has mail facilities. The main components available in Exchange Server are shown in Figure 6.2.

Figure 6.2
Structure of Microsoft Exchange Server (from Microsoft Exchange Server, Planning, Design, and Implementation, *with permission of Digital Press)*

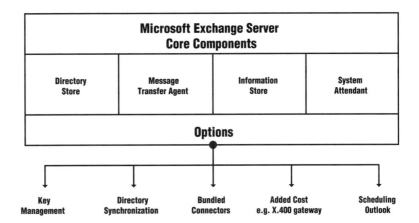

Details of the main components of Exchange Server are as follows:

a. The Information Store is effectively a message database divided into messages for registered users which are stored in personal folders and messages in public folders which can be shared between users. The messages may also act as containers for documents.

b. The Directory Store is important for lookup of user address information and addresses of other servers when operating in a distributed model. This store is replicated between servers.

c. The Exchange Administrator for user account administration and the System Attendant for systems management and configuration. This is closely integrated with Windows NT administration features; in fact each Exchange user has an NT account.

d. The Message Transfer Agent (MTA) is a messaging gateway component used to route messages to other mail systems such as SMTP or X.400. These are known as connectors in Exchange terminology.

In terms of platforms, Exchange Server is restricted to platforms supported by Windows NT, so it is available for Intel and Alpha processor based machines. This limitation presents a problem for companies with mixed hardware platforms who are aiming to adopt a corporate groupware standard. On the client side, client programs are available for different flavors of Windows and the Macintosh.

The groupware functionality offered by Exchange Server is similar to that of Lotus Notes, although the way the functions are achieved is different and consequently their strengths lie in different areas. Table 6.4 indicates Exchange Server's capabilities in a number of key areas of groupware functionality. The use of public folders is used to share information in discussions.

Table 6.4 *Exchange groupware capabilities. Reproduced from* Microsoft Exchange Server, Planning, Design and Implementation, *with permission of Digital Press.*

Groupware functions	Exchange capabilities
Interpersonal messaging	Strong, the basic function of an Exchange Server
Structured document repository (file cabinet)	Medium, based on mixture of public and private folders
Bulletin boards	Strong using read-only public folders
Workflow/electronic forms	Weak—electronic forms do not provide the type of comprehensive workflow functionality available in workflow-specific applications
Interactive conferencing	Strong, using writeable public folders
Time management/scheduling	Strong (Schedule+, Outlook)

With version 5.0, the second major release of Exchange, support of Internet protocols became significant. Supported standards include HTTP/HTML, NNTP, POP3, LDAP and IMAP4. The HTTP/HTML support enables access of the Exchange in-box from a web browser. Support for a wider range of e-mail standards enables access from a range of mail clients which support POP3 such as Eudora or Netscape mail. Other major additions are improved administration in areas such as management of mail users and wizards for setting up mail and news for a workgroup. One of the criticisms of Exchange Server 4.0 was the limit of 16Gb of data in a server's public folders. This capacity will be increased to 16Tb in a future release.

Although Exchange is targeted at basic messaging and ad hoc or collaborative workflow, administrative and production workflow are possible through integration with third-party products, such as Eastman Software's Workflow for NT. Figure 6.3. shows Exchange being used as part of a Staffware workflow application for the authorization of product designs. Work items showing jobs to be processed appear in the user's personal in-box and selecting the item displays the form shown. If appropriate, the item can be authorized. Jetform software also has a link option for use with Exchange. Microsoft is gradually adding limited workflow functionality such as a routing wizard which creates specific routes for parallel or serial tasks.

Microsoft Exchange Clients

With the release of version 5.0, Microsoft has rationalized the complex choice of clients available to access Exchange and has branded them using the Outlook name. The following Outlook clients exist:

▶ **Microsoft Outlook.** This is the replacement for the Microsoft Exchange clients and Schedule+. It provides support for the standard Exchange functions such as calendaring given above. It is included with Microsoft Office 97 and Microsoft Exchange Server 5.0. This product supports a wide range of standards: SMTP, POP3, IMAP4, LDAP, NNTP, MIME and S/MIME. Viewing of HTML is also supported. A Macintosh version and more limited 16-bit version for Windows 3.1 are available.

▶ **Outlook Web Access.** This is for Exchange users to access e-mail, calendaring and Exchange public folder data through a Web browser. This helps extend Exchange across platforms to unsupported UNIX environments.

▶ **Outlook Express.** A simple Internet e-mail client which includes calendaring and contact management and is integrated with Explorer 4.0 with which it is included. It replaces the mail client in previous versions of Explorer. It is targeted at SoHo users, not Exchange users who could only use it for Internet e-mail.

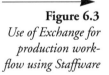

Figure 6.3
Use of Exchange for production work-flow using Staffware

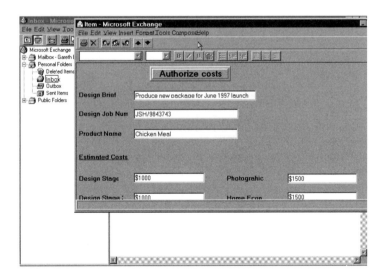

Microsoft Exchange clients (previous versions for 32-bit Windows, 16-bit Windows and Macintosh) will be supported but not improved.

Web reference: http://www. microsoft.com/exchange/

Novell Groupwise

Groupwise version 5.5 was released in 1998. It requires Netware 4.x or IntraNetware and has the standard messaging features you would expect in a competitor to Exchange and Notes. It has server replication and MTA gateway tools enabling a GroupWise server to communicate with Exchange and Notes. This makes it suitable for deployment in the Enterprise, particularly for companies which already operate with Netware. On the client side, Groupwise is similar to Exchange with a two- or three-paned windowed view similar to the Windows Explorer as shown in Chapter 1 and in Figure 6.4. By selecting an icon on the left which represents an in-box containing document, calendar/task list items, fax, e-mail or voice mail messages nested in a folder with the contents appearing on the pane in the right.

Support for workflow consists of a basic forms routing service with new work appearing in the user's list of tasks. These tasks can be assigned to roles. It has good built in document management facilities making it straightforward for different members of a team jointly authoring a document to book in and book out documents. Web support is currently less advanced than Notes and customization features through scripting do not exist as they do in Notes. Remote access is supported.

This is only a brief review of the main groupware packages. It does not include other less popular products such as Fujitsu-ICL TeamWARE used in

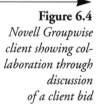

Figure 6.4
Novell Groupwise client showing collaboration through discussion of a client bid

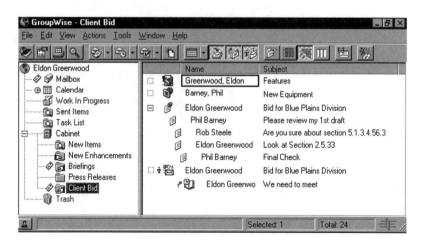

many larger organizations or packages for smaller organizations such as Attachmate Corp.'s OpenMind 3.0. Although the aim has been to indicate the general strengths and weaknesses of the product, the detailed features will change from release to release as the vendors play catch up, particularly in the area of web support. Frequent reviews of these products are included in *Byte, Datamation* and *PC Magazine.*

Web reference: http://www.novell.com/groupwise

Making the Decision

The three main contenders for the groupware crown are now all mature products and are at common version 5.0 (although not all started at 1.0!). Applications development in Notes is generally thought to be more straightforward and flexible than in Exchange or Groupwise. Notes ships with templates for simple form based applications and different views of the data once entered and many example templates are freely available. Applications with forms using Exchange such as Figure 6.3 require customization of forms using Visual Basic and they then need to be registered which can be unwieldy.

Lotus Script is available with Notes for building complex workflow applications, whereas Visual Basic is only available from within the forms of Exchange and it is not currently possible to build more complex production workflow applications. Groupwise has the Informs module so it scores well for forms based workflow. It potentially offers the most functions out of the box. This was the rationale behind international ad agency Saatchi and Saatchi adopting it for 5000 users worldwide.

Exchange and Groupwise seem to have the edge in ease of use in set up and administration. In Exchange, administration and security is tightly integrated with that for Windows NT. This may be an advantage or disadvantage depending on the existing operating system and skills in your company. Support of other messaging protocols is similar for all these products. In terms of platform, exchange servers only run on WindowsNT, Groupwise requires IntraNetware on PC, while Notes can run on OS/2, Windows 95, RS/6000Unix and AS/400, which is useful for large implementations.

For working in a distributed environment the replication in Notes is considered by most commentators to be superior, partly as a result of the number of years the feature has been in the product. Another consideration is the ease with which documents, messages and conferences stored in Exchange and Notes can be made available to a web audience and whether they can be secured. With its Domino release Lotus seems to be ahead, with Microsoft and Novell playing catchup.

Not Just Features

Given the similarity in features, many companies make the decision based on cost of ownership and which company they are already committed to. A 1997 user satisfaction study by Creative Networks Inc. showed that most users were basically happy with their products. This survey gives an interesting insight into the way in which the products are used at large corporations. The study covered 124 companies averaging 25,000 employees, with Notes serving up to 38,000 employees on average.

Notes scores best in overall system reliability and security while Exchange leads in its Internet mail integration and receives the highest overall consolidated performance ratings. Novell scores well on support and licensing flexibility. Significantly, the products receive their lowest scores for initial migration to the application—so expect difficulties in this area.

So which is the best option of the groupware heavyweights? If you are committed to Microsoft or Novell strategically then Exchange or Groupwise will probably be your preferred route. For example, British Telecommunications (BT) has recently selected Microsoft Exchange in a head to head competition with Lotus Notes with the desire to standardize on Microsoft products a key factor. Given a level playing field, Notes as the more established product with better intranet support will often be selected as is reflected by the installed base. As *Byte* magazine put it in their July 1996 review "Lotus Notes vs Microsoft Exchange—No Contest."

Choosing an E-mail Package

Many companies do not need all the functionality of a groupware package. If you fit this description, the facilities provided by an e-mail server may be sufficient for improved collaboration. In this section we briefly review the merits of the most widely used mail servers for mail on a LAN and Internet mail. Note that packages such as Groupwise, Exchange and Notes can be used just for their mail function initially. This allows room for expansion into other groupware functions later. On the end-user side important features to look out for are listed in the box "E-mail user features."

E-mail user features	
Feature	**Details**
1. Message composition	Can formats such as underline and bold be applied, can URLs be incorporated? The latest mail clients can send pages as HTML. Is a spell-checker integrated?

E-mail user features	
Feature	**Details**
2. Message management	Can messages be grouped by author or subject? Can they be placed in folders?
3. Add message to personal task list	Does e-mail package integrate with to do lists and calendaring functions?
4. Message tracking	Can notification occur when messages are opened or are not delivered?
5. Can files be attached to messages and viewed?	Are attachment standards such as MIME (Multipurpose Internet Mail Extension) supported? Can the decoded documents be viewed seamlessly? Which viewers are supported?
6. Reply features	Can title and original message be easily quoted and address filled in?
7. Rule based message handling	Can certain types of messages be deleted or placed in folders?
8. Addressing	Can shorthand addresses and groups be set up easily?
9. Fax and voicemail integration	Can message be faxed seamlessly if necessary?
10. Web browser integration	Is it possible to view URLs incorporated into body of mail message?

LAN Mail Servers

Lotus cc:Mail

Cc:Mail is a very widely used e-mail package with an installed base of over 13 million. It has evolved to provide a very rapid and popular service with support for the standards described in Chapter 3. It is now being replaced by the Notes Mail engine in many companies, but the two can co-exist and the mail engine is now available from a web client through the Lotus cc:Mail Web product. SMTP Internet gateways exist for this and all the LAN mail server products. Lotus recently announced cc:Mail Release 8 which allows access by any Internet standards based mail client, including Web browsers, Lotus Notes clients and POP3 and IMAP4 clients. NNTP and LDAP are not supported. The limit for the message store is 4 Gb, which using a mailbox limit of 20 Mb per user can give a maximum of 200 users per post office. Adding post offices increases administration. This consideration needs to be taken into account with all these mail servers. Lotus has announced plans to discontinue cc:Mail and hopes users will migrate to Notes mail.

Microsoft Mail Server

Like cc:Mail, this is a widely used well-established package which is gradually being replaced as sites migrate to Microsoft Exchange Server.

Banyan Systems BeyondMail

BeyondMail is a powerful e-mail system which, as you would expect from its name, offers more than mail, particularly through its use of Rules and Forms. It has a powerful interface with rules available to automatically delete mail or place mail or forms in certain folders which makes e-mail management more straightforward. The MessageMinder agent works using simple rules to file new messages in folders as soon as they arrive; AutoForward forwards new messages automatically and While I'm Out is designed to route new mail to a colleague or your home computer when you're not in the office. A range of pre-supplied forms include: Meeting, Customer Support, Phone Message and Request Form. BeyondMail also has options for an Internet SMTP and MHS compatible system.

Web reference: http://www.banyan.com

Internet SMTP Mail

There are many products in this sector; this listing indicates the main providers of mail servers specifically developed for Internet based e-mail, which will also work across company intranets. For these types of products, message tracking is an important feature to ensure receipt of mail.

Davinci SMTP E-mail

Davinci from On Technology is a package for NetWare available as a NetWare Loadable Module. It includes a built-in SMTP gateway and POP3 server for routing e-mail from the LAN across the Internet. Its attraction is based on its low resource requirements and relatively limited functionality—it is not forms capable and does not have groupware capabilities. It does support most essential functions such as private and public address lists, user defined folders, document attachment viewers and remote access.

Web reference: http://www.on.com

Netscape Messaging Server

Built on *Lightweight Directory Access Protocol* (LDAP) services, Messaging Server 3.0 provides *Simple Mail Transfer Protocol* (SMTP) message delivery and *Internet Mail Access Protocol* (IMAP4) mailboxes. It is part of the Netscape Suitespot range of server applications.

Web reference: http://home.netscape.com

Software.com PostOffice 3.0 and InterMail

PostOffice is widely used as a replacement for UNIX sendmail and also operates on Windows NT. Its main benefits are its security features to limit access to mail or administration features and List Manager for easier maintenance of listserv style mailing lists. These can be moderated or maintained from an e-mail or web browser client. PostOffice has an Auto-Reply feature for users who are on vacation or want to distribute information from a particular account. These products are good at using server administration features to remove unwanted e-mail.

Web reference: http://www.software.com

WorldTalk NetTalk

NetTalk has good interoperability standards, offering links to LAN based e-mail systems and groupware such as Microsoft Mail, Lotus cc:Mail and Microsoft Exchange, Novell GroupWise and Lotus Notes. NetTalk is built around an Intranet Message Transfer Agent (MTA), a POP3/IMAP4 Message Store, and a native X.500-based LDAP Directory.

Web reference: http://www.worldtalk.com

Sun Internet Mail Server

This UNIX based solution is widely used on Solaris systems. It is touted as a solution for the large enterprise, boasting the ability to comfortably handle 25,000 simultaneous active IMAP users on a single server. Through supporting a large number of users on a single server, this product can also help reduce the cost of ownership.

Web reference: http://www.sun.com

Choosing Group Discussion Software

In this section we do not distinguish between web versions and non-web versions since all products now also support web based access. This product area is now mature, so feature-sets of competing products tend to be similar. Text based conferencing is available as a function in the integrated groupware products such as Lotus Notes, Microsoft Exchange and Novell Groupwise and web based groupware such as Radnet Webshare and Opentext Livelink (Chapter 5). Features to look out for are shown in the box below.

Text based conferencing/discussion	
Feature	**Details**
1. What types of conferencing are supported?	Real time (Chat) versus asynchronous. Most products feature asynchronous text only.
2. Is a threaded discussion supported?	Are replies to an original posting indented clearly?
3. Is it possible to view main topics only?	Lotus Domino supports this well with options to expand or collapse discussions
4. Search	Is it possible to search all postings?
5. Can thread be exported to a word processor?	This is often difficult, but useful for summarizing a range of opinions
6. How easy is it to moderate?	Moderation is important for public discussions
7. Access control model	Can this allow unlimited public access, access to individuals or groups? Can specific passwords be set up for those replying?
8. Frequency of update	Does posting occur immediately or after a fixed length of time?

Internet Usenet groups and mailing lists can also be used to provide low cost conferencing within a company as described in Chapter 3. The main proprietary products for text based conferencing are:

FirstClass

FirstClass is one of the best established text based conferencing products used widely in colleges throughout the United States. The web version is powered by the FirstClass Intranet Server.

Web reference: http://www.softarc.com

Telefinder

This product is also widely used in education, particularly sites that are Macintosh based since the server software runs on Macintosh. Macintosh, Windows and Internet browser clients are available.

Web reference: http://www.spiderisland.com

Collabra

Collabra was one of the most successful business conferencing products before it was acquired by Netscape. It is now incorporated as one of the

SuiteSpot Server products and is available as part of Netscape Communicator as described in Chapter 5.

Web reference: http://home.netscape.com

TeamWARE

TeamWARE is a multiplatform groupware product from ICL. As well as discussion databases it also offers facilities for messaging, group scheduling, and document sharing. For enterprise wide solutions, TeamWARE can synchronize directories and replicate forums across sites of an organization.

Web reference: http://www.icl.com and www.icl.co.uk

TeamWave Workplace

TeamWave Workplace is a multiplatform solution for electronic meetings which provides whiteboarding. Like many of the new products for use on intranets it uses a room based metaphor with participants and documents visible in each room.

Web reference: http://www.teamwave.com

Video-Conferencing Solutions

There are three main players in the video-conferencing area. These are Intel with its Proshare product, White Pine software with CU-SeeMe and the longest established PictureTel with its high end systems and Live2000 series. These have been joined recently by the video-conferencing features in the Microsoft Netmeeting product.

Video-conferencing	
Feature	**Details**
1. Use for desktop or room conferencing?	Most desktop video-conferencing systems will not be very functional for a room meeting, while a room design system may be very costly for simple one-on-one desktop conferencing.
2. Support for a variety of bandwidth conditions	Is there support via modems, ISDN, LANs or whatever new communications transport that comes along? A product that can support multiple bandwidth environments today will have a better design for tomorrow's transports.
3. The ability to adjust the setting for optimized performance over highest quality	Every user will have their own specific bandwidth conditions so they should be able to choose quality over performance if desired.

Video-conferencing	
Feature	**Details**
4. Support for industry standards	Basic industry standards support is necessary for your video-conferencing to reach to other departments or organizations.
5. Address book	Video-conferencing is not as simple as dialing a phone to call someone, but a well designed address book should begin to help solve this problem.
6. Bandwidth management and billing functions	Bandwidth will always be a premium item for the high consumption needs of video-conferencing. So are there ways to conserve bandwith (multicasting) or bill departments or groups per usage?

CU-SeeMe

CU-SeeMe is a free Windows or Macintosh video-conferencing program originally developed at Cornell University. Using CU-SeeMe reflectors enables multiple parties at different locations to participate in a CU-SeeMe conference. This multisite facility is one of the key advantages of CU-SeeMe compared to other free or low-cost solutions. CU-SeeMe uses simple but efficient video frame-differencing and compression algorithms. Examples are given in Chapter 3.

Web reference: http://cu-seeme.cornell.edu/ The originators of Cu-SeeMe who provide the freeware version.

Web reference: http://www.cu-seeme.com/ White Pine software, developers and resellers of server and the advanced version of Cu-SeeMe known as Enhanced CU-SeeMe.

PictureTel

PictureTel is one of the main suppliers of video-conferencing products achieving sales of several hundred millions of dollars in each recent year. Over 50,000 PictureTel systems are installed worldwide. They began as suppliers of high-end video-conference suite systems such as the X.400 system.

The latest Concorde group video-conferencing systems now provide other facilities for group-working such as tools for electronic presentations, document conferencing, application sharing and whiteboarding. Revenues have been hit in recent years by competition from cheaper desktop conferencing systems. To compete PictureTel has introduced the Live and SwiftSite series of personal video-conferencing products. Internet based systems such as Picture-Tel 380 have also been released.

Web reference: http://www.picturetel.com

Intel

Intel is now a major provider of video-conferencing software and hardware which is branded as "ProShare." Products include both the conference room Business Video Conferencing product and desktop based ProShare systems. These products have more limited group-working facilities compared to Picture-Tel, but these can be provided by other products such as Microsoft NetMeeting.

Web reference: http://www.intel.com/proshare/conferencing/index.htm

Microsoft Netmeeting

Netmeeting is a relative newcomer to video-conferencing products which uses Internet standards. The switchable audio/video feature allows users to switch among participants they communicate with. To select participants to NetMeeting, you can either select by the IP address or through the white pages directory of Microsoft Universal Location server. To share an application, any currently running application can be selected and this will then appear on the screen of the person selected. Whiteboarding, text chat and Internet phone facilities are also available.

Web reference: http://www.microsoft.com

Scheduling and Calendaring Applications

The table below indicates key factors in the selection of this type of package.

Scheduling and calendaring	
1. Check for conflicts/find first time open for all	The main function of this software
2. Support for address books and calendars on different platforms	Both different hardware and software platforms. Chapter 3 describes efforts to allow interoperation between products
3. Number of views available	Day, week, month are standard
4. Ease of sending documents	Attachments such as agenda and minutes can be sent before and after meeting
5. Task management facilities	Can tasks be assigned to other users and attachments sent via e-mail
6. Facility to print out schedule	For an individual and across a workgroup

Products available for calendaring and scheduling include the features available in the three main groupware packages including Microsoft Exchange and the Outlook client, and the following specialist applications:

Lotus Organizer

An example of the application of this widely used workgroup product is given in Chapter 3.

> *Web reference*: http://www.lotus.com/organize

WorldTalk Meeting Maker

Meeting Maker from WorldTalk is a well established enterprise calendaring application. It runs on a wide range of platforms such as: Windows, Macintosh, UNIX, OS/2 and DOS or as a Netware Loadable Module.

> *Web reference*: http://www.worldtalk.com

OnTime

OnTime is a well established enterprise product available for Novell NetWare, Banyan VINES and Windows NT via a Windows client. OnTime is known as a scaleable architecture which is run by many enterprises operating across multiple sites. It has the benefit that it offers up-to-the-minute scheduling since it does not work by periodic replication of its calendar database which is the method used by other products such as Notes. Instead a separate OnTime service runs on a server in every local workgroup and requests timing and delegate information from the other servers as required. There is now also an intranet edition.

> *Web reference*: http://www.ontime.com

Crosswind

Synchronize from Crosswind Technologies is another enterprise level server which runs on many flavors of UNIX and on NT. It functions across TCP/IP networks in a similar way to OnTime, again giving "instant responses." Clients are available for Windows, Macintosh, Motif and character based terminals. The Internet client is known as CyberScheduler.

> *Web reference*: http://www.crosswind.com

Choosing a Workflow Management Product

Workflow tools are reviewed in terms of the different sophistication of workflow features they offer as described in detail in Chapter 4. As well as these packages which provide all the functions needed for a workflow implementation there is a range of tools available for process definition. These are also considered in this section.

The choice starts by deciding which sort of workflow you want to support now. If you need production then products such as Staffware, Flowmark, Inconcert should be considered. If it is administrative then forms based packages, or groupware packages can be used.

Simple Forms Based Products

These products provide support for ad hoc, collaborative or simple administrative workflows. They are based on mail enabled forms. The products include JetForm FormFlow and JetForms and Novell Informs. Features to look for are listed in the box "Forms based workflow features."

While most products now offer good graphical form designers, more variable features are the use of an audit trail for tracking forms and security to restrict access to forms. Security features must enable the security of the form to change as it is routed from one person to the next. This is not available in all products. The audit trail should capture date and time of action, who performed the action and a description of the action. Workflow activities: started, received, opened, closed, completed and viewed should be recordable and also document management features such as documents worked on, checked-out, created new versions.

Forms based workflow features	
Feature	**Details**
1. What tools are available?	For designing forms and defining method of routing workflow from person to person.
2. What types of routing are supported?	Serial routing, pre-defined routing lists, rules based routing lists.
3. What are notification features?	Can arrival, opening be notified? How is failed delivery notified?
4. What are security features?	Can individual fields be locked using a password, and can they be optionally hidden? Can security status be changed as form is directed to people with different roles?
5. Integration features	Which mail servers are supported for routing? Can forms be submitted via a web browser?
6. Tracking	Is it possible to find the current location of a form once sent?

Forms based workflow features	
Feature	**Details**
7. Database connectivity	Can the form use optional fields based on database records? JetForms performs well in this area.
8. Form designer	How easy are these to use? Are full range of interface elements available (radio buttons, selectable lists, action buttons)?
9. Detailed on form features	Can formulas be applied to perform calculations? For example, is there an autoincrement field which might be used to assign a new invoice number each time a new invoice form is generated? Validation facilities.

We now consider the main providers of forms based software. The number of such products has decreased recently to make JetForm and Novell the main suppliers. However these players are being challenged by new web based solutions from companies such as Action and Radnet which are described in Chapter 4.

JetForm Corporation JetForm

As with many of the forms based applications JetForms consists of a form filler deployed as a client and a form designer which is used to layout the forms and set up the routing rules. JetForms capabilities can be extended using the JetForm server product or JetForm Workflow which gives more advanced routing options and enables roles to be assigned to participants. Jet-Forms filler can now be deployed over the intranet or Internet using a plug-in, helper application or Java applet such as that shown in Figure 5.4.

A recent introduction from JetForm is InTempo which is targeted at the ad hoc and administrative workflow markets and offers more sophisticated definition of roles and rules than previous products.

Web reference: http//:www.jetform.com/

JetForm Corporation FormFlow

This is a widely used package, previously distributed by Delrina and Symantec. It shares many features with JetForm. It remains to be seen how the two products will be integrated. Its strong point is its Routing Designer which graphically maps business processes and allows tracking.

Groupwise Informs

This product is an integrated part of Groupwise, so it represents the best route for forms based workflow for users who are already using this product.

It has similar functions to JetForms and offers excellent security features and tracking features.

Web reference: http://www.novell.com

Caere Omniform

This product offers basic forms capabilities, but is more limited in areas of routing, security and tracking. Its strength is the handling of scanned paper based forms which are processed using OCR. An example form showing calculations performed on the form is shown in Figure 6.5.

Web reference: http//:www.caere.com/

Filenet Paragon Ensemble and
Paragon Integrated Document Management

FileNet is best known for Visual Workflo, its high end product, but it also offers Ensemble for project or document approval applications. Routing of tasks occurs by e-mail using either Microsoft Exchange or Novell GroupWise. As well as the standard "drag and drop" graphical process definition it also offers graphical status tracking so users can monitor work as it progresses. Ensemble can also be integrated with FileNet's production workflow product. Paragon ICM, a new product, focuses on document management following the takeover of Saros Mezzanine.

Web reference: http://www.filenet.com/prods/ensemble/

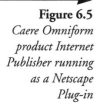

Figure 6.5
*Caere Omniform
product Internet
Publisher running
as a Netscape
Plug-in*

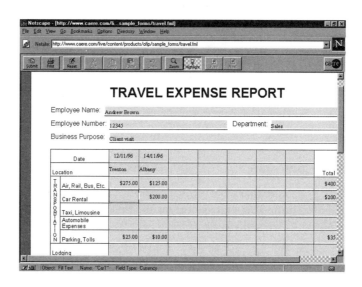

Keyfile Keyflow

Like Filenet, Keyflow is again integrated with MS Exchange server and Outlook for management of tasks and as a launch method for viewing documents. Keyfile has an approach that centers on documents which can either be forms for approval, or lengthier business documents. Keyfile also has another product, Keyfile, which has more advanced document management features such as simultaneous mark up and viewing. This has been extended by some companies for production workflow also.

Web reference: http://www.keyfile.com

Workflow in Generic Groupware Applications

Until recently packages such as Notes, Groupwise and Exchange were only suitable for ad hoc, collaborative workflow. Lotus Notes version 4.0 included Lotus Script which enables simple administrative workflow applications to be developed. This is also possible when Forms Designer and Visual Basic are added to Microsoft Exchange. Production Workflow Systems are not normally built with these products. TeamWare from ICL falls in this category also.

Production Workflow Systems

There are over twenty workflow management tools with a range of capabilities; some of the most widely used include Flowmark from IBM, Visual Workflow from Filenet, Viewstar from Viewstar Corp., Inconcert from Xerox/XSoft, Staffware from Staffware Corporation and products from Eastman Kodak/Wang. As well as these "workflow-only products" there are Enterprise Resource Planning applications from SAP, Peoplesoft and Baan which are either developing workflow and groupware features or being integrated with the workflow products. We briefly consider some of the major players in this section. For desirable features of a production workflow system, Chapter 8 can be consulted since this focuses on design features for large scale workflow applications.

IBM Flowmark

Flowmark has been positioned as part of an EDM suite from IBM which offers separate solutions for imaging, document management and workflow. Originally running only on OS/2 servers, it now also supports AIX and Windows NT. It can also be run in a host environment on MVS. There are two components, a buildtime client (available only on OS/2) and runtime client.

Buildtime is based on an object oriented process designer which offers reuse of parts of processes that have been defined before. An animation tool enables processes to be reviewed to highlight bottlenecks. A process monitor shows the status of individual processes as they occur. Recently it has been extended by Internet Connection which gives web browser access and it can also be accessed from a Lotus Notes client which gives the possibility of production workflow from within the Notes environment.

Web reference: http://www.software.ibm.com/flowmark

Eastman Software Workflow for Windows NT and UNIX

This system was originally developed by Wang, but has now been adopted by Eastman Software. It has the facilities which would be expected of a production workflow system, namely a graphical process definer (RouteBuilder), an application creation tool (FormBuilder) and an imaging module. It runs on Windows NT, IBM AIX, HP/UX and Sun Solaris versions of UNIX. An interesting feature of the NT system is the ability to spread the workload across different physical servers which are viewed by the application as a single logical workflow queue.

Web reference: http://www.eastmansoftware.com

Filenet

Paragon Visual Workflo is the product marketed by Filenet for production workflow. It is a well established product which is widely used in the financial services industry. As with other workflow products, it contains a process definer (WorkFlo/Composer), a runtime client for performing work items (WorkFlo/Performer) and a management tool for monitoring, (WorkFlo/Conductor). It has flexible development tools suitable for integration with imaging tools such as scanners and optical jukeboxes. It supports a range of UNIX based hardware platforms suitable for production workflow, namely: IBM RS/6000 AIX, HP/UX, Sun Solaris and also Windows NT. It can make use of the same database product that is used for the case data. For example, Oracle can be used for both workflow control data and case data.

Web reference: http://www.filenet.com

Staffware

Staffware is one of the best established production workflow systems from a company that originated in the UK, but is now multinational. The pages of this book contain many examples of its applications.

Web reference: http://www.staffware.com

Inconcert

Inconcert is a relative newcomer originating from research at Xerox PARC. It differs from most older products in that it uses an object model for defining workflow. As such it is considered in more detail in Chapter 10 in the section on the future shape of workflow.

Enterprise Resource Planning (ERP) Applications

ERP products are produced by companies such as Baan, SAP, JD Edwards and Peoplesoft. These are high-end products for supporting a range of business operations, particularly in manufacturing companies. Although these contain workflow functions and tools for collaboration, these are not the main focus for these applications. The functions supplied are for the planning and management of key business areas such as procurement, manufacturing, distribution, human resources and financial reporting. Since collaboration is not the focus of these applications and because they are often tailored to specific companies I do not propose to compare these products. However, the EPC process definition model for workflow within SAP is a significant process definition method, and is covered in Chapter 7.

Web reference: http://www.baan.com (Baan IVc for Backoffice is the latest release from this company)

Web reference: http://www.sap.com (R/3 is the flagship product of this German company)

Web reference: http://www.peoplesoft.com

Web reference: http//www.jdedwards.com

7

Process Analysis and Modeling

When undertaking analysis, the question business and systems analysts are trying to answer is *what* should the system do? The analysis phase of a project starts with an information capture stage in which we perform interviews, questionnaires and observation in order to understand the existing situation. A definition stage follows in which the information gathered is summarized in a specification. The requirements specification produced acts as an input to the next stage where system analysts design *how* the system will physically function.

In doing analysis for workflow systems we are aiming to specify the way business processes should work. This includes specifying the pieces of work staff need to complete and the order in which they need to occur. Whether specific roles such as "supervisor" are needed for some tasks and the roles of the people and other resources needed to perform them are also described.

There is no magic formula, or set of steps for performing workflow analysis. It is made more difficult since there are a range of process definition methods which exist from individual vendors and those promoted by industry groups such as the WfMC. These will be described and examples will illustrate how the most important methods can be used. You will then be able to select from a range of techniques as you see fit.

In This Chapter

This chapter shows how to specify what you want from your groupware or workflow system. That is, it defines how to specify the detailed requirements for collaborative systems. We look first at methods of capturing requirements, that is finding information from users, customers and managers. We then concentrate on how to define the process definitions for workflow systems.

These definitions can also be applied to rule based groupware. The three different methods of process definition that are considered are:

▶ activity based
▶ communication based
▶ object-oriented

Planning Analysis—An Overview

Analysis occurs within the setting of a feasibility study being recently completed with the go-ahead for the project. Some preliminary analysis will already have occurred to establish the main functions of the system, but additional work will be required to specify the details. The requirements specification includes the following:

▶ Business requirements
▶ Functional requirements (including process modeling)
▶ Data requirements (data modeling)
▶ Functional constraints on performance—number of users, throughput required and hardware

Process modeling is critical to workflow and groupware systems. Here we are establishing a map of the activities that need to be performed with the assistance of the system. Process modeling should define:

▶ tasks performed by different users and details of sub-tasks
▶ deliverables produced on task completion
▶ input data and resources needed by process and sub-tasks
▶ dependencies between tasks business rules which define when one task is complete and the next can start

In this coverage we concentrate on methods for defining the process since this is such an important aspect of analysis for collaborative systems. Other aspects of requirements analysis are covered in one of the many books on systems analysis, such as that by Yeates.

Data Capture Techniques for Analysis

To find out the requirements of a collaborative system a number of straightforward techniques are available. These techniques usually start by understanding the existing business practices and then documenting these. This is either accomplished by techniques such as interviews, questionnaires or observation centered on the users or process owners. It will also include analysis of documentation such as company standards and procedures manuals. As mentioned in Chapter 2, when reengineering it is best not to embark on detailed analysis of existing processes straight away since this may prevent new, innovative ideas.

Many of the analysis techniques are user centered, since it is obviously important to know what the potential users of a new system will want from it. Users will also be able to identify the faults of the present system readily since they have to cope with problems day by day.

Interviews and Questionnaires

Asking questions through interviews and questionnaires are the main techniques for gaining the users' view of how a new system should operate. Interviews can yield the most information since they are flexible, giving more opportunity to express views. Questionnaires tend to have a narrow focus. To maximize the value of interviews, these should have structured segments.

In one, different people are asked the same question and a range of opinion is collected. Other segments can be more free ranging, possibly to collect suggestions. A powerful technique is that of the "think aloud protocol" in which the user or manager will talk through the stages of the existing process, often while they conduct the task. This method usually ensures the process is described fully, but can also spark off comments about the problems of the system.

Questions should be asked in a variety if ways. Closed questions with a definite Yes or No answer are required for quantitative analysis. Open questions are useful for opinion seeking and probing questions for when further details are needed. A series of questions should be developed to identify and describe particular problems in a context and then establish what possible solutions there are to these. A useful model summarizing this is that of Yeates (Figure 7.1).

Questionnaires are useful for canvassing a larger number of people and providing quantitative feedback since all are asked the same question. They need to be clearly worded otherwise the questions may be misinterpreted resulting in unreliable information. Again, it is best if a combination of open

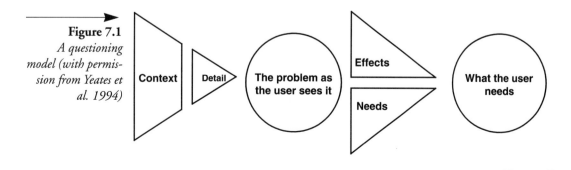

Figure 7.1
A questioning model (with permission from Yeates et al. 1994)

and closed questions are used since only asking closed questions may miss some important feedback.

Observation

The final user centered method is observation which used to be known as time and motion studies. In these, a team of observers review every action taken in performing the process and note down who it involves and how long it takes. This is particularly useful for process analysis since it can be used to identify inefficiencies in the existing process such as tasks that are taking too long. The output of this type of an analysis will be a flow process chart, an example of which appears in a later section (Table 7.3).

Documentation Reviews

Documentation is useful for collecting the details the users miss. For any systems developer, "the devil is in the detail." For example, a standards manual will list all the stages that a loan application passes through, but a person may miss some. Similarly, all the information that is collected from a customer is best abstracted from the application form they submit or the screen of an existing system that is used to take down customer details over the phone. Documents available may include:

▶ Office procedures manual
▶ Quality system manual
▶ Printed or on screen forms used to enter information
▶ Records of customer complaints

A common issue facing business analysts is whether to start with user centered analysis or documentation reviews. I think most analysts, myself included, would prefer to hear the human view first to help build a picture of the process and will then use the paper documentation to corroborate what has been said or fill in details that have been missed. For specialized applications, initial familiarization with a procedures manual is useful to become familiar with the terminology—the interview session is less effective if the interviewer is interrupting the interviewee frequently to ask for explanation of terms.

System Audits

Most processes are likely to have been partly automated with a computer system already, so a further source of information is to look at how the system is used. This is useful for similar reasons to documentation reviews in that details missed by users can be identified.

As well as considering the screen content and navigation of the existing system there are many examples of supporting documentation that will be very useful in building a new system. These include:

► requirements specifications

► process diagrams from analysis for a previous system

► design documentation

► user and administrator manuals change requests, support calls or bug lists of problems found with the system

► printed output from the system—useful for defining metrics

To summarize, the following guidelines are based on my personal experience of using these techniques.

1. Use a combination of interviews and questionnaires with both common structured questions and open questions encouraging comment.

2. Interview a range of staff—managers and users who will be aware of the detail.

3. Use observation to highlight inefficiencies in the existing processes.

4. Do not allow your analysis to prevent innovative ideas as to how the process can be improved.

5. Integrate the analysis with prototyping (Chapter 9).

An Introduction to Workflow Analysis

Workflow analysis or process definition tools are used early during a project to define the existing or baseline workflow of a business process. If modification or reengineering is required, alternative scenarios can then be defined. The *process or workflow definition* acts as an input into the design and implementation phases of development in which the workflow is enacted in a workflow scheduler. The process definition tools may also be linked into simulation models which enable us to make a selection of the best candidate processes based on the volume of workflow.

There are a wide variety of process definition tools or diagramming methods available to choose from. This reflects the relative newness of workflow systems, with no standards being established, but also reflects borrowing from a range of existing methodologies. Methods range from traditional methodologies such as the Structured Systems Analysis and Design Method (SSADM) and object-oriented methods such as *Object Modeling*

Technique (OMT) through to new tools recommended by workflow vendors. We look at the range of these to get an indication of how these methods are used.

What Information Defines a Workflow?

The information which defines a workflow has been explained in Chapter 4. Let's recap here by relating the workflow elements to a familiar process: a software project. Here, the output of the process is the delivered software which is built through structured tasks performed by the development team. Each member of the team has a series of tasks or *work items* to perform, usually in a set order to produce a particular outcome or deliverable. Thus, a programmer may perform the tasks of writing pseudocode before coding in a programming language, performing a unit test before finally releasing a deliverable of a module of compiled and tested object code.

Note that the tasks are part of a hierarchy where the main task is to complete the project and this is decomposed in the task breakdown structure into analysis, design, coding and so on. Each of these phases such as coding is then broken down further. Such a divide and conquer strategy is applicable to many business processes and is appropriate for use in workflow management.

The project manager has a series of *resources* that are available to assist in the project. No surprise that these are also known as resources, workers or actors in WFM terminology. These resources will have different *roles* and responsibilities such as analyst, designer and programmer. To summarize, the main information that needs to be collected to define the workflow enacted in a WFMS is:

▶ tasks (processes, activities or functions) and details of subtasks and time to completion

▶ deliverables produced when tasks are completed

▶ dependencies between tasks (or sequences of tasks)

▶ resources to perform the tasks and their roles or responsibilities

An example of a workflow within a development shop is how a change request is processed. This involves the tasks and dependencies shown in Figure 7.2. Note that this diagram is essentially a Data Flow Diagram which would be used in a methodology such as SSADM (with intermediate data stores omitted). Since Data Flow Diagrams show the processes and the order in which they occur, they

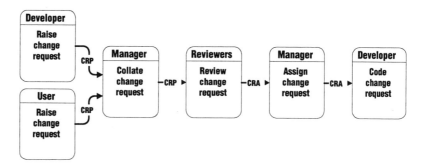

Figure 7.2
Data flow diagram indicating tasks and resources for processing software change requests (CRP and CRA—pending and authorized change requests)

are ideally suited to diagramming a workflow. Similarly, traditional flow charts are also used for this purpose; an example is given in the case study later.

Process Definition Methods

Traditional approaches to process definition borrow from well established systems analysis and design methods such as that promoted by Yourdon. This approach uses diagrams familiar to systems analysts such as data flow diagrams and state transition diagrams. It is based on a combination of different diagramming methods we will consider in turn. These define:

▶ the processes and their constituent sub-processes

▶ the dependencies between processes

▶ the inputs (resources) needed by the processes and the outputs

These traditional methods are sometimes known as *activity based methods* since they focus on defining the work that needs to be performed during the processes. Activity based methods predominate in commercial products. The precise notation used by different products vary so a range of examples will be considered. A small number of vendors have adopted an alternative approach which is based on the contracts established between the different participants involved in the workflow. This is known as the *communication based approach* and is best known in the Action Technologies product.

Finally, the object-oriented approach is being used for process definition by some tools vendors, but these are in the minority. As an introduction to examining the different methods of process analysis, Table 7.1 summarizes the differences between the main methods. Note that for each "method" there are a range of alternatives recommended by different product vendors and analysts.

Table 7.1 *A summary of the main process analysis methods*

Analysis method	Distinguishing feature	Best for	Used by
Activity or traditional methods	Defines processes, dependencies and resources using a range of methods such as IDEF, EPC and DFD methods	All degrees of workflow complexity, particularly production workflow	Majority of workflow vendors, e.g. SAP, Filenet and Staffware
Communication based	Based on contracts drawn-up between workflow participants	Straightforward administrative workflows	Action Workflow
Object-oriented	Each workflow object incorporates both data and methods operating on it	All degrees of complexity	Limited number of vendors such as ObjectFlow and Inconcert (can also use activity method)

Activity Based Process Definition Methods

Activity Based Process Definition: Process Mapping

At an early stage, before detailed activities are identified, we need to identify where in the organization processes occur and who is responsible for them. This procedure is often known as process mapping. Table 7.2 illustrates the activities which occur across functions in a business. Such a process mapping is clearly important for identifying potential users of a new collaborative system and the order in which they will perform their activities.

Table 7.2 *Process map for activities with process "prepare proposal"*

Process activity	Marketing	Engineering	Finance	Senior management
1. Cost estimation		M		
2. Assess financial risk		m	M	
3. Publicity presentation	M	m		
4. Review	M	M	M	m
5. Authorization			m	M
M = Major role in function, m = Minor role in function				

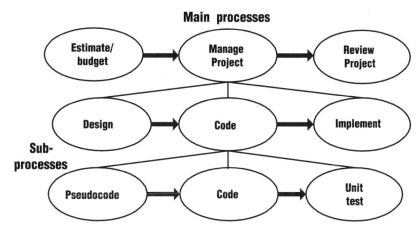

Figure 7.3
Workflow task decomposition for coding phase of project

Activity Based Process Definition: Functional Decomposition

A good starting point for defining existing or new business processes involves a functional decomposition of the tasks that occur within a business process. Figure 7.3 continues our example of a software project by looking at the decomposition of the different tasks which make up a software project. The decomposition of the code stage is shown in three further parts. Note that although there is some indication of the sequence of tasks, this is shown in a more rigorous way in the next stage through a network diagram.

A problem with this process decomposition is that there are no hard and fast rules for what to call the different levels of decomposition or how far to decompose the process. The number of levels and the terminology used for the different levels will vary according to the application you are using and the consultant you may be working with.

Georgakoupoulos and coauthors in their excellent 1995 summary of state of the art workflow management talk about "task nesting" of tasks broken down into subtasks as part of the activity based method for describing workflows. They give the example of a workflow process for procurement where the task "procure materials" is broken down further into the subtasks of "verify status," "get bids" and "place order." Curtis et al. (1992) provide a useful framework, referring to *process units* or *elements* at each process level as follows:

Level 1 *business processes* are decomposed into:

   Level 2 *activities* which are further divided to:

      Level 3 *tasks* and finally:

         Level 4 *subtasks.*

Each process element such as a level 2 activity has *actor(s)* which perform the process, *object(s)* such as customer which the process acts on and a *conclusion* which is a state transition of the object when the process element is complete (an *event* recorded in the WFM) together with initiation of a subsequent process. The box "example of a level 4 process definition for the real estate business" gives a real world example of applying this decomposition.

A significant point to note is that at level 3 there are a huge number of tasks—more than could be practically used in a system. In this workflow implementation the tasks performed by negotiators were prompted by the system at level 2. One of the main tricks in performing process analysis is to identify a suitable level of tasks for the system. The types of tasks chosen should be confirmed by discussions with users, managers and using these tasks in a prototype of the system. A good rule of thumb is to define tasks as the level at which they cause a significant object state transition.

An example of a four-level process definition for the real estate business

Level 1: **Business Processes** (5)—one of the main business processes. Defining processes at this level is important to ensure that the tasks lower in the hierarchy correspond to the business objectives and CSFs. For the real estate business the main processes involved with selling a house are *obtain listing* of property, *market property, facilitate sale* and *provide financial services.* Davenport (1993), notes that even for large multinational organizations the number of main processes will rarely exceed ten.

Level 2: **Activities** (34)—a significant negotiator operation to partially fulfill a particular business process and usually associated with an object state transition. The activity is recognized by managers and negotiators as one of the main stages in house sale, for example "arrange viewing" for a potential purchaser. The number of process elements and their description at this level is such that end users can easily understand them and complete them in a few minutes. This level of detail was that typically used in the WFMS task list in this case.

Level 3: **Tasks** (136)—a piece of work which is part of the activity that can usually be completed immediately, but can be broken down further. Some tasks in the workflow task list were specified at this level, but there were too many in total to be specified.

Level 4: **Sub-tasks** (many)—the smallest division of work used in work measurement. This would be at the level of "walk to filing cabinet, retrieve card, return to desk." Clearly it was not practical to specify tasks in the workflow task list at this level.

I have found it useful to record further details of the tasks which are helpful in system design. These include the following which can be attached at level 2 or 3:

| ⊕ | Reminder required for negotiator (prompt needed in task list) |
| ✍ | Record information (data input via an onscreen form) |

🗁   Retrieve information (data output)

🖥   IT system used to perform activity

☒   Letter or form needs to be produced by the system.

Illustration of the use of these symbols is shown in the box: "An example of the four process levels for the *Obtain listing* business process."

Following completion of this system it was found that 85% process coverage occurred for sales activities performed by negotiators at level 2, i.e. 85% of activities were conducted using the system. Other activities tended to be those that occurred out of the office.

An example of the four process levels for the *Obtain listing* business process

Level 1. Business process:
Obtain listings

    Level 2. Activities:
    1. Register vendor
    2. Inspection preparation
    3. Inspection appointment
    4a. Follow up Inspection—IF listing instructions obtained
    4b. Follow up Inspection—IF listing instructions NOT obtained (exception)
    5. Ensure listing obtained

        Level 3. Tasks for "ensure listing obtained"
        🗁 ✍   *1. Prepare initial property particulars (48 hours)*
        🕒   *2. Remind negotiator to handle sale to contact vendor*
        ☒   *3. Send property particulars*
        ☒   *4. Instruction to sell with draft PMA details*
        🕒 🗁 ✍ *5. Contact vendor to obtain PMA on particulars*

            Level 4. Subtasks
            ☒ *1. PMA chase*
            ☒ *2. Tenure details*
            ☒ *3. Amended details*

Key
   🕒   Reminder required for negotiator
   ✍   Record information (data input)
   🗁   Retrieve information (data output)
   🖥   IT system used to perform activity
   ☒   Letter or form produced (level 4)

Although the previous example showed a four tier hierarchy, it is most common for products and consultants to adopt a two tier hierarchy for implementation with *business processes* at the top level and *activities* or *tasks* at the next level. Owing to the number of tasks in a real business, decomposition of the process into more than two tiers is necessary to clearly represent the processes during analysis. These can then be simplified as required.

To help distinguish between subprocesses or work items, ask these questions:

1. Is there a change in performer of the work or the customer?

2. Is there a change of resources or documents used (either as input or output)?

3. Is there a different objective for the subprocess?

4. Is there a change in object state transition?

If the answer to any of these questions is "yes" then you have identified a new subprocess.

We finish this section with the terminology recommended by the Workflow Management Coalition (see the box "WfMC reference standard process element definition"). As this becomes well established the varying use of terms may improve, although the difficulty is that it is very easy to use the terms activity, task or work item interchangeably. The WfMC definition has the advantage that it is a simple, three level definition distinguishing between the main business processes and the activities that occur as part of the process. The smallest level of definition is the work item which are the daily tasks performed by end users.

WfMC reference standard process element definition
From Issue 2.0. June 96.

1. **Business Process**
   A set of one or more linked procedures or activities which collectively realize a business objective or policy goal, normally within the context of an organizational structure defining functional roles and relationships.

2. **Activity**
   A description of a piece of work that forms one logical step within a process. An activity may be a manual activity, which does not support computer automation, or a workflow (automated) activity. A workflow activity requires human and/or machine resources(s) to support process execution; where human resource is required an activity is allocated to a workflow participant.

3. **Work Item**
   The representation of the work to be processed (by a workflow participant) in the context of an activity within a process instance. An activity typically generates one or more work items which together constitute the task to be undertaken by the user (a workflow participant) within this activity.

Activity Based Process Definition: Process Dependencies

Process dependencies simply indicate the order in which activities occur according to the business rules that govern the processes. Normally, activities occur in a sequence and are *serial*, sometimes activities can occur in parallel when they are known as *parallel*. We now look at several methods for showing dependencies; flow process charts, data flow diagrams and the IDEF techniques and network diagrams including the EPC standard used by the SAP product.

Data Flow Diagrams and flow charts can both be used to define these dependencies. Dependencies can be shown by using a simple Data Flow Diagram such as that of Figure 7.2. In this example, different actors are involved in different serial activities involved in updating software as a result of a change request.

Case Study of Flow Process Charts

A simple flowchart is another good starting point for describing the work flow and dependencies of an existing process. Despite their simplicity, flow charts are effective in that they are easy to understand by nontechnical staff and also highlight bottlenecks and inefficiencies. Flow process charts are used commonly when solving operational management problems, both in the factory and in the back office. An example of a flow process chart is given at the start of Chapter 8.

This case study of using a flow chart is based on a simple example of invoice processing. Table 7.3 has been drawn up following observation during a systems analysis project. It shows the workflow for invoice processing within a company of 500 staff. The main problem is the delay currently occurring when the CFO has to authorize an invoice of more than $10,000. The company can obtain a discount of 10% from the supplier if payment is made in 10 days. This is not achievable currently and the CFO wants to use a workflow system to make this possible. All staff are already connected to a LAN and are using PCs, but currently all mail is transported from desk to desk using a team of office mail collectors who distribute mail every five hours on average. As part of reengineering, restructuring should also be possible—the CFO believes that fewer staff are needed for invoice payment.

It is apparent from Table 7.3 that there are many inefficiencies in the company. These include separate people performing tasks that could be performed by one individual and unnecessary steps. Another problem is that the CFO is often out of the office, so authorization by him takes as long as two days on average. It can be seen that each time a new person is involved there is a delay while the item is transported via the manual mail system and then waits in their in-tray; the process chart symbols for processing, transportation and delay repeat again and again. Such is the extent of this problem that the total time for the whole process is nearly 90 hours, but with staff working nine through five this would stretch to over ten working days.

Table 7.3 *Flow process chart for invoice processing—original*

	Task description	Chart symbols	Dist (m)	Avg time (hours)
1.	Receive invoice, stamp date	● ⇨ □ D ▼	–	0.1
2.	To first payable clerks	○ ➡ □ D ▽	50	1
3.	On first payable clerk's desk	○ ⇨ □ ▶ ▽	–	0.1
4.	Write and attach purchase order	● ⇨ □ D ▽	–	5
5.	To cost accountant	○ ➡ □ D ▽	20	5
6.	On cost accountant's desk	○ ⇨ □ ▶ ▽	–	
7.	Code to appropriate job number	● ⇨ □ D ▽	–	0.1
8.	Return to first payable clerks	○ ➡ □ D ▽	2	
9.	On first payable clerk's desk	○ ⇨ □ ▶ ▽	–	1
10.	Make copies	● ⇨ □ D ▽	–	0.1
11.	To CFO	○ ➡ □ D ▽	200	5
12.	On CFO desk	○ ⇨ □ ▶ ▽	–	48
13.	Reviewed and approved by CFO	● ⇨ □ D ▽	–	0.1
14.	To second payable clerk	○ ➡ □ D ▽	200	5
15.	On second payable clerk's desk	○ ⇨ □ ▶ ▽	–	1
16.	Add vendor number and due date	● ⇨ □ D ▽	–	0.1
17.	Write to accounts payable ledger in accounting systems	● ⇨ □ D ▽	–	0.5
18.	Pay invoice–write cheque	● ⇨ □ D ▽	–	0.1
19.	To file clerk's desk	○ ➡ □ D ▽	20	5
20.	On file clerk's desk	○ ⇨ □ ▶ ▽	–	1
21.	File Invoice	● ⇨ □ D ▽	–	0.1

○	⇨	□	D	▽
Processing	Transportation	Inspection measurement	Delay	Inbound goods

Key to Symbols on Flow Process Chart

A suggestion for improving the workflow is shown in Table 7.4. An important change is in the role of the clerks; they have been empowered by giving them the responsibility to perform tasks such as assigning an invoice to an account number—this was originally the job of the cost accountant. Steps such as returning the invoice to the first payable clerk and that of the file clerk are then removed. Through making these changes to the process vast improvements have been made before using any technology or workflow system.

Through using technology further changes can be made. For such an application a full functioned workflow system is probably unnecessary, rather, a forms enabled e-mail system can be used to route information from one person to the next. So, the first payable clerk will pass a scanned copy of the invoice onto the CFO as an e-mail attachment which can be accessed remotely via modem when the CFO is mobile. Using forms enabled workflow has two key benefits, first it will drastically reduce the time for the transportation stages and secondly it will reduce the time while the item is waiting in the in tray—an item that needs prompt action can be notified as urgent immediately. Through making all these changes the total time has been reduced from nearly 90 hours to just over 20 hours although the efficiency is still low due to time awaiting processing when an item is in the worklist.

Table 7.4 *Flow process chart for invoice processing—reengineered process*

	Task description	Chart symbols	Dist (m)	Avg time (hours)
1.	Receive invoice, stamp and scan	● ⇨ ☐ D ▼	–	0.1
2.	E-mail to first payable clerk	○ ➡ ☐ D ▽	–	0.1
3.	In worklist of first payable clerk	○ ⇨ ☐ ▶ ▽	–	5
4.	Fill in purchase order, code job number	● ⇨ ☐ D ▽	–	0.5
5.	E-mail to CFO	○ ➡ ☐ D ▽	–	0.1
6.	In CFO's worklist	○ ⇨ ☐ ▶ ▽	–	12
7.	Review and approval by CFO	● ⇨ ☐ D ▽	–	0.1
8.	E-mail to second payable clerk	○ ➡ ☐ D ▽	–	0.1
9.	In worklist of second payable clerk	○ ⇨ ☐ ▶ ▽	–	5
10.	Add vendor number and due date	● ⇨ ☐ D ▽	–	0.1
11.	Key into accounting system	● ⇨ ☐ D ▽	–	0.1
12.	Pay invoice and mark task as complete	● ⇨ ☐ D ▽	–	0.1

Effort Duration Analysis

Effort duration analysis is an analytical tool that can be used to calculate the overall efficiency of a process when we have done a detailed analysis such as that of Table 7.3 and Table 7.4. To do this, sum the average time it takes workers to complete every activity making up the overall process, then divide this by the total length of time the whole process takes to occur. The total process time is often much longer since this includes time when the task is not being worked on. Here this is during transport of the forms, and when they are waiting in out trays and in trays. The efficiency relationship can be given as:

$$\text{Efficiency} = \Sigma \ (T_{(\text{effort on tasks})}) \ / \ T_{(\text{total process time})}$$

If we apply effort duration analysis to the first scenario, with delays and transport not contributing to the overall process, we can see that the efficiency of this extremely inefficient process is barely 2%! This measure can be extended by noting the activities which add value to the customer rather than being clerical.

IDEF Techniques

IDEF stands for ICAM DEFinition where ICAM is an acronym for Computer Aided Manufacture (developed by the U.S. Air Force). The different IDEF methods are evaluated by Plaia and Carrie (1995). IDEF gives a number of diagramming techniques which divide into those that are used for descriptive purposes, and those that can also be used for modeling. Mayer and Painter (1991) give a detailed definition of the IDEF suite.

IDEF is a standard method of diagramming processes which are also used by many software developers. They are similar to Data Flow Diagrams which show processes as boxes and arrows indicating inputs and outputs to and from datastores. IDEF0 is the IDEF method used to decompose processes into their activities, controls, inputs and outputs. IDEF0 provides a simple visual vocabulary for describing business processes as follows:

▶ activities or processes are represented by boxes

▶ inputs and outputs to each process are shown by arrows from the left and to the right

▶ resources required by each activity are indicated by an arrow from beneath the box (mechanism arrows)

▶ triggers and control arrows which govern the transformation can also be shown

An example of a procurement process described using this method is shown in Figure 7.4. Here the system requirements form the input into the first stage of planning. The output from this first stage is the requirements

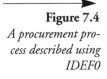

Figure 7.4

A procurement process described using IDEF0

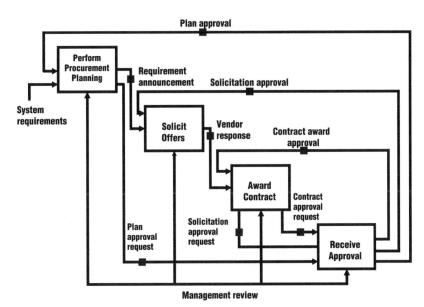

announcement which forms the input into the second stage of soliciting bid offers. For each process to be closed there is a feedback from a later process. For example, the award contract process isn't complete until the input contract award approval occurs.

In common with data flow diagrams, the IDEF models are usually used in a hierarchical manner, showing different levels of abstraction. A level 0 model shows the overall context whereas a level 1 diagram such as Figure 7.4 describes the main processes. A more detailed level 2 diagram would show the subprocesses occurring within the "solicit offers" or "award contract" processes.

IDEF3 extends IDEF0 by allowing us to show causality through object-state transition diagrams and process flow diagrams. Plaia and Carrie (1995) explain that IDEF3 is a process description capture method which is used to summarize the knowledge of a domain expert about the behavioral aspects of a system such as the sequence of tasks and the events that require them.

Metasoftware uses the IDEF notation in its WorkFlow Modeler which is widely used and interfaces with workflow products such as Visual Workflow. WorkFlow Modeler is part of Workflow Analyzer that also includes Workflow Simulator which gives modelling facilities to perform what-if scenarios with workflows.

Web reference: http://www.metasoftware.com/

Network Diagrams

While data flow diagrams and process charts may give a good indication of the sequence in which activities and tasks occur, they often do not provide a sufficiently tight, formal definition of the process sequence necessary for input into a workflow system. To do this, we can use a network diagram such as a GAN (Generalized Activity Network). Here, nodes are added between the boxes representing the tasks, to define precisely the alternatives that exist following completion of a task.

The most common situation is that one activity must follow another, for example a check on customer identity must be followed by a credit check. Where alternatives exist, the logic is defined at the node as follows: where a

Table 7.5 *Workflow dependencies at a node on a network diagram*

Node type	Description	Summary
AND-SPLIT	Workflow splits into two or more parallel activities which all execute	
OR-SPLIT	Workflow splits into multiple branches of which only one is followed	
AND-JOIN	Multiple executing activities join into a single thread of control	
OR-JOIN	An exclusive alternative activity joins into a single thread of execution	
Iteration	Repetition of one or more workflow activity(s) until a condition is met	
Must follow	No alternative paths exist	

single pathway is taken from two or more alternatives, the node is defined a an OR node, and when several pathways may be followed this is an AND node. Join nodes combine previous activities, and splits determine which activities occur next. Where there are alternatives, business rules are defined as pre-conditions or post-conditions. A summary of the alternative dependencies appears in Table 7.5.

Event Driven Process Chain (EPC) Model

One of the most widely used traditional methods for describing business events and processes is the *Event Driven Process Chain* (EPC) method. This has been popularized by its application to re-engineering of enterprises performed using the SAP R/3 product which accounts for world-wide sales of several billion dollars. Over 800 standard business EPCs are defined to support the SAP R/3 system. Originally described in a German text by Keller, they are intended to illustrate business rules clearly for interpretation by business users before enactment in the software. As with many process definition methods they suffer from the problem that the definition cannot be readily converted to a software specification. The different elements of the EPC model are shown in Table 7.6, these include the different types of dependencies previously reviewed in Table 7.5. Figure 7.5 is an EPC metamodel illustrating how the different elements relate to one another. This figure shows

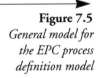

Figure 7.5

General model for the EPC process definition model

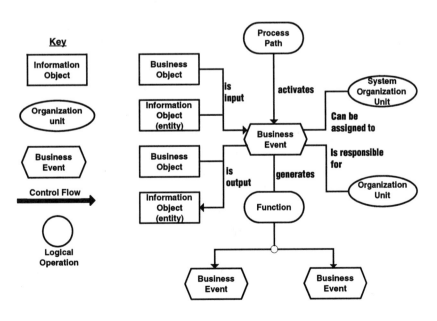

how business functions are triggered through transactions on *business objects* which also lead to a *business event. Control flows* link the activities, events and logical operators. Entities or information objects are items such as sales orders or invoices.

Table 7.6 *Elements of the Event Driven Process Chain (EPC) model*

EPC symbol	Description of EPC element
Business Event	An event occurs when there is a change in the status of a process. It occurs in response to completion of a function.
Business Function	A function is an activity or task that is usually completed by a person in the organizational unit responsible for the function. Alternately it can be completed automatically through the workflow system.
xor and or Logical operation	Control flow logic between processes is denoted by joins/splits as follows: • xor—a single activity follows the completed process(es) • and—an and-split gives rises to multiple subsequent functions • or—an or-split gives a multiple choice split
	control flow forming the process network
Information Object	Data needed for completion of a function and acting as input to subsequent functions (workflow relevant data in the WfMC definition). Also known as entity.
Organizational Unit	The unit responsible for the execution of a function

An example of an EPC model for a simple business process is shown in Figure 7.6. This shows that the method produces a complicated diagram for a simple process. This is necessary because the method has to describe the inputs and outputs explicitly so that they can be used as an input to the workflow model.

Activity Based Process Definition: Other Methods

The traditional method sometimes also utilizes entity or object life histories to indicate that when tasks are performed the state of the object on which they act may be modified. For example, if we consider the "test" subtask performed by a programmer, the completion of this task causes the state of the code to change from untested to tested. For certain situations it may be useful to show this dimension of the problem.

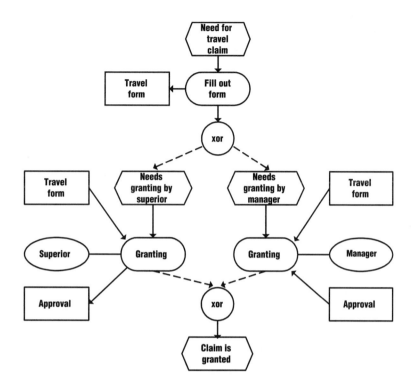

Figure 7.6
An EPC diagram for a simple travel claim process

An example of this would be the tasks performed by a real estate agent in selling a house; as tasks are completed the state of the house changes from not on market through awaiting inspection, available for viewing, under contract. Each of these state changes would be fundamental to a WFMS used for controlling the house sale process. These state changes will eventually be displayed in an activity log showing which tasks have been completed.

Communication Based Process Definition Method

This approach has been popularized by Winograd and Flores through their involvement in the development of the Action Workflow product and has been used by some other manufacturers subsequently. It is based on the common sense assumption that improving business processes is about improving process quality and customer satisfaction. To help this, the model involves defining a series of contracts between a *customer* and *performer* of a task in which a deliverable, time scale and completion criteria are agreed on. The model for each contract involves four stages which together define a workflow loop as shown in Figure 7.7.

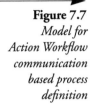

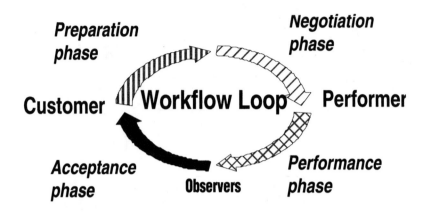

The four stages in the communication model are:

1. **Preparation**—The customer requests that a task be performed.

2. **Negotiation**—The customer and the performer agree on the terms of acceptance for the task.

3. **Performance**—The performer undertakes the task.

4. **Acceptance**—If appropriate, the customer agrees acceptance when work is complete.

We now look at an example of the Action Workflow method in action. This is similar to the flow process chart example involving a workflow for an expense authorization. Here, the process involves four employees in different roles: employee, supervisor, the accounting department and the divisional chief. All expense reports are approved by the employee's supervisor before they are sent to accounting for processing. Where an employee has extraordinary expenses these must be authorized by the divisional head first. The process definition for this example is shown in Figure 7.8.

The main workflow loop here is between an employee as the customer and accounts as the performer. The condition of satisfaction for this workflow is to pay the total amount of the expense report within two weeks of submission. Dependencies within Action workflow work by specifying triggering actions such as C(ustomer):Request will then invoke the links set up between workflow loops. AND-Joins can be defined through using a "rendezvous" node and AND-Splits through "splitters." Subprocesses in this example are Approve Expense Report and Approve Extraordinary

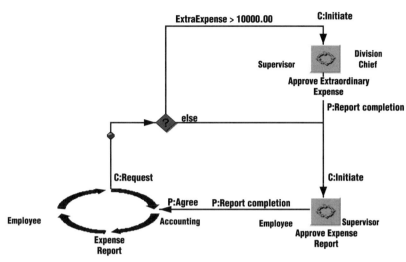

Figure 7.8
*Example of Action
workflow process
definition
for expense
authorization
process*

Report. The condition for special authorization is when the expense report is more than $10,000.

Proponents of the communication based method argue that it is a natural way of working since it mirrors the agreements that occur in a business between different employees and is a natural way to represent workflow. It does not just focus on the tasks, but on people and deliverables also. While this is valid, it has some disadvantages. Namely, it requires learning a new model which is not supported by the majority of workflow tool vendors and is generally not considered to be practical for complex production workflows. Additionally, it does not provide a suitable model for those business processes which are not customer focused such as transaction workflow monitors.

Object-Oriented Process Definition Methods

Object-oriented analysis and design is now widely used in software development, but the majority of workflow vendors do not support a true object-oriented paradigm. InConcert and ObjectFlow provide true object-oriented tools for defining the process definition.

In a business workflow context a simple model for the use of objects is given in Figure 7.9. Here task objects are the means by which business objectives objects are achieved. The tasks in turn are achieved by organizational resources and IS resources.

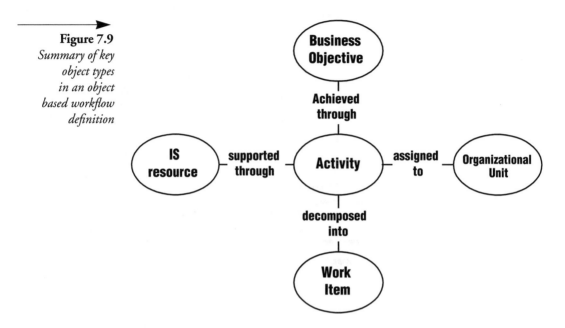

Figure 7.9
*Summary of key
object types
in an object
based workflow
definition*

An OMT Based Metamodel

A more detailed metamodel using the OMT method is shown in Figure 7.10.
This model describes how objects can be used to represent the components of
a Workflow Management System described in Chapter 3.

Figure 7.10
*A detailed OMT
metamodel for
workflow analysis
(from Rohloff, M.
1996)*

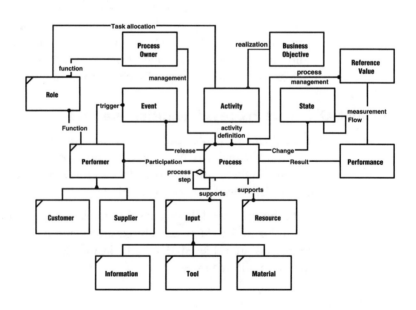

The process is at the center of this metamodel and receives input in the form of information and other resources. Performers participate in the process and two subclasses of these are customer and supplier. It is these performers who trigger different events which will affect the process and cause a change in its state. The level of achievement of business objectives is also included in the model.

The Use-Case Method

Despite its relative lack of adoption, there is good potential for applying these techniques to workflow definition. Indeed Jacobsen, one of the advocates of the use of object orientation in a business context offers many examples of the "use-case" model which are applicable to workflow applications. The use-case model is essentially another method of process definition, but uses an external perspective, that is, it considers the process from the customer's point of view.

To a customer or "actor" which may be a human or a machine, the process is simply a "black box" providing a service. In some ways, therefore, it is similar to the communication model defining an agreed service between the process and its customers. Jacobsen describes a use case as a grouping of a course of events in a business which can be related to a process such as "selling" Jacobsen identifies different categories of objects which are defined in the Use Case. These include:

▶ interface objects which represent tasks in the business and involve communication with the customer such as providing details on the progression of a loan in application at a call center

▶ control objects also represent operations in the business, but this time controlling the flow of operations, usually without direct interaction with the customer. Examples of control objects include a supervisor in a loan brokers or a department head

▶ entity or information objects represent physical objects that are used as part of the process. These would include a loan request or an invoice

▶ actors who make up the use-case are the customers and workers involved in delivering a service

When performing analysis to define use-cases we will ask questions such as "who are the actors for this process?"; "What services does the process provide?"; "What are the actor's tasks?" and "What changes will they cause to the status of the process?" Use-case can be integrated with object-oriented methodologies such as Rumbaugh's *Object Modeling Technique* (OMT) as described by Don Kavanagh. Rumbaugh OMT methodology is defined in detail in Rumbaugh's seminal text.

Object orientation represents the future of workflow. It is considered in more detail in Chapter 10.

Validating a New Process Model

Whichever method has been used at to arrive at the process definition, we need to check that the process definition is realistic. When developing a wish list of process capabilities and corresponding business rules the stages described by David Taylor in his book on concurrent engineering may be useful. He suggests that once new processes have been established they are sanity checked by performing a "talk-through, walk-through and run-through."

Here, the design team will describe the proposed business process as a model in which different business objects interact and in the talk-through stage will run through different business scenarios using cards to describe the objects and the services they provide to other business objects. Once the model has been adjusted the walk-through stage involves more detail in the scenario and the design team will role play the services the objects provide. The final run-through stage is a quality check in which no on-the-spot debugging occurs—just the interactions between the objects are described.

Figure 7.11
An example of a use-case for a loan application

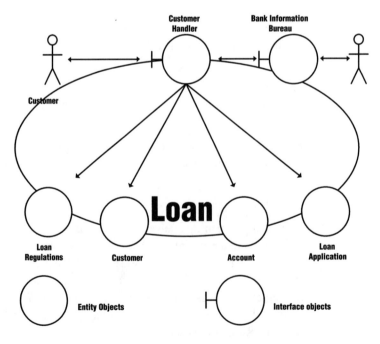

This method is similar to the class responsibility collaboration (CRC) model proposed by Kent Beck and also described by Kavanagh (1994). CRC modelling uses OMT to identify nouns which may define classes and verbs which define services or tasks. CRC considers classes and services and then asks the following questions:

▶ Class—What should objects be called? (Name from the noun search)

▶ Responsibility—How is the work of the system divided between the objects?

▶ Collaborators —Which objects are required (colloborated with), for the object to provide its service?

Similar talk-throughs and walk-throughs are used to those advocated by Taylor to check the validity of the object model developed in this way. The Object model developed by use-cases and CRC scenarios is then developed further by using "event trace diagrams." Kavanagh (1994) summarizes OMT analysis as consisting of the following stages:

1. a problem statement

2. a context diagram

3. an object and relationships pick list

4. use-cases with text descriptions

5. scenarios and event trace diagrams

6. an Object Model

7. an event flow diagram

8. dynamic model for important and interesting classes

Data Analysis for Workflow and Groupware Systems

Traditional systems development places great emphasis on data modeling to understand the data used by the system in order to build a rational database structure as a repository. With workflow systems the process analysis defines the key control data which is used to define the business rules. In addition to this data, there is also the case data such as customer details which will vary from system to system.

In many production workflow systems this data will be stored in a separate legacy system or in tables defined by the developers. This case data requires normal analysis techniques such as normalization according to Codd's rules and representation in Entity Relationship diagrams and data dictionaries. The analysis required for case data is similar to that for many information systems and since it is not specific to collaborative systems is not considered here.

Analysis of Duration of Development

Estimating the duration of the development of any software system is fraught with difficulties and as a result of under-estimating, many project overruns occur. Staffware have developed a useful scheme to relate the different degrees of complexity of a workflow system to the length of time it will take to develop. This can be performed once detailed process analysis has occurred.

Three main factors are used together to estimate the duration which are shown in the box "Factors in estimation of a workflow system."

Factors in estimation of a workflow system

From Staffware White Paper "Workflow Desktop Development Metrics"

1. Degree of automation.
Level 1 automation involves simple workflow routing with tasks delivered to the appropriate individual such as "Verify customer" or "Send acceptance letter."
Level 2 automation again involves simple routing, but also includes triggers which invoke an external application such as a legacy application with the relevant information to hand.
Level 3 is fully automated procedures which in addition to the functions of levels 1 and 2 also uses forms to enter all information relevant to the completion of each task, which is then available for future use. Other facilities such as automated letter generation may be included also.

2. Complexity.
Each level of automation can be broken down further according to its estimate complexity as follows:
A. Simple Process such as change of address.
B. Moderate Process such as notification of death.
C. Complex process such as new customer registered on system.

3. Development tasks.
These are the standard stages in a software development. They are defined as:
- Analysis and modeling
- Prototyping
- Development
- Integration
- User review
- Implementation

Table 7.7 shows how the three factors described in the box can then be evaluated for each new workflow system and then be used to derive an estimate of total effort across the project.

Table 7.7   *A matrix of estimated effort against tasks. From Staffware White Paper Workflow Desktop Development Metrics, 1996. (Complexity is measured from A simple to C complex.)*

Task	Level 1 automation			Level 2 automation			Level 3 automation		
	1/A	1/B	1/C	2/A	2/B	2/C	3/A	3/B	3/C
Analysis and modeling	2	4	8	4	8	16	6	12	24
Prototyping	–	–	–	–	–	–	6	12	24
Development	2	4	6	4	7	14	5	10	20
Integration	–	–	–	–	–	–	4	8	16
User Review	1	2	3	1	2	3	2	4	6
Implementation	1	2	3	2	3	4	3	4	5
Total	**6**	**12**	**20**	**11**	**20**	**37**	**26**	**50**	**95**

8

Designing Collaborative Applications

The design representation of how a system will work forms the input specification for the final stage of building the system. Some developers find it too easy to move straight from analysis to development, skipping design. This is a bad move, since by producing a clear design "spec," time spent in configuring and testing the system at later stages can be greatly reduced. By design I mean the definition of *how* the WFMS or groupware system will operate within its implementation environment. For example, the design must include the architecture of the system; how security will be implemented; methods for entry, storage, retrieval and display of data and how this is achieved through the user interface.

How you approach the design of a groupware or workflow system will vary greatly according to the package you are using to implement your chosen solution. In this description of design we are not considering design of a new WFMS or groupware system, but design for an implementation based on an existing product. Note though, that many products require considerable tailoring and configuration before use. Given this, many of the comments also apply to a custom made system developed from scratch.

In This Chapter

We start by reviewing what is involved in designing the architecture of the system, that is, what arrangement of hardware and software components is required. Key elements of system design are then considered. These include user interface design, security and specific issues for the design of modules of collaborative systems. A case study illustrating some of the design challenges of a workflow system concludes the chapter.

General Aspects of System Design

Top Down or Bottom Up?

Given that collaborative systems are often made from pre-built components that need to be constructed, the approach that is most commonly employed is a top-down strategy. Given this, it is best to consider the overall architecture first and then perform the detailed design on the individual functional modules of the system. The divide and conquer approach can then be used to assign the design and implementation tasks for each module to different development team members. The description here follows this approach by looking at the overall design first and then the detailed module design.

Validation and Verification

An aspect of the design that is quite easy to overlook is testing that the design we produce is the right one. Checking the design involves validation and verification. In validation we check against the requirements specification and ask *"Are we building the right product?"* When undertaking verification we walk through the design and ask *"Are we building the product right?"* These two questions should be considered throughout the design process and also form the basis for producing a test specification to be used at the implementation stage.

Moving from Analysis to Design of Workflow Applications

Figure 8.1 places design in the context of other stages of workflow development. From the analysis stage in which the requirements are developed, a new business process is defined and formalized in the workflow definition. This definition then forms the basis for the workflow implementation. However, this is not a smooth transition.

Figure 8.1
The links between the analysis and design stages of workflow implementation

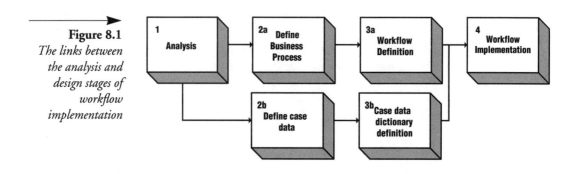

This transition is problematic since the logical design of the revised business process in the workflow definition has to be transformed to the physical process definition in the software used to implement the business process. Most standalone process definition tools do not provide the facility to transit directly from stage 3a to stage 4 directly. The workflow must be redefined in the language of the package.

Increasingly, tools are permitting this transition. For example, the Metasoftware workflow analyzer referred to in the previous chapter now interfaces directly to the Filenet workflow products. Products such as Action workflow, Staffware, Flowmark and Inconcert now have integrated process definers which allow direct transition from stage 3a to 4. So, it is well worth checking this feature when buying analysis tools and workflow systems. The definition of case data such as customer details which is usually stored in a database occurs as a separate process with the data dictionary being used to construct the database at the implementation stage

Elements of Design

Getting the design of the collaborative system right covers a lot of seemingly unrelated areas. We will cover all the important ones such as: how to give the right levels of functionality and ease of use at the interface, setting up administration, security, multiuser access, transaction processing features and automation. We will look at design elements in three key areas:

▶ Design of system architecture (overall design)—What is the best client/ server infrastructure and how should the application functions be partitioned between client and server? The system architecture will define an overall, high level design of how the system will operate. Integration methods between the collaborative system and support applications such as scanning and links to legacy applications are also included. These methods include the methods of invoking applications and APIs to transfer information between them.

▶ Design of modules and user interface components (detailed design)— This covers how the system will operate and the details of what will be displayed as the user enters and reviews information. This is reviewed by looking at standard user interface components and how they are used to interact with the data required by collaborative systems.

▶ Design of administrative features—Includes security measures for restricting access to data and safeguarding data. Since many systems are based on database engines, this includes standard resilience features of databases.

System Architecture Design

Designing the overall architecture involves specification of how the different hardware and software components of the system fit together. To produce this design a good starting point is to consider the business process definition that indicates which high level tasks are performed using the different components of the system. These functions can be summarized using a flow process chart as shown in Figure 8.2.

Figure 8.2 does not show the detailed tasks performed by workers and supervisors, rather it is a generalized walk-through of how a typical case is handled. This example shows how a home loan is handled. From inspection of Figure 8.2, we can decide which hardware and software components are needed to support the keying-in of new applications, scanning of applications and the workflow functions of prioritizing, assigning and completing tasks. Completion of tasks may involve telephony integration for talking to customers and a workgroup printer for customer letters. A link to a mainframe legacy application is necessary to check the credit rating of the individual, so software must be provided on the client to achieve this. A first cut at the architec-

Figure 8.2
Flow process chart
for home loan
application process

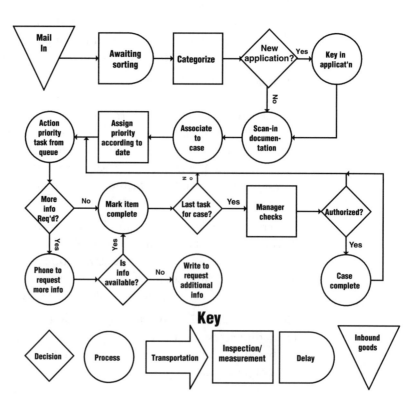

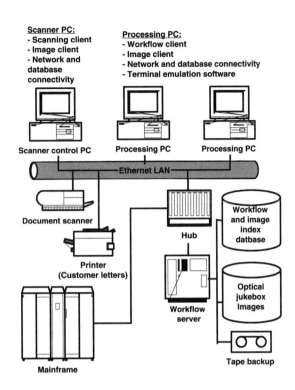

Figure 8.3
System architecture for a home loan workflow management system

ture is then possible through diagramming the software and hardware components necessary to perform and support these functions. Figure 8.3 shows how this might be achieved.

Figure 8.3 shows a simple client/server arrangement in which the workflow engine resides on the server with the client application which is used by the user to review and complete tasks running on the client PCs or workstations. Groupware systems typically comprise a similar structure. For example, a mail system will have a mail database of all incoming and outgoing messages residing on the server and this will be accessed via the client which is running on a PC. Since the client/server model is now pervasive in collaborative computing and there are more sophisticated ways of splitting up the software functions between client and server we will now examine the client/server model in more detail.

The Client/Server Model of Computing

Most groupware, workflow and intranet systems conform to the client/server model of computing. In producing the overall system design and planning the physical layout of equipment you will be guided by this. In the client/

server model, the clients are typically desktop PCs which give the "front end" access point to business applications. The clients are connected to a "back end" server computer via a local or wide-area network. When introduced, the client/server model represented a radically new architecture compared with the traditional centralized processing method of a mainframe with character based "dumb terminals."

Client/server offers the opportunity for processing tasks to be shared between one or more servers and the desktop clients. This offers the potential for faster execution as processing is shared between many clients and the server(s), rather than all occurring on a single server. Client/server also provides good opportunities for customization at the client end with the end user empowered through being able to modify rules and settings at runtime. Centralized control of the user administration and data security and archiving can still be retained.

With these advantages, there are a host of system management problems which were not seen at the outset. These have been partly responsible for the reduced costs promised with downsizing not materializing. To some extent there is now a backlash in which the new network-centric model is being suggested as a means of reducing these management problems.

A client/server architecture design is prevalent for the development of collaborative systems since this permits partitioning of tasks between the client computer accessed by the end user and the more powerful server. The design decision which must be made is how best to partition the tasks such as:

▶ data storage

▶ query processing

▶ display

▶ application logic including business rules

A range of options are available for partitioning the tasks between client and server. Today, the options are largely simplified down to the "thin client" which only handles display and the "fat client" which handles both display and application logic. Most typically the client handles the display and local processing with the server holding the data typically in a database and responsible for handling processing of queries on the back end. This model, which is known as two tier client/server is still widely used but more recently the three tier client/server is becoming widespread.

Figure 8.4 shows a simple two tier client/server arrangement. In this, a client application directly accesses the server to retrieve information requested by the

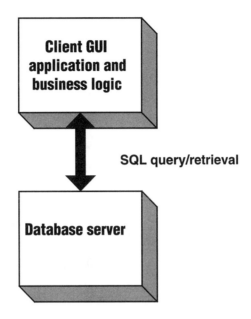

Figure 8.4
*Two tier client/
server
architecture*

user such as "show me my outstanding tasks on the workflow queue." In many workflow systems, this is mediated through SQL with an SQL request being passed to the server as a parameter which is processed by the server and the result of the query returned to the client. In this two tier model, the client handles all application logic such as control flow, the display of dialogs and formatting of views. Typically, the business rules will also be contained in the "fat" client application, although these could also be held on the database as stored procedures. The two tier model has the advantage of simplicity, but it has the major problem that the business rules become bound in with the user interface code. This makes maintenance difficult. It was also found that two tier client/server did not scale very well to larger implementations.

In a three tier client/server model (Figure 8.5) the GUI or thin client forms the first tier with the application and function logic separated out as a second tier and the data source forming the third tier. In this model there may be a separate application and database server, although these could reside on the same machine. Two tier may be the most rapid to develop in a RAD project, but it will not be the most efficient at runtime or the easiest to update. Through separating out the display coding and the business application, it is much easier to update the application as business rules change. It also offers better security through fine-tuning according to the service required. The three tier model has been extended further by the Butler group as explained below. For mission critical workflow applications the three tier client/server model is often implemented using the *Distributed Computing Environment* (DCE) as a standard

Figure 8.5
*Three tier client/
server architecture*

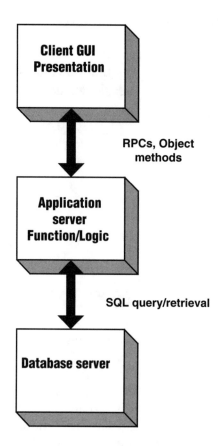

which gives interoperation between the different processes. In this, the different servers are connected using Remote Procedure Calls.

Separating Out the Business Logic

When defining the overall architecture for a collaborative system, it is important to separate out the application logic from the business logic. The reason? Business rules vary often, and when they change it will be difficult to make amendments if they are tightly tied in with the code and data structures of the application. It is one of the benefits of object-oriented programming that the business objects can be separated from the application interface objects while the business objects are integrated well with the business data.

An extended version of the three tier client/server model has been developed by the Butler group to highlight the importance of separating out the business logic (Figure 8.6). In this model, the business model at the top of the pyramid

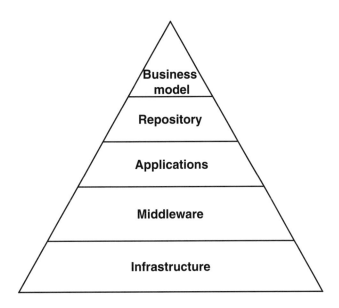

Figure 8.6
*The Butler Group
value added layers
model*

exists separately from the technologies on which it is built. This contrasts with the situation in many organizations where the computer program and the business model evolved together and are now irreparably intertwined. The repository layer in this model is a formal process definition of the business model and in a workflow system would be defined as a workflow definition.

Applications are the executable components which execute the business processes and are linked to the resources they use through a middleware layer. The middleware enables the applications to be independent of the infrastructure that is used. The resources of the infrastructure layer include operating systems, networks, user interfaces and relational databases. Butler refers to this model as "added value," since business benefits mainly accrue from the value added components beyond the infrastructure. Many companies agonize over the infrastructure, whereas it is having the right applications and a coherent business model which is most important.

Function Placement

Bakman (1995) provides some practical guidelines for partitioning functions between client and server. He recommends that designers should review:

1. **Function frequency and scope.** If a function is called frequently during execution it should be placed in proximity to its caller to minimize network traffic. This becomes difficult to achieve when it has a broad scope. That is, the function is called by a large number of other functions.

2. **Location of data.** If data exists on the server, then placing the function which acts on it on the server is the best option. The use of stored procedures or packaged queries that occur on a database server is a good example of this principle being followed.

3. **Process allocation.** This guideline indicates that tasks should be shared equally between processors as far as possible. For example, a collaborative system involving a large volume of printing of customers' letters should have a separate print server and a scanning component may have a dedicated client/server for the scanning process.

4. **Application development tool.** Critical components of the system that need to execute rapidly such as a TP monitor will be written in a low level language that has good performance. Interface components can be written in higher level languages and 4gls.

Thin Clients, Fat Clients and NCs?

This does not refer to the eating habits of your customers, rather the amount of functionality placed in the application running on the client PC or workstation. Currently, most groupware and workflow technologies use relatively fat clients with many functions packed into the executable running on the client. There is a trend away from fat clients with the advent of intranets which can support a thin client running as part of a web browser. The Action Technology Metro product uses this method. The Netscape SuiteSpot intranet applications involve using a thin web browser client with a lot of functionality on the server. Further details on the use of intranets for running collaborative applications appear in Chapter 5.

The use of thin clients running on low cost Network Computers (NCs) has been put forward as a method of reducing the cost and complexity of support on the client side leading to a dramatic decrease in the cost of ownership. When using an NC the bulk of processing will occur on the server, with the client mainly being used for display. NCs are normally based on Java as the operating environment rather than Microsoft Windows. Upgrades to applications which may be required for maintenance purposes or perhaps when there are changes in the business rules are easier to perform in the NC thin client model, since the application will only need to be updated on the server.

It is now several years since NCs were first proposed, and they are starting to be used by large corporations. In the UK, for example, food retailers such as Safeway have committed to purchasing hundreds of NCs as have some finance institutions. In the US, Boeing is said to be planning the purchase of thousands of NCs. With such a potential threat, Microsoft and Intel—the main companies with an interest in the dominance of the PC market—have responded by a specification for a "Net PC" which is positioned between a PC and an NC in functions and cost of purchase and ownership, but will still run Windows. A further development is the use of Windows terminals or "Winterms" from companies such as Wyse.

NCs will likely be an important means of deploying production workflow applications since here the user does not need the extra features of a PC. With production workflow, the user simply needs the workflow application plus a means of generating letters and viewing digital images. The complexity of a PC is unnecessary and only adds to the cost of purchase and ownership. For ad hoc workflow and groupware, it will be different. With these applications, users need access to a range of programs, and need the flexibility of the PC or Net PC. With these developments, the choice for implementing workflow and groupware systems has certainly become more complicated, but it offers the chance for more choice and lower prices.

Scalability

When designing groupware and workflow systems, the design target must always be for the maximum anticipated number of users. Many implementations have failed, or have had to use a new approach because the system used in the development and test environment with a small number of users does not scale to the live system with many more users. If the system does not scale, there may be major problems with performance which make the system unusable. Volume testing in which the anticipated workload of the live environment is simulated can help foresee problems of scalability.

The increased popularity of three tier client/server results from its ability to scale better to enterprise-level systems. When purchasing or designing applications for the enterprise it is necessary to check with vendors and other adopters on the scale of their implementations—what are the maximum number of users and transactions that are supported. This is particularly true for groupware and messaging systems, since many products originally developed for the workgroup market may then evolve into enterprise offerings.

Time Synchronization

Time is a further aspect to be considered in the design of enterprise client/server systems, particularly for the multinational company working across time zones. The normal practice is for local times to be used on local servers. The implications of this for a workflow system which requires tasks to be completed at a particular time or date should be carefully worked through. A further issue is that in a distributed client/server system working within a single time zone, each server's system clock is liable to be different. These should be synchronized if required.

Message-Oriented Middleware (MOM)

The use of message-oriented middleware (MOM) helps reduce the problem of time synchronization. MOM operates in an asynchronous mode, suitable for a distributed environment with servers or clients requesting information on demand from other servers. This publish then request mechanism from a server managing events is known as "publish and subscribe." MOM is often used in transaction processing (TP) monitor implementations where the messages in question are queued workflow tasks.

TP Monitors and Transactional Workflow Managers

TP monitors are commonly used today in the implementation of production workflow, so it is worth pausing a while to review their role. TP monitors originate from the mainframe world for managing database transactions that occur in large scale transaction processing applications such as a network of bank autoteller machines. The main role of these TP monitors is to manage data commits and enable recovery from failed transactions. Additionally, they provide a means of integrating the many different processes or services which make up a large scale system.

The TP monitor allocates requests from the many clients between different processes to achieve load balancing. It is apparent that both these functions of TP monitors must also be achieved by large scale production workflow systems. A full coverage of TP monitors is beyond the scope of this book, but they are significant in that they are now widely used when designing large scale, three tier client/server applications. You can read more on TP monitor applications in *Three-tier Client/Server at Work* by Jeri Edwards.

User Interface Component Design

This section describes the detail of how individual modules are configured to display the relevant information for your application. The input to this stage will be the information collected in analysis on the process definition, user roles and administration features of the software. For a workflow system this information will include control data such as the process definition and application relevant (case) data such as customer details or documents used in the system.

For a groupware system the data types divide into user administration data and the data that users exchange such as messages and documents. If routing and workflow is included, then a process definition and control data is also required.

There are two basic approaches that can be taken for tackling the different elements of detailed design. The first is to structure the detailed design on the interface components such as the task list or user administration dialogs. For a workflow system, these will correspond to those of the WfMC model in Chapter 4. This approach to modular design is most commonly used since this provides a good way of breaking down the problem. Each module can be broken down further into interface elements such as *dialogs* which are used to enter and update information such as rules or user details, and *views* which tabulate or graphically display related information such as a to do list, a process definition or a list of all data and *documents* such as a letter to a customer.

A second approach is to design the interaction with the different types of data that are used by the user and the system. The different categories of data used by a workflow system have been reviewed in Chapter 4. They include:

1. Process definition. The activities, rules and dependencies which define the business process. Most systems will also allow modification of the process definition at runtime via the user interface.

2. Workflow control data. Data that is used internally by the workflow engine, not modified via user interface.

3. Workflow relevant data. Data such as dependency rules which may be updated via the interface.

4. Application relevant or case data include the objects that are acted on, usually customers. Although case data is not interacted with directly by the workflow engine, this is often a major component of analysis, design and configuration of the user interface.

Elements of User Interface Design

Since groupware and workflow applications are meant to enhance productivity it is important that users are not hindered by poor user interface design! This sometimes can happen if the development team spends most time in developing the rules and workflow engine. I outline here some design principles based on those used by the UK software company AIT in guiding the design of their own workflow systems.

AIT User Interface Design Principles

Functionality
The major purpose of the user interface is to allow operators to complete their tasks effectively, quickly and without frustration. The system must meet the needs and requirements of the users.

Consistency
Consistent systems are easier to use because similar operations are performed in a similar manner in different modules. There needs to be consistency in presentation of information and operation.

Navigation and Control
The way the system works and information is structured should be clearly revealed to the user. Users should be guided through the interaction process in an efficient manner. Users should know which module or mode they are using at any stage.

Modes
A mode is where the system allows a restricted set of actions. Modes force users to focus on the way the system works rather than on the task at hand. Try to avoid using modes. If modes cannot be avoided, provide the user with visual cues to make it clear to them which mode they are in.

Relevancy
It is important that only relevant and useful information is displayed.

Visual Clarity
- Users need to be able to find information they require easily. Each screen needs to be easy to read and users' attention should be focused on important information.
- Present all information required by users to complete a task effectively at any stage.
- Similar information should be grouped together to improve readability and highlight relationships. Lower case text is easier to read, decreasing search times. Serif fonts are more difficult to read on displays, particularly when displayed in a small point size.
- Important information needs to be highlighted to attract the user's attention.

Feedback
Feedback helps users understand what the system is doing and to determine what is required next.

Terminology
Every word and phrase that appears on the computer screen should be meaningful and helpful in the completion of the user's task. Technical terms and computer jargon should be avoided. Abbreviations, acronyms and codes should only be used if they are meaningful to target users and used consistently.

Help
Users should be encouraged to learn about the system. This will ensure that they are using full functionality. Users need to be able to use a help facility quickly and easily.

Data Input
Users must be able to enter information easily. Fields should be formatted to cue users to information required. This minimizes potential errors. Validation of data input should occur.

> *Error Handling*
> The system should minimize the possibility of user error. All input should be validated before processing. The system should clearly inform the user when an error is detected and include information which enables the error to be traced.
>
> *Web reference*: http://www.ait.co.uk (with permission)

Main Modules of a Collaborative System

Each interface component will function as a separate window (view) within the main client window or as a separate application. If they are all started as separate applications there will be a separate control program giving a menu which allows other modules to be started. It should be possible to see each module simultaneously if necessary. The exact way in which the functions are divided into modules varies from product to product, but the modules described here are usually present. In an intranet web environment, these modules may appear as different screens or windows within frames within the browser accessed by selecting different hyperlinks. In future each module will run as a separate Java applet in a separate window.

Process Definition Tool

This is used for on screen design of the business processes that will be enacted in the system. It is usually a graphical means of specifying processes, used extensively during the physical design and implementation of a system. Examples of workflow tools include either Action Workflow (Chapter 7) or InConcert Process Designer. In the process definition tool it is possible to set up event action triggers which are fired if a certain condition is met. This facility is provided by most products. Similarly notifications can be set up as reminders of deadlines for important tasks. In a groupware application this module will provide rules for routing e-mail or forms to different users.

Work Management Module

This important module is used for managing the work performed by the user such as reading documents or completing tasks. In a workflow system this is the worklist handler which displays the list of tasks for an individual sorted by urgency and will give details on the status of the case. It may also give access to a more detailed checklist of subtasks that are involved in completing a task. Little tailoring will be required during the design of this module since the tasks and subtasks will have already been entered in the process definition tool.

As part of the worklist module there will be various functions for acting on tasks. These will include:

▶ display further information relating to a task (case data module)

▶ complete a task

▶ reassign or reroute a task to another worker, possibly overriding the rule for that task

▶ create a follow up task

▶ abort, suspend or defer a task (and add details of why this is necessary)

In a groupware application this module will also display a list of tasks entered by the user, often in the form of a diary or calendar. These can be modified to enforce corporate standard tasks. Groupware tools also use a list metaphor for managing all the messages and documents used for collaboration. This is usually in the form of an in-box showing messages in and out and related documents.

Application Data Modules

Common to all systems are modules for displaying information needed by the user to complete tasks. This will vary greatly according to the application. Often this module will be invoked as a separate application such as image viewer or a word processor. For a workflow system data will include a case data module displaying information on customer and related documents. For a groupware system this will include details of messages, documents or tasks.

Group Monitoring and Review Module

This will provide an overall view of the appointments or outstanding tasks across a workgroup. It may also have drill down to show the various performance measures indicating the productivity of individual workers. It should also be able to provide a task history or audit trail for each customer or job showing when work started, when finished and outcome.

Administration Module

This tool is used to create new user accounts and to change the roles of users. It is usually run on the server, although it may be possible to log in remotely from a client. It may also contain monitoring tools and will provide facilities for correcting any inconsistencies in the workflow queue or failed message deliveries. To do this options to create, suspend, abort, defer or reroute a task may be available here. Options to backup or restore data may also be included in the administration tool.

Invocation of Other Applications

There are a wide range of invoked applications that may need to be linked to a collaborative system. These hooks are usually provided by the product vendor in the form of APIs which require scripting or coding to make the call from the parent client application and pass parameters such as the name of a template for a standard word processing document. The design aspects of application invocation include identifying the required applications and specifying the triggers or actions which cause invocation together with the parameters and return codes on completion of the invoked application. A standard API for the interface to invoked workflow applications has been set up by the WfMC (Interface 3).

The types of application that are invoked to run on the client of a collaborative system include:

▶ Links to legacy systems running on UNIX or mainframe systems. These may often be character based and will contain application case data such as customer details. A straightforward text based 3270-style terminal emulation may be sufficient. If a GUI front end is to be provided this can be provided by "screen-scraping" using the Emulator High Level API (EHLLAPI) standard. An example of a traditional terminal emulator showing case data concerning the policy details on a car insurance claim is shown in Figure 8.7.

Figure 8.7
IBM 3270 terminal emulation showing insurance policy data

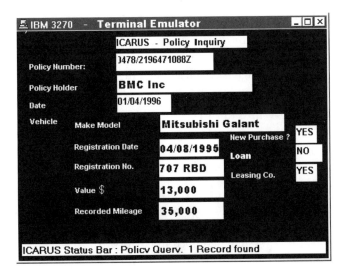

▶ Word processors for generating standard letters or forms to customers. An interface needs to be setup to specify the name of the template forming the standard letter and to pass information such as name, address and case details which are required in fields in the letter. If there are a large volume of letters, for example in a call center, the design must permit a batch process to run overnight to achieve this.

▶ Document viewers for previewing scanned images. These provide the user with a view of a scanned customer letter, for example. The interface should enable any scanned document associated with a case to be easily viewed in a separate window (Figure 4.5).

▶ Notepad for storing additional text information about the case. Staffware uses this approach to store information about insurance claims, for example.

▶ E-mail. This could pass the users and recipients e-mail address and any application data to the e-mail client. (Some workflow systems use e-mail as a basis for all communications.)

▶ Reporting tools to show the status of workflow for administrators often exist as separate standard business graphing packages. An interface to these will need to be designed according to the type of information which is required.

Security Design

Data security is a key design issue, since collaborative systems often deal with mission critical or confidential data. The four main attributes of security which must be achieved through design are:

▶ **Authentication.** Authentication ensures that the sender of the message, or the person trying to access the system is who they claim to be. Passwords are one way of providing authentication, but are open to abuse. Digital certificates and digital signatures offer a higher level of security.

▶ **Authorization.** Authorization checks that the user has the right permissions to access the information they are seeking. In a workflow system the concept of roles such as manager and administrator are used to ensure that the right people can authorize important transactions such as a loan issue.

▶ **Privacy.** In a security context, privacy equates to scrambling or encryption of messages, so they cannot be easily decrypted if intercepted during transmission. This can be achieved through the PGP public key system described in Chapter 3.

▶ **Data integrity.** Security is also necessary to ensure that the message sent is the same as the one received. A security system can use a checksum digit to ensure that this is the case and the data packet has not been modified.

Data must be secure in the sense of not being subject to deletion, or available to people who don't have the "need to know." When designing a collaborative system there are a number of critical security functions which must be "designed in." These must be checked with vendors of the collaborative system, database server and operating system between which data management functions will be shared. Most groupware products such as Lotus Notes integrate proprietary access control. Those that are more integrated with the operating systems such as Microsoft Exchange base security on the host operating system. To prevent prying eyes or deletion, the majority of commercial collaborative systems offer access control or password protection.

Owing to the range of operating systems supported by workflow systems, these tend to implement their own access control. In workflow systems the user identifier is required for an assignment of the roles they can perform. Additionally, users may be assigned to a group of people who work together (a pool in Inconcert terminology). There is a tendency for user names and passwords to be shared between coworkers. This should be discouraged, not only because of risks to data, but using a different user name may confer the wrong role to that person. In intranet and Internet based systems a company is potentially exposed to outside attack. How to overcome this threat through use of a firewall is explained in Chapter 5.

Database Integrity

Since collaborative systems tend to be based on database engines, many design issues for these systems are common to database construction. Some of these features may be part of the database functions and be poorly supported by the vendors of the collaborative system. Quiz the vendor to find out which of the following features are supported. The importance of these issues makes employing a competent *Database Administrator* (DBA) for database design, construction and maintainance a good investment.

Significant database design issues include:

1. *Database performance optimization*

   If tailoring a product, the use of indexes or stored procedures to accelerate the display of commonly used views such as a task list are useful. Query optimization is important here. To verify the design is good, volume testing is essential to ensure the system can cope when it is ramped up from testing to release.

2. *Multiuser access/concurrency control*

Assessing how the product you are using deals with the situation when two users are accessing the same data should be part of the design process. If access to records is unlimited, then there will be irregular data in the database if users save data at different times. It will not be common for operators to be dealing with the same customer data, but it should be accommodated. Since multiuser access will occur the best method for dealing with it will be to implement record locking. Here, the first user to access a record will cause the database to restrict subsequent users to read only access to the record rather than read-write. Subsequent users should be informed that a lock is in place and access is read only.

3. *Planning for failed transactions*

Recovery methods can be specified in the design for how to deal with failed transactions. Some products are poor at handling these or require a manual intervention. Databases which support automatic two phases commits of inserted records are best at dealing with this. TP monitors also control failed transactions. Further details on these is given below. Situations that may occur in a workflow system include a partially completed task that can not be completed due to a system error such as a bug or hardware failure and also a task that is cancelled by user intervention. With these situations there are two basic choices, either to allow completion or to abort the task and undo the task. The second option is preferable as otherwise an erroneous "complete" task is still included in the work list.

4. *Database referential integrity constraints*

The database must be designed that when aborted transactions are deleted, the change must be propagated back to all other tables which the transactions refers to. This also applies to other tables stored in the database such as activity dependencies or roles.

5. *Media, hardware or power failure*

A backup strategy should be designed to ensure minimal disruption occurs if the database server fails. The main design decision is whether a point-in-time backup is required or whether the previous day will be sufficient. Frequently, a point-in-time backup will be required. Of course a backup strategy is not much use if it can not be used to restore the data, so backup and recovery must be well tested. To reduce the likelihood of having to fall back on a backup using a fault tolerant server is important. Specifying a server with an uninterruptible power supply, disk mirroring or RAID level 2 is essential for any corporate workflow or groupware system

6. *Replication*

Duplication and distribution of data to servers at different company locations and for mobile users is supported to different degrees by different vendors. For example, field level replication is more efficient than record level replication.

7. *Database sizing*

The DBA will size the database and perform capacity planning to ensure sufficient space is available on the server for the system to remain functional. This can be a particular problem with workflow systems, because of the large number of transactions that are generated as tasks are created and completed. Additionally, if storing scanned images to magnetic media, these can soon also use up a server's storage capacity. Disruption to messaging systems can also occur as users retain mail and the server capacity is reached. Planning ahead will avoid this.

Error Handling and Exceptions

The design will include a strategy for dealing with bugs in the system or problems resulting from changes to the operating environment such as a network failure. Collaborative systems built on products will use the exception handling features of the product and there is not usually a necessity for an input to this as the standard messages will keep the user informed. It is a useful feature to check before product purchase however.

Help and Documentation

After configuration the collaborative system will need additional guidance on how to use the system with specific customer or company information. Help and training is important here. It is straightforward to construct a Windows Help file based on a word processed document. Intranet and groupware make providing system documentation easy and interactive help desk conferences can also be constructed.

Object-Oriented Design

Design for object-oriented collaborative systems will involve similar design problems to those raised already, although the approach is different. Object-oriented analysis and design techniques are covered in the latter part of Chapter 7. An introduction to these type of workflow systems, which will become more common in the future, is covered in Chapter 10.

Workflow System Design Issues—
A Loan Issue Case Study

As a conclusion to this section we look at a case study to illustrate some detailed design issues involved with the development of a workflow automation system which uses document image processing. In this case study a bank is looking to remove the responsibility of processing mortgage applications (loans) from branches in different towns to a centralized lending unit. It is hoped this will result in better customer service and less need for staff training and troubleshooting within the branch. A workflow system will be used in the centralized unit.

Figure 8.2 shows the relevant flow process chart which summarizes the workflow. Each individual stage is not shown here by the diagram, rather it is the overall workflow structure. The mortgage applications are received at the unit in the first post at 8 A.M. It is then necessary to identify *new applications* and supporting documentation for applications already received (*return post*). New applications are keyed into the workflow system as a new *case* and the original form scanned in for reference. Supporting material such as ID (driving licenses) and letters from employers are also scanned in. A team member will then assign or associate all scanned images of material which has been scanned in to a particular case. Assigning new documents (*assignment tasks*) is always the most important task so these are automatically placed at the head of the workflow queue. After assigned, the documents will need to be actioned (*action tasks*) by the operator. According to the type of document and when it needs to be chased the workflow system will assign a priority to the task and place it on the workflow queue. Team members will then have to action tasks from the workflow queue which are prioritized according to date.

Design of Scanning Process

A potential bottleneck in all Document Image Processing (DIP) systems is when mail is first delivered in the morning. This will need to be scanned in as quickly as possible as a batch. To reduce this bottleneck the scanning and association process must be well designed and supported by appropriate hardware. The scanning stage involves converting the document to a bit-mapped representation which can be stored digitally. To achieve a high speed design the image scanner will usually be a high throughput machine with a flatbed feeder accepting several sheets per minute. A duplex facility is necessary for double-sided sheets. This performance is necessary since many documents will need to be scanned as soon as the post arrives and it is a potential bottleneck in the system if this stage takes a long time.

Design of Storage Method for Scanned Images

The image will normally be stored as a black and white image since most of the sources will be in this form and this reduces the storage requirements compared to a color image. To further reduce the storage requirements the design should specify that image should be processed by a digital compression algorithm to a standard format such as GIF or JPEG.

Design of Text Recognition

In advanced DIP systems the images may be stored as text following Optical Character Recognition (OCR). This is not common for several practical reasons. Not the least of which is that given the accuracy of OCR, manual intervention for confirmation or correction will still be required. Many documents such as handwritten customer letters or birth certificates for example cannot be interpreted. If preprinted forms are scanned however the accuracy may be sufficient for identifying the case number or reference code.

Association Design

Association involves assigning images to a particular case or customer within the workflow system. This is necessary since if images have not been OCR processed they are "dumb" in that they contain no information on their context. This means that as soon as they are scanned they must be associated with a particular customer case. Thus the first stage in workflow is to associate a scanned image with a case. Several alternatives are available at design:

1. If OCR is used the case or customer reference number can be automatically identified and the image automatically associated with case. If manual confirmation is necessary as a precaution, automatic association is not really worthwhile.

2. With a small volume of documents it may be most efficient to do association on the scanning workstation as each individual document is scanned.

3. With a larger volume of images this will not be practical since the images must be scanned in rapidly in large batches. In this case images are associated by workers after rapid scanning of a batch. To do this paper documents will need to be retained to do association, because it may not be apparent from a single onscreen document to which case they relate—other documents are required for context. To help this the

scan process can be designed to scan in batches of documents related to a single case to keep them together. Marker sheets can be inserted between cases to achieve this.

4. A further compromise solution is to use barcoding to identify each case document. This will rely on forms printed for customers each containing a unique barcode or sticky labels can be added to letters before scanning. This does introduce an extra step, but will save time in association.

Design of Case Ownership

When designing a workflow system the way in which the different cases are assigned to staff needs to be considered. The following options are available:

▶ Case ownership where a single team member owns the case throughout the activities performed as part of the business process.

▶ Role ownership where team members have a number of roles and can only undertake an activity when they have been granted the right privilege.

▶ Shared ownership when any member of the team can perform the next activity when they are free.

Often some combination of these approaches is employed. When using case ownership, authorization by a different person with a supervisor role is usually required. The case ownership approach is often best in terms of customer service since this enables the member of staff to become familiar with the case. However, this is only usually practical for small implementations since the workflow will not be as efficient if each case has to wait for a particular individual to become free.

CTI Integration Design

Since processing an action task will usually involve phoning the customer for clarification or writing a letter to request additional information, the design for this system needs to consider the viability of *Computer Telephony Integration* (CTI). When an operator has a case on screen, CTI can be used to autodial the customer and repeat until an answer is received. With incoming calls CTI can use Caller Line Identification to automatically bring up the customer case on screen using the phone number of the caller as an identifier. Both of these features can help in improving customer service and increasing the number of calls an operator can handle.

Design of Worklist and Follow Up Actions

When the operator marks the item as complete a new workflow task can be automatically created if necessary. For example to follow up by calling the customer if a letter is not received within five days. To indicate the amount of detail involved with processing an application, Table 8.1 shows the checklist that must be completed for each item. If the tasks have not been completed after the case has been on the system a certain number of days, then a task to "chase customer" for the item will be automatically created. This checklist appears on the user's screen to indicate how far an application has progressed.

Table 8.1 *Workflow item checklist for mortgage processing*

Risk assessment *Priority ordered checklist*	*Chase after n days*
1. Risk assessment interview with branch staff	3
2. Credit reference check	4
3. Proof of ID (birth certificate)	4
4. Proof of employment	4
5. Current lenders reference	4
6. Current employers reference	4
7. Current landlords reference	4
8. Credit commitments	4
9. Previous lenders reference (if < 6 months)	5
10. Previous landlords reference (if < 6 months)	5
11. Valuation of property by branch staff	6
12. Proof of deposit	6
13. Proof of insurance for property	6
14. Proof of residency	6

9

Implementation—Development, Deployment and Human Factors

Implementation—the final development and deployment of a system is built on successful completion of previous stages of the project. So it could be thought of as straightforward since many technical problems will already have been dealt with. However, there are significant non-technical factors which are important at this stage. Understanding how people will be affected by the new system, why they may resist change and how they can be encouraged to use the system is critical. We consider how resistance can be countered by encouraging user involvement throughout the project.

The scope of implementation is described here to include all activities necessary to get the system up and running and on the user's desktop after the system has been designed. This includes technical work such as configuration, coding, database population, testing and documentation which are collectively termed the build process. It also includes management activities such as procuring kit and managing the change in the organization that is associated with the bringing the new system in. Finally, it includes methods of deploying the software once everything else is in place.

In This Chapter

Here we cover both technical and non-technical aspects of implementation. Since human factors are so important and sometimes neglected these are considered first. This includes particular problems with introducing groupware into the organization. Then the importance of prototyping in involving users is covered. We then go on to consider the specific problems of implementation such as testing and planning deployment. Finally, general guidelines for avoiding failure at this stage are given.

The Human Factor

How a new system affects the working day of the people using it should be at the front of the mind of all developers. This is particularly true with the introduction of systems associated with BPR since very often they will not be automating the existing way of work, but changing the way work is performed and also peoples' job functions. If we do not explain the rationale behind the change and how it will effect the individual, then when the system is installed, all the classic symptoms of resistance to change will be apparent.

While outright hostility manifesting itself as sabotage of the system is not unheard of, what is more common is that users will try to project blame onto the system and will identify major faults where only minor bugs exists. This will obviously damage the reputation of the system and senior managers will want to know what went wrong with the project. Another problem that can occur if the system has not been introduced well is that avoidance of the system will occur with users working around the system to continue their previous ways of working. Careful management is necessary to ensure that this does not happen.

The Psychology of Group Working

When planning the design and deployment of all types of collaborative software it is useful to appreciate some of the theoretical background describing what governs group behavior and interaction. This is particularly important with groupware which involves active decision making and negotiation such as meetings support software and decision support software.

Normal face to face communication occurs through visual channels and audio channels, each of which can be subdivided into further channels such as language content and vocalizations and body movement or gestures. When using software other than video-conferencing we are reduced to a single channel and we lose the visual clues to communication such as facial expression, body movement or other responses—a yawn, eye contact or a fist thumping the desk usually signify something! The audio channel is simplified to the language content only, missing out on the vocalizations, such as pauses and hesitation. Despite losing this information, we do not lose all emphasis since some of it can be replaced by the use of numbering, indentation, CAPs or direct language.

McGrath (1984) proposes a framework for the study of group dynamics which includes the following elements:

▶ properties of individuals

▶ relationship between individuals

▶ properties of the environment in which the group functions

▶ task to be carried out by the group

▶ the "behavior setting"—the fit between the group structure and the task

Computer resources are obviously directed at assisting the task to be performed by the group and provide part of the environment in which it is conducted. Although groupware tools cannot affect the properties of the individual such as their age, experience, temper or whether they are introvert or extrovert, it can moderate the effect of these characteristics. For example, using groupware, the introvert has a better platform, with more opportunity to make their views known. Conversely, the extrovert is not able to exert such a powerful influence.

It has been shown that this can result in more balanced decisions from a group. It has also been shown that more ideas can be generated when anonymity of participants occurs (Valacich et al., 1991), although for practical reasons many group systems use named participants. However, dominant managers may well see this as a problem with groupware as they may feel that they are losing their power and will be less likely to sanction groupware purchases.

Barriers to Group Behavior

It is also useful to consider impediments to successful group behavior. Such dysfunctions in group processes were labeled by Steiner (1972) as process losses. It will be seen from the list of losses below that groupware can encourage contribution by members and reduce the losses which include:

▶ **Unequal airtime** occurs as groups become larger or individuals dominate, thus monopolizing the discussion. Asynchronous meetings hosted via groupware can reduce this problem since it is easier to participate—there are not the barriers of interrupting someone else. When individuals dominate some team members may "free ride" and not get involved because they won't be noticed.

▶ **Production blocking** is a result of only one member being able to speak at a time. This can reduce the capability of the group to generate new ideas as ideas may be forgotten by individuals if they cannot state them immediately or other new ideas may be blocked while they are remembering what they want to say! Again such problems may be reduced by asynchronous meetings—ideas can be contributed as soon as they are thought of.

▶ **Evaluation apprehension** causes people to withhold valid ideas for fear of the opinions of others. The relative anonymity of remote meetings can help here also.

▶ **Cognitive inertia** is well known to meeting participants as the way in which meetings tend to follow one line of thought or "go round in circles." Groupware can again help break out of this.

These are the main process blocks, but there are others such as the loss of socializing that can occur before and after meetings, but tends to be useful. All is not rosy in the garden (or in the electronic meeting), since other authors argue that computer mediated communication can exaggerate some of the problems described above. They argue that groupware can cause a loss of individuality and social cues and that there are technological barriers caused by the inefficiency of typing and reviewing many comments on a screen

Another well known model for group behavior is that of Richard Weber. This suggests the four stages of effectiveness shown in Table 9.1 which are all likely to be experienced when groupware is introduced. With good leadership and support from groupware teams should develop to the efficient performing stage. Without either they may not get beyond the Forming or Storming stage.

Groupware and the Organization—Avoiding Problems

The Flame-Mail Phenomenon

Despite the brave new world promoted by groupware and e-mail, not everyone likes working in this way. Recent research conducted by Novell of over 1000 e-mail users in the UK showed that e-mail can lead to lower productivity, and raise stress because of e-mail bullying. "Flame-mail," or abusive, bullying messages, often from superiors were said to be experienced by at least half the staff. This shows that a change in culture caused by the introduction

Table 9.1 *The stages of group dynamics. Richard C. Weber.* The Group: A Cycle from Birth to Death, *pp. 68–71.*

Issue/stage	1. Forming	2. Storming	3. Norming	4. Performing
Group behavior	Superficial, polite, ambiguity	Frustration, anger, attacks on leadership	Negotiation, agreement, cohesion	Growth, insight and collaboration
Group tasks	Define membership, Define objectives	Decision making	Functional	Productive
Leadership	Dependence	Counter-dependence		Interdependence
Interpersonal	Inclusion	Control		Affection

of e-mail is not being well handled by some companies. Under time pressure, or when staff want to avoid a face to face confrontation, they may lash out using e-mail rather than discussing the problem. This phenomenon highlights the need for training and policies on e-mail use.

A further problem of e-mail illustrated by this survey is the time it takes to read e-mail. Almost all respondents (94%) said they wasted up to an hour a day reading and replying to messages. The results of the survey were mixed, with 70% of respondents saying that they could not now do without e-mail.

E-mail Best Practices

The following best practices for e-mail implementation include guidelines contained with the report and other tips for managing e-mail.

▶ Think before you send an e-mail rather than rashly sending an e-mail in anger.

▶ Don't use e-mail instead of discussing a problem.

▶ Don't SHOUT or use capital letters, this can cause "e-mail rage."

▶ Ensure e-mail is clear and not open to misinterpretation.

▶ Encourage meetings to reduce e-mail traffic.

▶ Do not send messages to everyone, just in case they are interested.

▶ Set up formal channels for dealing with flame-mail, such as a reporting mechanism and, if necessary, disciplinary action.

▶ Use a structured approach to archive all e-mail after a certain length of time (say six months). E-mail is transient, if it is left solely to users important company information may be deleted without being archived. Systems should be purchased which facilitate this.

▶ Discourage printing of e-mail, encourage use of archive facilities.

A final problem of e-mail stems from it being so easy to use—a large number of messages sent to one person can result in insufficient time for them to deal with them and a backlog develops. As well as this causing problems for the individual, large volume of messages on the server can cause performance problems, particularly as the server nears its capacity. Without guidelines e-mail can severely stress a company's network. E-mail messages and attachments that are sent to all company staff may be duplicated many times on the server. All these copies unnecessarily use up network bandwidth and server storage. Many readers will have experienced support staff visits asking them to clear out their in- and out-boxes so the server won't go down again when it reaches capacity for e-mail storage.

Are You Making the Most of Your Groupware?

Surveys of industry practice indicate that many companies do not make use of all available groupware functions. Some, such as e-mail are more widely used. A recent press release from a UCLA/Arthur Andersen study conducted in 1996 which surveyed 1500 users of Lotus Notes showed that while groupware has the power to give companies an edge, most aren't using it to its full potential. Instead, they use it primarily for its most basic communication function—sending and receiving e-mail.

The study found that 80% used e-mail an average of 23 times a week, with 50% using discussion databases eight times a week on average, while 14% used workflow applications three times per week. According to the study, an organization with the highest quality implementation of groupware tended to deliver more benefits than those with lower quality implementations. In high quality implementations groupware had twice the impact on individual job performance and nearly three times the impact on customer satisfaction.

How to Manage Change

To avoid the problems associated with change, the guidelines below stress involvement of all parties. These problems are commonly presented, but also commonly ignored as apparently pressing technical problems arise. Ignore them at your peril!

▶ Use senior managers as *sponsors* who want the system to work and will fire up staff with their enthusiasm and stress why introducing the system is important to the business and its workers.

▶ Involve potential users early in development and treat them as customers. Involve them in all stages of specification, prototyping and testing. Use a range of users from clerks to supervisors and their managers. Some companies make the mistake of only using managers to specify the system who are removed from the day to day intricacies of the process or their knowledge of them is five years out of date.

▶ Ensure there are *stakeholders* at every location the system will be used who are respected by their co-workers and will again act as a source of enthusiasm for the system. The user representatives used in specification and testing are ideal candidates for this role.

▶ Use appropriate education and training. A lot of companies make the mistake of not training staff sufficiently for a new system, of those that do train, the training is often the wrong sort. Training in how to use the software—which menu options are available and which buttons to press is common. What is sometimes missing is an explanation of why the system is being brought in—why are the staff's existing ways of working being overturned? This educational part of training is very important.

Aside from the cultural problems that stem from the introduction of a new computer system groupware poses its own problems. The introduction of groupware and collaborative systems are often associated with reengineering of a company and always herald a new way of communicating. If currently there is a rigid, autocratic way of working then groupware will give a more flexible, open way of communicating.

This may be resented by senior managers as they may feel this will erode their chain of command and the freedom in exchange of information will reduce their knowledge base in comparison with other workers. As a result it will be the more senior staff members who will find readjustment hardest so the training and education plan should allow for this. It may also be best to introduce the system first to senior managers so they can become familiar and comfortable with it so they can then use it to manage their workgroups effectively. Companies who already have a relatively flat structure with high information availability and team work will find the transition easier, but probably have fewer gains to be made.

Who Owns the Problems?

For the system to be used effectively, clearly defined responsibilities are needed for the parties involved. This becomes particularly important when problems arise, which they will and probably often!

A clear route must be available for escalating support problems. These will be made either to an internal help desk or a help desk run by the systems integrator. Owing to the complexity of some workflow systems, it may be necessary to set up a temporary help desk when the system is first introduced and there are a higher volume of queries.

Once the nature of the problem has been identified at the help desk, what action to be taken and by who should be defined. If a problem results from a failing in the design or operation of the software then review must occur to decide on the severity of the problem. Often there is a five tier classification of severity:

1. Critical problem, system not operational. This may occur due to power or server failure. Level 1 problems need to be resolved immediately.

2. Critical problem making part of the system unusable or causing data corruption. These would normally need to be resolved within 12 to 24 hours depending on the nature of the problem.

3. Problem causing intermittent system failure or data corruption. Resolve within 48 hours.

4. Non-severe problem not requiring modification to software until next release.

5. Trivial problem or suggestion which can be considered for future releases.

During development there is often a simpler three point scale which can be used to cut through protracted discussion of the desirability of making the fix. The three point scale is:

▶ Priority 1—Must fix

▶ Priority 2—Fix if time available

▶ Priority 3—No time to fix

If the system has been tailored by a systems integrator these will be the responsibility of the system integrator to fix and this will be specified in the contract or *Service Level Agreement* (SLA), together with the time that will be taken for the change to be made. If the system has been developed or tailored internally by the IS department or even within a department an SLA is still a good idea. If the problem occurs from a problem with packaged software you will have to hope that a patch to the problem exists and you will have to lobby the supplier for a fix if none exists yet.

Apart from solving problems someone needs to be responsible for making sure that the system is being used effectively. Checks need to be made that the system is being used and that staff are not persisting with previous methods of working. This is where the stakeholders are important.

As a summary of the important human issues in the implementation of groupware the box "Critical factors in groupware implementation" shows recommendations by Arthur Andersen Business Consulting.

Prototyping

Since prototyping is widely used in workflow implementations we will briefly consider why this is the case and suggest methods for approaching it. Prototyping was introduced in response to the problems caused by the traditional extended software life cycle, giving rise to often inappropriate systems, delivered late. This involved a prescriptive, highly structured approach with distinct stages of analysis, design and build (coding), each taking up to several months. Systems could be delivered to users months or years after their inception without the users being involved apart from the initial specification.

Critical Factors in Groupware Implementation

Best practice guidelines have been produced by Arthur Andersen to reduce the problems referred to in the UCLA/Arthur Andersen survey referred to above. Christopher P. Andrus, Director of Collaborative Systems with the Advanced Technology Group of Arthur Andersen Business Consulting advises that: "Organizations should study how groupware can add value to work tasks, and keep it relevant to company strategy. They must also understand existing usage patterns, norms and attitudes about sharing, learning and cooperation before implementing groupware. By understanding the existing culture, conflict and misunderstandings can be avoided." He also recommends that companies use small experimental projects to expand groupware usage.

Web reference: http://www.arthurandersen.com/aabc (Arthur Andersen business consulting resources)

Arthur Andersen Business Consulting's groupware management framework helps to ensure that organizations embrace five critical factors in groupware implementation and usage:

1. "Socialization: Create early positive user awareness about groupware. Provide formal and continuous training.

2. Commitment: Generate a sense of ownership and need for groupware by allowing users to try it before implementation. Provide significant user involvement in adoption or implementation decisions.

3. Reward: Formally recognize and reward groupware use. Encourage a learning culture in which cooperation and sharing are valued.

4. Feedback: Implement and promote formal feedback mechanisms. Allow employees significant involvement in growth activities.

5. Legitimacy: Ensure users develop a feeling that groupware is an appropriate way to get work done. Publicize success stories and continually demonstrate how groupware improves job performance and ease."

In the time it took for the system to be developed, business practices had moved on and the system was no longer appropriate. When users were trying to explain to the analysts what they wanted it was difficult to understand what the analyst's Data Flow Diagrams and Entity-Relationship diagrams would mean in terms of the software. Prototyping is intended to break the life cycle into shorter stages in which the users are more actively involved.

The main elements of prototyping are that it is:

▶ Rapid—Prototyping is often referred to as *Rapid Application Development* (RAD) since the time from inception to completion is reduced to months rather than years. More rapid development is achieved through reducing the length of time of the analysis, design and build stages by combining them in conjunction with the use of graphical software tools with which applications can be built quickly from pre-assembled components.

▶ Simple—Skeleton applications are produced as prototypes that do not contain all the functions of a system but are a framework which gives a good indication to users of the look and feel of an application so they can comment on it and say "we like that feature, but it would be nice to do that also" or "that feature isn't necessary, it is not what we meant." The prototype may initially be storyboarded as a "paper prototype" but is usually produced using RAD tools such as Sybase/Powersoft Powerbuilder, Centura, Microsoft Visual Studio or Borland Delphi.

▶ Iterative—Prototypes are produced often at a frequency of once every few weeks so that the comments from the last review can be fed into the evolving system.

▶ User centered—Users are involved at all stages of development, in describing the existing system, reviewing the prototypes and testing the system.

The stages involved with prototyping are to first identify the user requirements in outline and then rapidly develop a working prototype which the users operate to check the software proposed is in line with their needs. Once the first prototype has been produced there are several alternatives:

▶ Iterate and produce further refinements, this often occurs throughout the specification stage, when a satisfactory version has been produced other alternatives may follow.

▶ Develop module prototypes—prototype key views of the data from a workflow system or Lotus Notes or important data entry dialogs.

▶ Throwaway the prototype and develop a more robust version of the software for the production version. This is often prudent, since in rapid prototyping some corners have to be cut so it may not be optimized for performance or may not have exception handling features.

A frequent general problem with prototyping is to do "demonstration prototyping" rather than "hands-on" prototyping. Often prototypes are merely shown by developers to clients for general feedback and not used "hands-on" until several iterations of the prototype when many more features are integrated. This causes delays because problems that could have been trapped earlier will only become apparent at a late stage.

Prototyping Workflow Implementations

Workflow systems are usually not developed from the ground up as entirely customized packages, but are usually produced by customization in tools such as Staffware, Visual Workflo or Flowmark. Prototyping is still used to test out the suitability of the process definitions, worklists and reports. Prototyping is particularly important in workflow applications to:

▶ test the process definitions and business rules have been captured correctly in analysis and converted into a workable process enactment in the workflow engine

▶ test the volume of workflow is manageable by the existing staff—can workflow volume be managed by the human resources

▶ check performance on processing transactions and performing the queries which generate the worklist—can workflow volume be managed by the hardware and software resources

▶ test the integration of the different views of the data in the client application—is it easy to move from the workflow list to the case data? This process is often cumbersome

▶ workers may well not have used software with this method of working and prototyping offers a method of gradually introducing it to some of them

I was involved in a project for real estate agents where the volume of workflow generated was found to be too high in prototyping. This analysis stage had identified approximately 40 activities which were thought necessary to produce a good level of customer service. On prototyping it was found, however, that the staff in branches were having to work one to two hours extra each night to clear down their task list. Here prototyping identified that the process definition had been over-specified and that the activities could be reduced by eight to ten activities without degrading service. Take care not to make prototypes too simple, and therefore unrepresentative. Another project I am aware of did not undertake volume testing during prototyping with a sufficiently large representative number of customers—it was not scalable to the number of customer cases held on the system. This was a call center, CTI system and it resulted in customers phoning have to wait too many seconds before their customer details were retrieved.

Prototyping Groupware Implementations

Prototyping groupware before deployment is less common than for production workflow systems since less tailoring is required. The main benefit prototyping could give for applications such as video-conferencing, electronic meetings or document management systems is to show *how* to use the system. In this case, prototyping of the processes is really what will happen and it is part of training and procedure development. If ad hoc workflow functions in groupware such as Notes or Exchange are being developed it is natural to perform prototyping of the applications to check that the software supports the processes that are being automated.

Is There a Prototyping Nirvana?

Although prototyping is described as causing the end of systems development problems, many, many problems still exist. In the UK a 1995 survey by Cooper & Lybrand of Top 100 companies showed that 61% had significant cost overruns or failed to meet the deadlines with 42% not achieving business benefits. There are many possible reasons for this, a few of the most important ones, which can be avoided with experience are:

▶ The success of prototyping encourages unrealistic estimates which never can be achieved, production systems need the time spent on them in areas of performance optimization and testing, these cannot be short-circuited.

▶ Prototyping can be used to rapidly produce functional software, but it can equally lead to software with too many errors since design did not have enough time devoted to it—this cannot be skimped on without consequences!

▶ Client/server technology is still relatively immature, so trying to integrate new software and hardware from different manufacturers often leads to delays as incompatibilities have to be worked around.

▶ Poor project management with insufficient risk analysis and escalation to solve problems when they occur will also cause delays.

To counter these problems, which partly arise from there not being a methodology to assist prototyping, an industry group has been set up to develop and promote a more structured method of prototyping. The method developed is known as the *Dynamic Systems Development Method* or DSDM.

Dynamic Systems Development Method

One of the difficulties with RAD is that it is radically different from traditional systems development (no pun intended). It lacks rules which means that corners can be cut and essential work such as design and testing can be missed out! To overcome this problem a group of suppliers and customers in the UK and US have formed an organization to promote structured RAD under the banner DSDM—the Dynamic Systems Development Method. DSDM provides a valuable set of guiding principles:

1. Active user involvement is imperative (this needs to occur daily if possible)

2. DSDM teams must be empowered to make decisions

3. Product delivery should be frequent

4. Fitness for business purpose is the basis on which products should be assessed

5. Iterative and incremental development is necessary to give convergence to an accurate business solution

6. All changes during development must be reversible

7. Requirements are baselined at a high level

8. Testing occurs throughout the life-cycle

9. A collaborative and cooperative approach between all stakeholders is essential

Web reference: http://www.dsdm.org

Planning Deployment

A deployment plan takes the system architecture design and requirements specification and plan procurement to get everything in place in time for user acceptance testing. This is not a trivial task because of the range of equipment required from a variety of manufacturers. A deployment plan should list every piece of software and hardware required, when it needs to arrive and when it needs to be connected.

When planning deployment, advanced planning is required due to possible delays in purchasing and delivery, particularly for new technologies which may be in high demand. I remember an implementation being delayed because an optical jukebox model was so new it required a new type of SCSI cable to connect to the server which was not available in the country (at least according to the supplier). The burden of planning will often be taken by a systems integrator, but it may be shared by the purchasing department of the company installing the new groupware system. This needs careful liaison between both groups.

Deployment Options—Advantages and Disadvantages

Moving from a previous system to a new system is possible in four different ways regardless of whether the previous system is paper based or computer based. These are often used in combination through the course of project. The options are:

1. Pilot system

2. Phased implementation

3. Parallel running

4. Big bang or immediate cutover method

In a national or international implementation of a new workflow system it is customary to trial the project in a single region or country using a pilot system. If a pilot system is considered successful there is then a choice for either immediately implementing the system elsewhere using the big bang approach or running the new and old system in parallel until it is certain the new system is stable enough. If the new system is modular in construction it is possible for the implementation to be phased with new modules gradually being introduced as they are completed and the users become familiar with the existing system.

Due to the scale of production workflow a combination of these methods is used with an initial pilot system deployed in one area with different modules phased in. Parallel running will probably also occur in this instance in case there is a need to revert to the old system in the event of failure of the new system. Once the system is proved in this area then further rollout will probably occur through the big bang approach.

With installation of new hardware, a particular problem is where changes to infrastructure are required; for example, upgrading cabling to a higher bandwidth for video-conferencing or installing a new router. This can take a considerable time and cause a lot of disruption to users of existing systems. Since workflow and groupware systems are often introduced as part of reengineering there is often an associated investment in new hardware which means new hardware is purchased for the installation, increasing logistical problems.

Documentation and Training

These must be phased in with the deployment plan. Often part of the new system will need to be in place far in advance of the live date for prototyping, testing or training. Documentation and training materials will have to be available for these dates.

Testing

In this section we looked at the types of testing that should occur for workflow systems. Testing should be performed against a *test specification* which details tests in different areas. Too often users perform only a general usability test of the system where they perform common functions chosen by themselves. While this is valid and is necessary, it does not give a good coverage of all the areas of the system. Systematic tests should also be performed using a *test script* which covers, in detail, functions to be tested. For workflow this will include separate test scripts for case management, task list, handling case data and administrative functions.

Given the variety of tests that need to be performed, large implementations will also use a *test plan* which describes what testing will be performed when, and by whom. Testing is always a compromise between the number of tests that can be performed against the time available. The test plan will specify the scope of the testing and agree coverage of the software alternatives that should be chosen. It will also describe the mechanics of how the test is performed. This is the method I have adopted:

▶ Testers perform tests. Those completed are checked off on a *test-log* to ensure good coverage (users don't like structured testing) and results written to a *Change Request* log or form.

▶ Change requests are reviewed daily by team manager. Major problems escalated to development team for correction.

▶ Change requests are reviewed at least weekly by team manager and customer. Fixes categorized as Priority 1—Fix immediately; Priority 2—fix before final release; and Priority 3—will not fix before final release.

▶ Agreed changes are made for next release of software and cycle then repeats.

We now look in more detail at some of the types of test that should be performed. These are reviewed according to the tests that are typically performed by developers and end users or a testing team.

Developer Tests

Module Tests

These are performed on individual modules of the system. The module can be treated as a "black box" and we can check that expected outputs are generated for given inputs.

Module Interaction Testing

Expected interactions between modules are assessed. Interaction between all modules is assessed in the system test.

Database Testing

This is a test to determine that the connectivity between the application and the database is correct. Can a user log in to database? Can a record be inserted, deleted or updated, i.e. are transactions executing? Are cascading deletes working as expected? Are two phase commits executing as designed.

Volume Testing

This is linked to capacity planning. For workflow systems, simulation tools can be used to assess how the system will react to different levels of usage anticipated from the requirements and design specifications. Methods of indexing or performing queries may need to be updated if the software fails this test.

Performance Testing

This involves timing how long different functions or transactions take to occur. These are usually important so they may be specified in a contract and will certainly affect users' perceptions of the system.

Confidence Test Script

A short script which may take a few hours to run through which tests all the main functions of the software. It should be run before all releases to users to ensure their time is not wasted on a prototype that has major failings which mean the test will have to be aborted and a new release made.

Automated Tests

Tools specifically for automatically testing workflow and groupware systems are rare due to the relative newness of the technology. However automated testing tools normally used by software developers can be used for this. Automated tools simulate user inputs through the mouse or keyboard and can be used to check for the correct action. Scripts can be set up for these and are particularly useful for performing regression tests.

Regression Testing

This testing should be performed before a release to ensure that the software performance is consistent with previous test results. It is usually performed with automated tools.

End User Tests

For ease of assessing the results the users should be asked to write down for each request:

1. Module affected

2. Description of problem (any error messages to be written in full)

3. Relevant data—particular message or record affected

4. Severity of problem on three point scale

Different types of end user tests that can be adopted include:

▶ Scenario testing—in this particular business scenarios are followed with realistic case data. For collaborative software these should be constructed so that several users are involved in performing a task.

▶ Functional testing—users are told to concentrate on testing particular functions or modules such as the process definition model in detail either following a test script or working through the modules systematically.

▶ General testing—here users depart from the test specification and test according to their random preferences. Sometimes this is the only type of testing used which results in poor coverage of the functions in the software!

▶ Multiuser testing—the effect of different users accessing the same message or case data are simulated in this case. The software should behave as specified, i.e. not permitting two users to modify the same data. Tests should also be made to ensure that users with different permissions and rules are treated as they should be, i.e. they are locked out of data where appropriate.

▶ User acceptance testing—this is the final stage of testing which occurs before the software is signed off as fit for purpose and the system can go live.

Avoiding Failure at Implementation

As a summary to this section we look at reasons why collaborative systems may go wrong in the implementation. These are the rules to avoid failure at the implementation stage:

1. *Don't forget the people*

You are likely introducing a new way of working, so explain to your people why the change is happening and then train them adequately in the use of the system.

2. *RAD is too rapid*

Some corners cannot be cut, especially process design, optimizing system performance and testing.

3. *Make sure computer resources are adequate*

Ensure the server can handle the load at critical times of the day such as when scanning is occurring or at peak times in a call center. Ensure also that the system performance does not degrade as the number of users of the systems or customers record held ramp up.

4. *Good project managers make it happen*

To make sure that the project is controlled and that corners aren't cut, the need for a good project manager is evident.

5. *Support from the top*

Top management must support the cultural changes necessary to introduce collaborative products.

10

Designing for the Future

Groupware and workflow systems are relatively new software technologies, although PC based groupware has been used by some organizations for nearly ten years. Given this, and their ever increasing usage in business, there are many ways in which they will develop further. Key influences are likely to be the growth in use of the Internet and distributed computing and the role that software objects play in this. We also will see more incorporation of groupware features into all types of software applications whose primary function is not group working. For example, accounting software was traditionally software for individuals. Today it has functions to enable accountants to work together as a team.

In This Chapter

We look into the future by considering the likely future of groupware and workflow software separately. We then consider significant technologies and techniques for the future. These include the Internet, software objects and artificial intelligence. When looking into the future, the intention is to identify technologies which are likely to become extensions to the current systems in business. This should help in building systems which can grow with the business. Finally, I present a set of tips to plan for the future which will help to avoid building in obsolescence to current systems.

The Future of Groupware

In Chapter 1 we started by reviewing the evolution of groupware. We now try to predict future trends and ask where do we head next? Figure 10.1 shows the current and near future situation. The most significant trend is the use of the TCP/IP based intranets for the deployment of applications using web servers and browsers. This will not destroy group working functions. Rather,

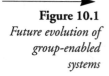

Figure 10.1
Future evolution of group-enabled systems

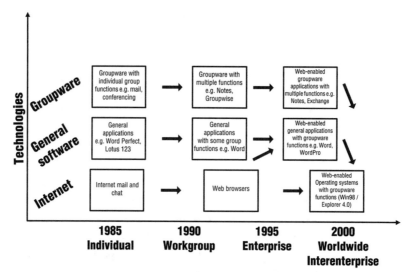

they will be included within the intranet. Or as one magazine recently put it "Groupware is dead, long live the intranet."

The main trends evident from Figure 10.1 are:

▶ all general business applications will include group working functions

▶ web browsers accessing data across TCP/IP based networks will become the primary means of deploying group applications

▶ applications which are accessed from web browsers will be incorporated as plug-in functions and Java or Active-X applets

▶ operating systems will incorporate group working functions such as e-mail, news and conferencing

There is plenty of evidence for these trends already. For example, in Chapter 5, there are examples of prototypes of forms based software such as Form-Flow which are already available as Java applets. Java rather than Active-X currently seems to be the preferred language for developing these applications. New increments of operating systems such as Microsoft Windows 98 have the option of using the web browser as the main means of accessing applications and data from the desktop.

The rapid increase in users attached to the Internet is clear from Chapter 5 that showed web users predicted to increase from 46 million in 1997 to 152 million by the year 2000. But will this change lead to the eventual disappearance of monolithic groupware applications such as Lotus Notes and

Microsoft Exchange? I believe this is unlikely since the well tested server technology on which these products are based has been essential to their success. New products are unlikely to be able to compete in areas of security, scalability and reliability without the foundation of years of previous improvement.

What will change is that the proprietary groupware clients will disappear to be replaced by applets running in the web browser and that all communications from the applet with the server will be established over the TCP/IP protocol. Lotus has developed its eSuite (Kona) applications suite which will include both personal applications and group scheduling and calendaring. Meanwhile Oracle has produced its "Hat-Trick" applications. Both suites have been significantly delayed which is indicative of the problem of optimizing such Java applications.

With the advent of components and continually evolving standards to assist interoperation, a real implementation headache will be to get this componentware to function in a coherent way. This isn't likely to happen anytime soon and we may see several steps backwards before we move forwards in this area.

What is the future for relative newcomers who have introduced intranet based groupware products such as Opentext Livelink and Radnet Webshare? Judging by their reference sites, these companies are achieving some success. These are likely to remain niche products, however, due to the huge installed base of Exchange, Notes and Groupwise and the speed at which the companies which produce these products have embraced the Internet.

The Future of E-mail

E-mail and groupware were software tools which supposedly heralded the arrival of "the paperless office." As we know, this hasn't happened. In the 1970s in the UK, consumption of office paper was running at 70 million tons per year. In the 1990s this has reached 200 million tons per year. The reason for this increase in paper usage is that the antiquated "edit, print, copy and circulate" method of publishing business information has been made more efficient at each stage by computer systems. E-mail made easier editing, faster printing and copying all possible.

E-mail has not replaced paper because people believe it is reliable and secure—people don't like virtual documents. The growth in e-mail is now slowing in comparison with the web. E-mail users were shown in Chapter 5 to be expected to increase from 80 million in 1997 to 200 million in 2000.

Increasingly, there is a blurring between where e-mail ends and other forms of groupware and workflow begin. This is particularly true for forms based e-mail which can be used for simple workflow applications such as purchase order processing. This trend will continue with e-mail functions becoming incorporated within other applications and the operating system. Evidence that this is already happening is provided by Lotus cc:Mail Web. With this product a user's mailbox and all its functions are accessible from any forms capable web browser.

In the intermediate period, before web based e-mail clients become predominant, there will be a lot of confusion over e-mail choice. Lotus has different clients for Lotus cc:mail, Notes mail and Domino mail and Java and Active-X versions for browser integration. Meanwhile Microsoft is offering several mail clients including Microsoft mail, Exchange clients and Outlook. Browsers such as Netscape Navigator also offer POP3 based mail.

The Future for Workflow

Many of the trends identified for groupware also hold true for workflow. Workflow applications such as Staffware and IBM Flowmark already offer web based clients for end users accessing workflow queues. This pattern will be repeated for all workflow vendors. Since production workflow applications occupy a more specialized business need than e-mail and groupware functions, it is very unlikely that the functions of these types of systems will be incorporated into operating systems.

At the other end of the workflow spectrum, the same does not hold true. Administrative or ad hoc workflow functions that involve routing forms between users using e-mail as transport could well become an operating system function. These changes should make workflow more accessible to small and medium companies. A future challenge for workflow vendors is to integrate different types of *Electronic Document Management Systems* (EDMS) since EDMS has the following overlapping functions:

▶ Document management

▶ Imaging

▶ Workflow

▶ Computer output to laser disk (COLD)

Possible Reasons for the Slow Adoption of Workflow Systems

Despite strong promotion of workflow by vendors and industry analysts during the 1990s, the level of adoption of workflow by companies has been low.

Sales predictions have consistently been lower than those estimated by analysts. This has been particularly true for small and medium companies.

The reasons why workflow growth have not been as rapid as expected are unclear. The root cause must be that businesses have not thought that workflow will deliver significant savings in comparison with existing processes. The value proposition has not been clearly demonstrated. The sentiment expressed is "why bother changing an existing method of administration, if it already works?" The cost of many early workflow solutions was also high and required a lot of development effort to tailor the workflow software to the needs of the company.

A further reason may be that the time is not right. Workflow is only one technology which is competing with others as possible ways of improving a company. Many small or medium companies will only have recently migrated to a LAN environment and may be experimenting with e-mail and document sharing. There are then strong pressures for obtaining Internet access and setting up an intranet. Workflow is of secondary interest in comparison with these other initiatives. It is in the large companies where workflow can help mission critical processes such as a call center in a financial services provider that increase in use of workflow has been most dramatic. There are also limitations to current WFMS which need to be solved in the future to increase acceptance of the technology. Georgakopoulos et al. (1995) identify the following limitations:

▶ Lack of interoperability between workflow management systems and other applications such as legacy systems. This should improve as vendors adhere to standards such as those proposed by the WfMC which are described in Chapter 4;

▶ Inadequate performance in high volume transaction based systems;

▶ Lack of support for standard database resilience features such as rollback/recovery;

▶ Relatively weak support for analysis, testing and debugging within the workflow products.

There are a number of reasons why, in the future, the barriers to entry for workflow applications may fall. Firstly, workflow is becoming available through web clients which are more straightforward to configure than proprietary applications. So, the technological difficulties will be reduced.

Secondly, as products have evolved, the user interface tends to facilitate the creation of the business rules and process definitions needed to make the product work. Growing competition between products, with lower cost web based applications from intranet vendors and groupware vendors will also drive the price of workflow products down, which again will reduce barriers to entry.

Summary of Future Workflow Trends

In the future, the main developments in workflow software are likely to be counter measures to the problems described above. Predictions of these and other future changes include:

1. A further blurring of the distinction between document management systems, workflow and groupware will occur as the functionality and interoperability of each type of application is enhanced. It will become easier to integrate administrative form and document based workflow products with production workflow systems where necessary. For example, Filenet now offers Ensemble and Visual Workflo to cover both bases.

2. Web browsers will become established as the main end user and administrative clients for workflow applications. Messaging will be achieved over TCP/IP based networks and will increasingly occur between businesses and/or customers across the Internet. Currently, web based workflow is mostly restricted to intranet use.

3. Increased adoption of object-oriented techniques will occur in the workflow products. But it does not seem likely that object-oriented databases will become widespread for storing process definitions or workflow transactions.

4. More interoperability both between components of workflow applications such as process definers, monitoring tools and the workflow engine together with better interoperability with other applications.

5. Improved interactive development environments for workflow applications will become available similar to those popularized by products like Borland Delphi and Microsoft Visual Studio.

6. Increasingly sophisticated process analysis tools such as Metasoftware's process analyzer will be used which have a more seamless transition from process model to the process definition required by the WFMS.

7. The appearance of *customized transaction management* (CTM) functionality will help support transaction correctness and reliability. These functions will be part of TP monitors which are commonly found on mainframe databases, but will be found more in client/server applications in future. A TP monitor manages a transaction from where it originates on a client across servers and back to the client. When the transaction completes, all servers confer to ensure it completed successfully.

8. A protracted period of discussion between proposers of rival workflow standards. This will not be helped by attempts by rival standards bodies such as the Document Management Alliance of AIIM, the Object Management Group and the Microsoft/Wang/Eastman software alliance to define standards which will dilute the work of the WfMC. It is difficult to establish what the outcome of these standards wars will be, although the WfMC currently seems to have support from the widest range of vendors.

Changing Working Practices Through Virtual Teams and the Virtual Organization

The virtual organization is now suggested as the shape of the future business by many authors such as James Martin in his book *Cybercorp*. A virtual organization makes use of networking to set up communication between its employees, suppliers and customers in such a way that there are no physical boundaries or constraints on the company. Employees may work anywhere in the world and customers are able to purchase tailored products from any location. The absence of any rigid boundary or hierarchy within the organization should lead to a more responsive and flexible company. This extends to "virtual products" where mass production is replaced by the ability to tailor the product to the customer's need. The Internet and wide-area networks are used to set up the links between the players in the virtual organization. Software such as e-mail, groupware and workflow will all be used to aid collaboration between people in this type of organization.

Important Technologies for the Future

In this chapter, we have already described how TCP/IP based intranets and the Internet will become the future platform for workflow and groupware applications. This will leverage technologies such as Java and ActiveX based applications which will run in a web browser accessing data on a database server which is served up by a web server. Internet and web based technology will itself change dramatically. "Push" technology, which is described in Chapter 5, is now changing the way content is provided and accessed on the web. Rather than users having to search the web to find what they want, users can now subscribe to services providing content they are interested in and this information is broadcast to them. This is also known as web or "netcasting."

An example of the use of push technology in a corporate setting was reported in June 1997 by *Computing* which described how Unilever is rolling out an intranet news system to broadcast news to 7,000 staff across Europe.

Pointcast will be used to display information on the desktop which is normally contained in the company Lotus Notes system, but users have to look for it proactively. This is interesting as an example of fusion of traditional groupware and new Internet technologies. In this section we look at two particular technologies which will have a particular impact on workflow and groupware products.

Object-Oriented Technology

Many software products including workflow products are labeled "object-oriented." Although some functions such as the user interface of the process definition tool may be object-oriented, this does not underpin their entire operation. The reason why most workflow products are not fundamentally object-oriented is that they are based on traditional relational databases and programming languages such as "C." It is not the intention here to revisit the widely known fundamental terms of object orientation. Instead, we will show how object-orientated principles can confer benefits on workflow systems.

The main benefits of using object-orientation are those common to all object-oriented software, namely more rapid development and lower costs achieved through greater reuse of code. Reuse in object-oriented systems is a consequence of the ease with which generic objects can be incorporated into code. This is a consequence of inheritance, where a new object can be derived from an existing object and its behavior modified (polymorphism). Experience of early adopters has shown, however, that these benefits do not come until later releases of the product and the first development may be more expensive than traditional methods. Reuse is a great prospect for workflow and groupware since the majority of business processes are common at a large scale for different companies and industries. The details, in particular the data items and structures, will be different for different companies.

Many of the benefits of object-orientation can and are delivered by existing workflow products that are not fully object-oriented. For example, SAP with its R/3 business workflow product provides several hundred standard business process modules for areas such as procurement or finance which can assist in rapid implementation of the system for new users. The business processes and the objects they act on are stored in an object repository. For example, an invoice is defined as an object with the standard methods:

▶ Create (constructor)

▶ Revise

▶ Release

▶ Post

▶ Delete (destructor)

When executed, each of these methods will automatically generate an event which can be used for generating subsequent actions or monitoring workflow status. Since it is not practical to modify the standard objects to a great extent, a consequence of this approach is that adopters of the SAP system tend to follow the standard processes provided by the software. Similarly Action Technologies products operate by assuming a similarity between business processes, assuming a simple situation which is only overridden when necessary when designing new processes.

InConcert is one of the few WFMS products claiming a pure object-oriented model, and we will consider the operation of this product in a little more detail. The object model of InConcert is based on a process which is a collaborative activity consisting of:

▶ tasks—the individual work units which comprise the process

▶ roles—the participants such as users or programs performing tasks

▶ references—to documents or other data objects that are used during the process

This process is a data object, rather than a program or script. A process and its related objects can be modified at runtime to adapt to the circumstances arising during its execution. These modifications might include changing the task structure of a process, or changing role and reference assignments.

As in many activity-based models, tasks have a hierarchical structure as many levels of decomposition are required. The InConcert model assumes that tasks execute in parallel unless task dependencies are specified. Dependencies can be specified through events which trigger subsequent actions.

The process definition is a template that gives a reusable template of tasks, roles and references for a category of business processes. An executing workflow process instance is created from a process definition object. At the time of starting the process instance, or during the course of its execution, the roles and references in the process are bound to specific users and document objects for that particular process instance. Standard processes for different business applications are provided with the product; because of the object-oriented manner in which they are defined it is straightforward to modify them.

The object-oriented nature of InConcert is evident since its API consists of C++ object classes such as process, task, role and related methods of each class. Methods include object creation, object update and retrieving information such as properties, attributes and relationships about an object. Queries can also be performed across collections of objects, so the number of outstanding tasks of a particular type could be identified.

InConcert provides modular tools for managing the development and operation of applications:

▶ An administration module allows object classes and attributes including users and groups to be defined.

▶ The process designer module provides a graphical means of producing hierarchical process definitions defining tasks and their dependencies, roles and document references.

▶ A task user interface designer module can be used to tailor the interface (see below) that is presented to the user performing a given task.

▶ The process manager controls initiation of new process instances and provides status reporting of executing processes such as time to completion.

▶ The task organizer module is for end users to view and work on their tasks. It can be sorted to show higher priority tasks first. The user can select a task to work on and is then given a task user interface which shows task status, checklist of sub-tasks and the associated documents. Run-time modification is possible to delegate the task to another user or modify the task structure

Distributed Object Management

The collaborative systems of the future will be designed using *Distributed Object Management* (DOM) techniques. Georgakopoulos et al. (1995) describe advantages which are conferred by DOM systems:

1. DOM can integrate with distributed legacy systems.

2. The object model provides reuse.

3. The object model gives flexibility in maintenance. As the business evolves new objects can be readily incorporated.

Distributed object management standards are coordinated and promoted by the Object Management Group (OMG), a group of more than 450 industry players. The important standard they have produced is CORBA 2.0.

This builds on the existing client/server model, but marries this with object-oriented techniques. Java applications are increasingly being integrated with CORBA based applications.

The workhorses in a DOM environment are ORBs or *Object Request Brokers*. In the future, object-oriented workflow on a distributed client/server system will be mediated by ORBs. Objects can exist on any server or client in the network environment and can provide a range of services. Through ORBs clients can invoke methods on remote objects. The job of the ORB is to locate the named template (i.e. the object), start the specified operation (i.e. the method), and pass it parameters. Because objects can exist anywhere on a network, there is a name service and a unique identifier to locate objects.

ORBs promote interoperability in two ways. First, they are readily portable since communications between ORBS is specified in the CORBA 2.0 standard interface definition language (IDL). This is a programming language independent method used to specify methods, attributes and relationships with other ORBs. Second, when methods of ORBs are called the caller does not have to worry about the location of the object, whether it is on the same machine, a local server or a server elsewhere. This is managed by the ORB.

Methods of ORBs are invoked using the standard EXECUTE command:

EXECUTE [object-name, method, parameter1, parameter2... parametern].

When invoking a method of an ORB, the mechanisms are similar to invoking remote procedure calls (RPCs) except that when invoking a method of an ORB you are referring to a specific object and its data. ORBs can exhibit polymorphism also, so specific actions can be taken for an individual object. This is not possible with RPCs which are not polymorphic. ORBs can exact a performance penalty if they are implemented via RPC since this introduces another layer of complexity.

CORBA 2.0 augments the *Distributed Computing Environment* (DCE) which defined the standard for RPCs. A further choice is the Microsoft and Digital distributed object model known as DCOM. This does not have such wide industry support and this grouping is often in conflict with the OMG. It does, however, have the installed base from wide use of earlier OLE and more recent Active-X object models. The way in which this dispute is resolved, will have great consequences for the future adoption of object technology. Although a single standard would spur the adoption, I feel this is unlikely in the near future and both standards are likely to coexist for some time.

Web reference: http://www.omg.org

Artificial Intelligence and Expert Systems

There is also potential for the application of artificial intelligence to collaborative systems. This will probably take the form of different software agents which monitor the operation of the system and then suggest how collaboration can be made to work better. The full power of expert systems will not be necessary; rather it is the introduction of monitoring using agents which operate according to simple rules which will be important. Groupware agents may perform the following actions:

▶ suggest decisions based on the views of participants in a group meeting

▶ search the web or intranet to assist in gathering information to help decision making and then display results using push

▶ prompt workers to complete tasks that have been neglected in a pull system

▶ provide guidance on how collaboration should occur

For workflow systems agents will:

▶ compare the process definition with the tasks that are most commonly performed and suggest modifications to the process definition and the workflow to improve performance

▶ provide tutoring to novice users

▶ compare existing system performance to simulated system performance and suggest adjustments

▶ constantly monitor the task list of workers and highlight problems to the manager, for example when work levels fall below a threshold

▶ reassign tasks on worklist according to the availability and performance of staff

The New Zealand immigration service has recently developed a workflow system where expert systems are being applied to improve workflow. In this workflow system, which is used for processing immigration applications, there are frequent changes to the business rules, i.e. the immigration regulations. The new system allows senior officers to modify the business rules as soon as new laws are introduced. Another facility provided in this system which will become more common in workflow systems is a training mode. Rather than operators needing to memorize regulations and different codes for application forms, the system electronically walks a new officer through the job. This system is based on Attar systems XpertRule software which can turn case rules and procedural requirements into branches on a decision tree and then into the system rules.

Web reference: http://www.attar.com

Guidelines for Future-Proofing Systems

As a summary of this chapter, here are tips for building collaborative systems which can grow with the business. These guidelines should assist in planning systems that will survive the future.

1. Use the Internet and intranets as a platform for deploying group and workflow applications within the company and beyond to its customers and suppliers.

2. Use group-enabled intranets as a mechanism to increase information availability to staff using push technology which integrates groupware and workflow.

3. Build in flexibility to change, so the system can accommodate changes in business structure, communication and decision making.

4. Use object-oriented techniques to enable this flexibility and reuse of processes in different parts of the organization.

5. Ensure the products you purchase support evolving standards and workflow specifications and APIs which will have the widest industry support.

6. Products purchased should have an architecture which permits interoperability through links to legacy and new systems.

7. Build in metrics to measure process performance and act on the results to continuously improve the business.

8. Ensure the users are at the heart of introduction of new systems by actively involving them in specification, prototyping, testing and steering future developments.

9. Integrate simulation of performance with metrics to allow optimization of the process.

10. Use configurable workflow tools which enable user modifications at run-time. These changes can be automated through software agents.

Further Reading

Bakman, A. 1995. *Delivering Client/Server Applications That Work.* Greenwich, CT: Manning.

Boehm, B. W. 1988. A Spiral Model of Software Development and Enhancement. *IEEE Computer,* May, pp. 61–72.

Chaffey, D. 1996. Integration of IT Strategy, Process Analysis and System Implementation in an Office Automation Based Process Improvement Programme. In *Business Process Modeling.* Edited by Scholz-Reiter, B. and Stickel, E. Berlin: Springer Verlag.

Coleman, D. 1995. *Groupware: Technologies and Applications.* Englewood Cliffs, NJ: Prentice-Hall.

Curtis, B., Kellner, M., and Over, J. 1995. Processing Modeling. *Communications of the ACM.* 35, no. 9, pp. 75–90.

Davenport, T. H. 1993. *Process Innovation: Reengineering Work Through Information Technology.* Boston: Harvard Business School Press.

Davenport, T. H. 1995. Will Participative Makeovers of Business Processes Succeed Where Reengineering Failed? *Planning Review,* January, p. 24.

Dahm, K. 1995. Leveraging Middleware Standards for Distributed Database Access. In *Integrating Personal Computers in a Distributed Client-Server Environment.* Edited by Khanna, R. Englewood Cliffs, NJ: Prentice-Hall.

Edwards, J. and DeVoe, D. 1997 *3-Tier Client/Server at Work.* New York: John Wiley and Sons.

Georgakopoulos, D., Hornick, M. and Sheth, A. 1995. An Overview of Workflow Management: From Process Modeling to Workflow Automation Infrastructure. *Distributed and Parallel Databases,* Vol. 3, pp. 119–153.

Hammer, M. and Champy, J. 1993. *Reengineering the Corporation: A Manifesto for Business Revolution.* New York: Harper Collins.

Hiltz, S. R. and Turoff, M. 1978. *The Network Nation. Human Communication via Computer.* Reading, MA: Addison-Wesley.

Jacobsen, I., Ericsson, M. and Jacobsen, A. 1994. *The Object Advantage. Business Process Reengineering with Object Technology.* Wokingham, England.: Addison-Wesley.

Jay, A. 1976. How to Run a Meeting. *Harvard Business Review,* 54, Mar./Apr., pp. 43–57.

Kaplan, R. S. and Norton, D. P. 1993. Putting the Balanced Scorecard to Work. *Harvard Business Review,* 70, Jan./Feb., pp. 71–80.

Kavanagh, D. 1994. OMT Development Process, Vintage. In *Business Objects: Software Solutions.* Edited by Spurr, K., Layzell, P., Jennison, L. and Richards, N., New York: John Wiley and Sons, pp. 90–105.

Keller, G., Nuettgens, M., Scheer, A.-W. 1992. Seman-tische Prozessmodellierung Auf Der Basis "Ereignisgesteuerter Prozessketten (EPK)," in: Scheer, A-W. (Hrsg.), *Veroeffentlichungen Des Instituts fuer Wirtschaftsinformatik.* Heft 89. Saarbruecken.

Krallmann, H. and Derszteler, G. 1996. Workflow Management Cycle—An Integrated Approach to the Modeling, Execution and Monitoring of Workflow Based Processes. In *Business Process Modeling,* pp. 23–42. Edited by Scholz-Reiter, B. and Stickel, E. Berlin, Springer Verlag.

Martin, J. 1996. *Cybercorp. The New Business Revolution.* AMACOM. New York: American Management Association.

Mayer, R. J. and Painter, M. K. 1991. *The IDEF Suite of Methods for System Development and Evolution.* College Station, TX: KBSI.

McGrath, J.E.1984. *Groups: Interaction and Performance.* Englewood Cliffs, NJ: Prentice-Hall.

Miller, J., Sheth, A., Kochut, K., Wang, X. and Murugan, A. 1995. Simulation Modeling Within Workflow Technology. *Proceedings of the 1995 Winter Simulation Conference,* pp. 612–619. Edited by C. Alexopoulous, K. Kang, W. Lilegdon and D. Goldsman.

Nunamaker, J., Dennis, J., Valacich, J. Vogel, D. and George, J. 1991. Electronic Meeting Systems Tool to Support Group Work. *Communications of the ACM.* 34, 7. pp. 40–61.

Obolensky, N. 1994. *Practical Business Reengineering. Tools and Techniques for Achieving Effective Change.* London: Kogan Page.

Plaia, A., and Carrie, A. 1995. Application and assessment of IDEF3—process flow description capture method. *International Journal of Operations and Production Management,* 15, no. 1, pp. 63–73.

Robson, W. 1997. *Strategic Management and Information Systems.* Second Edition. London: Pitman Publishing.

Rohloff, M. 1996. An Object Oriented Approach to Business Process Modeling, pp. 251–264. In *Business Process Modeling.* Edited by Scholz-Reiter, B. and Stickel, E. Berlin, Springer Verlag.

Taylor, D. 1995. *Business Engineering with Object Technology.* New York: John Wiley and Sons.

Rumbaugh, J. 1991. *Object Oriented Modeling and Design* (OMT). Englewood Cliffs, NJ: Prentice-Hall.

Steiner, I. 1972. *Group Processes and Productivity.* New York: *Academic Press.*

Valacich, J. S., Dennis, A. R. and Nunamaker, J. F. 1991. Electronic Meeting Support: the GroupSystems Concept. In *Computer-Supported Cooperative Work and Groupware.* Edited by Greenberg, S. London: Academic Press, pp. 133–154.

Weber, R. C. 1982. The Group: A Cycle from Birth to Death. In *Reading Book for Human Relations Training.* Edited by Porter, L. and Mohr, M., NTL Institute, pp. 68–71.

Workflow Management Coalition (WfMC). 1996a. Reference Model. Version 1. In *The Workflow Management Coalition Specification. Terminology and Glossary.* Brusssels: Workflow Management Coalition.

Workflow Management Coalition (WfMC). 1996b. In *The Workflow Management Coalition Specification. Interface 1: Process Definition Interchange.* Document Number WfMC TC-1016. Brussels: Workflow Management Coalition.

Yeates, D., Shields, M. and Helmy, D. 1994. *Systems Analysis and Design.* London: Pitman Publishing.

Index